Design Strategies for Reimagining the City

Design Strategies for Reimagining the City is situated between projective geometry, optical science and architectural design. It draws together seemingly unrelated fields in a series of new digital design tools and techniques underpinned by tested prototypes.

The book reveals how the relationship between architectural design and the ubiquitous urban camera can be used to question established structures of control and ownership inherent within the visual model of the Western canon. Using key moments from the broad trajectory of historical and contemporary representational mechanisms and techniques, it describes the image's impact on city form from the inception of linear perspective geometry to the digital turn. The discussion draws upon combined fields of digital geometry, the pictorial adaptation of human optical cues of colour brightness and shape, and modern image-capture technology (webcams, mobile phones and UAVs) to demonstrate how the permeation of contemporary urban space by digital networks calls for new architectural design tools and techniques. A series of speculative drawings and architectural interventions that apply the new design tools and techniques complete the book.

Aimed at researchers, academics and upper-level students in digital design and theory, it makes a timely contribution to the ongoing and broadly debated relationship between representation and architecture.

Linda Matthews is the Co-director of the UTS Visualisation Institute and a Senior Lecturer in the School of Architecture at the University of Technology, Sydney. Her research interests draw upon the history, politics and techniques of representation to explore new architectural and urban design methodologies that utilise the optics of digital visioning systems. The research aims to use virtual urban spaces as a source of qualitative and quantitative data to generate non-traditional modes of architectural and urban form. Linda has won several significant academic awards, including the prestigious Design Medal from the NSW Chapter of the Royal Australian Institute of Architects and the University Medal from the University of Technology, Sydney.

Routledge Research in Architecture

The *Routledge Research in Architecture* series provides the reader with the latest scholarship in the field of architecture. The series publishes research from across the globe and covers areas as diverse as architectural history and theory, technology, digital architecture, structures, materials, details, design, monographs of architects, interior design and much more. By making these studies available to the worldwide academic community, the series aims to promote quality architectural research.

Radical Functionalism
A Social Architecture for Mexico
Luis E. Carranza

The Architect and the Academy
Essays on Research and Environment
Dean Hawkes

Architecture of Threshold Spaces
A Critique of the Ideologies of Hyperconnectivity and Segregation in the Socio-Political Context
Laurence Kimmel

Pyrotechnic Cities
Architecture, Fire-Safety and Standardisation
Liam Ross

Architecture and the Housing Question
Edited by Can Bilsel and Juliana Maxim

Architecture and the Housing Question
Edited by Can Bilsel and Juliana Maxim

Mies at Home
From Am Karlsbad to the Tugendhat House
Xiangnan Xiong

For more information about this series, please visit: https://www.routledge.com/Routledge-Research-in-Architecture/book-series/RRARCH

Design Strategies for Reimagining the City
The Disruptive Image

Linda Matthews

LONDON AND NEW YORK

Cover image: Bill Kopitz/Lower Manhattan at Night/Getty

First published 2022
by Routledge
4 Park Square, Milton Park, Abingdon, Oxon OX14 4RN

and by Routledge
605 Third Avenue, New York, NY 10158

Routledge is an imprint of the Taylor & Francis Group, an informa business

© 2022 Linda Matthews

The right of Linda Matthews to be identified as author of this work has been asserted in accordance with sections 77 and 78 of the Copyright, Designs and Patents Act 1988.

All rights reserved. No part of this book may be reprinted or reproduced or utilised in any form or by any electronic, mechanical, or other means, now known or hereafter invented, including photocopying and recording, or in any information storage or retrieval system, without permission in writing from the publishers.

Trademark notice: Product or corporate names may be trademarks or registered trademarks, and are used only for identification and explanation without intent to infringe.

British Library Cataloguing-in-Publication Data
A catalogue record for this book is available from the British Library

Library of Congress Cataloguing-in-Publication Data
Names: Matthews, Linda (Linda M.), author.
Title: Design strategies for reimagining the city : the disruptive image / Linda Matthews.
Description: Abingdon, Oxon : Routledge, 2022. | Series: Routledge research in architecture | Includes bibliographical references and index. |
Identifiers: LCCN 2021061465 (print) | LCCN 2021061466 (ebook) | ISBN 9780367680176 (hardback) | ISBN 9780367680183 (paperback) | ISBN 9781003133872 (ebook)
Subjects: LCSH: Architecture and technology. | Architectural design--Data processing.
Classification: LCC NA2543.T43 M38 2022 (print) | LCC NA2543.T43 (ebook) | DDC 711/.40285--dc23/eng/20220210
LC record available at https://lccn.loc.gov/2021061465
LC ebook record available at https://lccn.loc.gov/2021061466

ISBN: 978-0-367-68017-6 (hbk)
ISBN: 978-0-367-68018-3 (pbk)
ISBN: 978-1-003-13387-2 (ebk)

DOI: 10.4324/9781003133872

Typeset in Sabon
by MPS Limited, Dehradun

Contents

List of figures ix
List of tables xii
List of abbreviations xiii
Acknowledgement xiv

PART I
Constructed fields of vision 1

   Introduction 3

1 The problem of the image of the city: From perspectival to digital space 8

   Disruptive techniques of spatial representation 8
   Singular or narrative spaces of representation 10
      The 'symbolic' intent of linear perspective geometry 10
      The perspectival city 11
      Photography as the bearer of truth 12
   Fragmentary spaces of representation 15
      Anamorphosis and the reversal of logic 15
      The Vertovian image: Issues of critique, representation and form-making 16
      Filmic space/architectural space 18
      Vertov in the digital image: Envisioning the contemporary city 19
      The qualitative image and affective space 22

2 The pixel's visual territory 28

   From analogue to digital 28
   Unique modes of digital assembly 30

    The discontinuous digital line 30
    Qualitative content is connected data 31
    The predictability of pixel relationships 32
Digital geometry's intersection with optical science 33
    Perceptual behaviours 33
The digital mediation of colour, brightness and shape 35
    Technological disruption 35
    Digital colour: Unique translations of digital technology 36
    Contrast perception, luminosity and the contextual advantages of pixel geometry 38
    Form perception and the inherent imperatives of pixel geometry 40
Representation and the pixel's 'symbolic form' 41
    Many authors 41

3 Seeing through digital image-making technology   46

Colour's transformation 46
Colour as form 47
The digital manipulation of colour 50
    Proprietary colour 50
    Colour by guesswork 52
New digital opportunities 53
    Non-proprietary colour and open-source code 53
    Exploiting CFAs 54
The digital perception of brightness 55
    Shifting the register: The pictorial application of brightness 55
    Eliminating the uncontrollable: Brightness as an artefact 58
    Fraunhofer diffraction as a productive aberration 59
Digital image legibility: Shape 60
    The human perception of shape 60
    The human visual system and scan path theory 61
    Saliency and the advantages of webcam technology 65
    The productive inclusion of digital artefacts 67

4 The new agency of distributed digital networks   74

Digital anamorphosis and the virtual picture plane 74
    Pre-digital anamorphic techniques 74
    The affective anamorphic network 76

Digital anamorphic techniques 77
The expanded image 80
    The distributed network and the multiplication of viewpoints 80
    An expanded temporal frame 84
    Responding to the digital city 86

PART II
New techniques of intervention and disruption   91

5   Generative techniques   93

New modes of practice 93
The qualitative image 95
The space within the image 98
    The anamorphic potential of digital technology 98
The dynamic image 103
    The image as a 3D volume 103
The synthesised landscape 106
    Transdisciplinary modes of activating digital colour and luminance (brightness) 106
    Colour and luminance (brightness) profiles as a generative procedure 108
Conclusion 110

6   **The building surface as a colour modifier**   113

Design templates for the built surface 113
Test strategies 114
    Colour 114
    Image artefacts 114
    Attention tracking 114
Validation methods 115
Series 1 tests overview 116
Test part 1: Strategies of pattern hierarchy 117
    Test technical data and conditions 119
    Test analysis methodology 120
    Test results 120
    Test summary and conclusions 121
Test part 2: Hierarchies of visibility – the shifting function of luminosity (brightness) 122
    Test results 122

Test summary and conclusions 123
Test part 3: The disruptive potential of additive colour 123
Test technical data and conditions 124
Test results and analysis 125
Test summary and conclusions 121
The data matrix 125

7 **Re-viewing diffraction** — 130

Series 2 tests overview 130
Patterns of disruption 132
Test technical data and conditions 132
Test analysis methodology 133
Test results and analysis 134
Test summary, conclusions and the data matrix 135

8 **New readings of the city** — 137

Series 3 tests overview 137
Scanning variants 138
Test technical data and conditions 138
Test analysis methodology 140
Test results and analysis 140
Test summary, conclusions and the data matrix 142
Concluding comments on the test series and the data matrices 144

9 **'La città ideale': Design drawings for the digital city** — 147

The digital Urbino Panel 147
Preliminary digital site mapping procedures 148
The digital Urbino Panel: A summary of visual effects 148
Intervention 1 150
Intervention 2 151
Intervention 3 152

Conclusion — 156

The new tools and techniques of architecture 156
The disciplinary shift 158

Glossary — 160
Bibliography — 162
Index — 171

Figures

2.1 Image of Bondi Beach, Australia, generated in PixelMath software. The image shows the distinct edges and the RGB value of each pixel   39
3.1 Antonio da Correggio, *Assumption of the Virgin*, 1526–1530   57
3.2 Piero della Francesca, *Annunciation (St Anthony)*, 1460–1470   64
4.1 Michelangelo Buonarotti, *The Last Supper* (1536–1541)   75
5.1 Digital glitch broadcasting error blue pixel noise ([golubovy]/Depositphotos.com) (left). Close-up of a section of the transmission error showing RGB pixel values of the artefact (right). (Image by author)   96
5.2 Emmanuel Maignan's fresco *San Francesco di Paola* (1642) in Trinità dei Monti, Rome, showing distorted image when viewed from frontal position (top left), image when viewed from 'correct' oblique viewing position (top right) and micro-landscapes embedded within the larger image visible from a viewing position perpendicular to the image surface (bottom). (Image by author)   100
5.3 Stationary camera viewpoints near Customs House, Circular Quay, Sydney (top left); catoptric anamorphic image generated from the same viewpoints (top right); Catoptric cylindrical anamorphic projections of Customs House, Circular Quay, Sydney, showing anamorphic projections, and 'corrected' Cartesian arrays in the reflective surface of the cylinder (bottom images). (Image by author)   102
5.4 Rotated time-lapse image stack (top left), intersecting orthogonal slice (top right) and conflated projection of an image stack along z axis (bottom) showing a view of Broadway looking towards Times Square, New York   104

x *Figures*

5.5 Montage of image slices selected from the *xz* (top) and *zy* (bottom) axes of an image stack showing a view of Broadway looking towards Times Square, New York   107

5.6 A single slice from the image stack (top) and a montage of slices selected from the image stack (bottom) showing a view of Broadway looking towards Times Square, New York   108

6.1 Patterns used in Series 1 tests. Column 1, top to bottom: Pattern 1 – Bayer CFA; Pattern 2 – pattern proposed by Lukac and Plationatis; Pattern 3 – Yamanaka CFA; Pattern 4 – diagonal stripe CFA; Pattern 5 – pseudo-random CFA. Column 2, top to bottom: Pattern 6 – HVS-based CFA; Pattern 7 – non-CFA pattern (red, blue); Pattern 8 – non-CFA pattern (blue, green); Pattern 9 – periodic hexagonal grid CFA; Pattern 10 – non-periodic hexagonal grid CFA. (Image by author)   118

6.2 Complementary colour variations of the Bayer array pattern, showing the effect of dynamic colour overlay, including areas of white. (Image by author)   124

6.3 Extract from example of an RGB transmission data matrix. (Image by author)   127

7.1 Patterns used in Series 2 tests. Column 1, top to bottom: Pattern 1 – standard horizontal raster scan-order pattern; Pattern 2 – standard horizontal raster scan-order pattern in a 45° rotated orientation; Pattern 3 – recursive Z scan-order pattern; Pattern 4 – hexagonal, HVS-based pattern; Pattern 5 – random or non-periodic pattern. Column 2, top to bottom: Patterns 1F–5F – Fraunhofer patterns produced from each of the Column 1 patterns. (Image by author)   131

8.1 Patterns used in Series 3 tests. Top row, left to right: Pattern 1 – standard raster scan-order pattern; Pattern 2 – standard raster scan-order pattern (45° rotated orientation); Pattern 3 – standard raster scan-order pattern (45° rotated and discontinuous); Pattern 4 – outward spiral; Pattern 5 – outward spiral (45° rotated orientation); Pattern 6 – outward spiral (45° rotated and discontinuous); Pattern 7 – recursive Z-pattern; Pattern 8 – recursive Z-pattern (45° rotated orientation); Pattern 9 – recursive Z-pattern (45° rotated and discontinuous); Pattern 10 – random or non-periodic pattern. (Image by author)   139

8.2 F-stop sequence of pattern 1 in horizontal orientation showing progression of visual blurring at f-6 aperture. (Image by author)   141

Figures xi

9.1	Rotated time-lapse image stack (top) and combined orthogonal view of image stack (bottom) showing a busy intersection in Times Square, New York	149
9.2	HVS-based CFA pattern building façade	151
9.3	Fraunhofer diffraction pattern derived from rotated raster-scan pattern used as building façade diffraction grating (left-hand column). Fraunhofer diffraction pattern derived from rotated recursive Z-pattern (right-hand column)	153
9.4	Raster-scan pattern façade diffraction grating (left-hand column). Recursive Z-pattern façade diffraction grating (right-hand column). (Image by author)	154

Tables

6.1 The total AVG, MAX RGB intensity, luminosity and particle data count values of Patterns 1–10   121
7.1 Unique colour count and particle data count values of Patterns 1–5 and 1F–5F   134
8.1 The total AVG, SUM and MAX luminosity and particle data count values of all versions of Patterns 1–10   143

Abbreviations

AIP	average intensity projection
CCD	couple charged device
CCTV	closed-circuit television
CFA	colour filter array
CIE	Commission International de l'Éclairage
CMOS	complementary metal-oxide-semiconductor
CYMK	cyan, magenta, yellow and key
FT	frame-transfer
HDR	high dynamic range
HVS	human visual system
IP	Internet protocol
IT	interline-transfer
LAN	local area network
MIP	maximum intensity projection
PTZ	pan-tilt-zoom
RGB	red, green and blue
sRGB	standard RGB
TV	television
3D	three-dimensional
2D	two-dimensional
US	United States

Acknowledgement

I should like to thank my editor, Dr Campbell Aitken, for his invaluable assistance in the production of this work.

Part I
Constructed Fields of Vision

Introduction

When addressing the impact of technological development upon art practice, Walter Benjamin drew a distinction between two of its practitioners – the painter and the cameraman. The distinction is defined by transformative conditions brought into being by the camera and by new ways the world could be experienced, understood and, ultimately, built. Inasmuch as linear perspective technology had for centuries constrained the viewer to a closed set of preordained viewing conditions, and thus a particular construct of urban space, so did the technology of the moving image instigate a new range of visual, experiential and formal conditions that exceeded the impact of its predecessor. The transformative effect of camera technology's 'plunging and soaring, its interrupting and isolating, its stretching and condensing of the process, its close-ups and its distance shots'[1] liberated the viewer from the constraints of the perspectival urban narrative.

Six years before Benjamin's essay, the revolutionary filmic techniques presented in Dziga Vertov's *Man with a Movie Camera* (1929) had already demonstrated what new viewing techniques might mean for conceiving a profoundly new kind of urban space.[2] Vertov used cinematic fragments (later described by Benjamin as 'a large number of pieces, which find their way back together by following a new law',[3]) to multiply rather than limit the urban viewing experience, thus unleashing the new potential of camera technology to draw the viewer's attention to the artifice and 'constructed' visual fields of previous urban narratives.

The awakening of the critical viewer was only one of the many newly enabled disruptive effects of Vertov's radical approach. Others, including a more inclusive and extended viewing field, contributed to undoing the visual conceit of spatial infinity, so intrinsic to the believability of perspectival space. With the new conditions for presenting urban space came new ways of producing this space. By penetrating deeply into the 'web' of reality, architects as 'surgeons' could avail themselves of these new technological conditions and apply them to the city.[4] Modern architectural counterparts of the multiple, fragmented spaces of Vertov's city can arguably be seen in the distributed programs of Tschumi and

DOI: 10.4324/9781003133872-2

Koolhaas,[5] among many others, whose overlapping and non-sequential programmatic distribution engenders disruptive effects similar to those produced by Vertovian filmic techniques.

The distinction Benjamin drew between the painter and the cameraman also applies to the transition from the analogue to the moving digital image, or, technologically speaking, from the film camera to the digital camera device. This technological transition creates a corresponding new set of viewing conditions according to which the contemporary world is now to be experienced, understood and once again, to be built. However, Benjamin's distinction requires updating if the extent of the new viewing conditions is to be considered and deployed comprehensively.

Addressing a more contemporary digital frame, Mario Carpo extended the role of Benjamin's cameraman beyond that of a single 'technician' at work in the making of images. New operational conditions requiring 'some form of almost collective decision-making'[6] exclusively initiated by the digital came into play, defining a very different type of urban experience: 'open-endedness, variability, interactivity, and participation are the technological quintessence of the digital age.'[7] Yet issues of authorship are only one aspect of the new operating conditions that confront those whose role it is to represent urban space and those who attend to the design and production of its form. It is the geometry that underpins digital technology and its close alignment with the way the principal perceptual properties of human vision are understood that determine the ways in which this technology can be deployed to represent the plural and fragmented space of the contemporary city. As an accompaniment to 'the traditional forms of architectural notations (plans, elevations and sections)',[8] the contemporary architect can draw upon the new effects and conditions of the digital – the numerical basis of the digital algorithm and the pixel – for the resources and techniques of architecture in an operational context of 'hitherto unimaginable venues and possibilities for openness and participation by even nontechnical agents in all stages of design'.[9]

The geometry of the digital image operates according to the three principal perceptual properties of the human visual system (HVS): colour, brightness and shape. Mediated by camera technology, these properties establish both the generative conditions for representational space and how it is perceived, understood and inhabited. The new, Internet-enabled presentation of virtual and real urban space thus offers a practical basis for the perception and assembly of material form. And, although the intrinsic instability of the digital ruptures the traditional 'indexical' link between design drawing and object, as Mario Carpo noted, 'digital variability may equally cut loose the indexical link that, under the old authorial paradigm, tied design notations to their material result in an object',[10] another replaces it that instead draws upon the numerical grid of the pictorial pixel array to assign qualitative properties to the city's viewed surfaces.

These new associations reinforce the city's ambiguity and complexity by directing the viewer's attention to the constructed nature of the image and its presentation of the city as an iconic and promotional space.

This book, therefore, investigates the interplay between digital geometry, camera technology and the HVS. It explores new ways in which the physical surfaces of the contemporary city can be linked to the interactive complexities of digital visioning systems. It also examines the consequences of this generative relationship for the role of the architect and the trajectory of the discipline.

The first chapter outlines the historical lineage of visioning technology's continuing effect upon urban building design from the Renaissance to the present, showing how architects have long been implicated in the way cities are represented and, consequently, built. The chapter reveals how architects and building design continue to reflect dominant visual regimes, tracing the historical influence of representational techniques and technologies upon urban form, from the viewing constraints of linear perspective construction to the disjunctive leaps of the moving image. With the digital's departure from the visual narrative of linear perspective in favour of the fragmented spatial effects of filmic montage, the chapter draws a parallel between the profound disciplinary shift brought about by the latter and that suggested by the pixel-based geometry of the digital image. It points to a link between Internet camera technology and the spatial understanding of the city, concluding that the digital image resituates representation, urban form and the architectural discipline within a new operational framework.

Chapters 2 and 3 explore the respective geometric and technological implications of this new operational framework. By outlining the perceptual effects of digital geometry's base unit, the pixel, chapter 2 identifies unique aspects of digital image-making that profoundly challenge the relationship between the viewer and the traditional representation of the physical world. It reveals how the geometric structure and composition of the digital image have a direct correspondence with the optical reception of an object's contextual colour, luminosity and shape. Privileging the qualitative properties of digital image content over the linear-dominant perspectival tradition establishes a new operational frame that draws upon the digital's unique properties for its generative potential. Furthermore, the chapter addresses the issue of multiple authorships and the emerging distinction between different types of viewers in relation to the broader disciplinary implications of digital image accessibility and the new operational conditions it initiates.

The new digital technological frame is the subject of chapter 3. It addresses the optical and spatial effects of visioning technology by first examining how the qualitative properties of the image, content and legibility (colour, brightness and shape) operate in relation to human optics, and how the digital camera mediates them. The chapter situates the discussion within

6   *Constructed Fields of Vision*

an historical context that reveals how the transition from analogue pictorial techniques and devices to the digital image-making device not only transforms the viewer's engagement with urban space but releases the city's qualitative properties to new modes of form-making.

Chapter 4 examines the spatial effects of user-based webcam technology on the viewer. It revisits historic, disruptive spatial frameworks, such as 17th-century anamorphosis, to reveal how this technology can profoundly disrupt the hierarchical, ideal view of the city. The chapter describes how releasing multiple, dynamic viewpoints allows its established systems of control and ownership to be interrogated and ultimately defines the new conditions according to which urban form can be realised.

Chapter 5 unveils a range of new techniques that draw directly upon the digital geometry and technology discussions in the previous chapters to establish new ways of generating architectural form. The techniques refer to the digital image assemblies that determine an object's visibility and the role these play in urban design development. The generative potential of their disciplinary contribution is explored in two ways.

The first describes new approaches to architectural site analysis and documentation offered by the digital camera's delineation of space and time. A combination of proprietary and non-proprietary scientific image analysis software is used to extrapolate and reassemble image data relating to the complex inhabitation of urban space and its many viewed surfaces. The reassembled data present a range of image-based procedures underpinning the digital's new generative urban design processes.

The second area of investigation, presented in chapters 6, 7 and 8, takes the form of a series of practical tests exploiting the technical capabilities of the digital camera and, in this case, the situated webcam. The tests refer to camera protocols associated with HVS optical cues, colour, brightness and shape. They seek to identify a range of image-based design procedures that draw directly upon digital image geometry and its numerical link with the city's viewed surfaces. The tests examine the effects of applying three pattern types unique to the camera's technical pathways to the viewed building surface. The intention is to exploit the pathways to establish a series of generative procedures that either use the viewed building surface to shift the image's hierarchy or disrupt the camera's production of a legible image of the city.

A further ambition of the practical tests is the production of a working document or matrix that can indexically link the receptive capacities of the camera and the pixel-based geometry of the digital image directly to the building surface. By correlating observed image effects with tabulated increments of the camera's aperture range acting in conjunction with its zoom mechanism, this predictive tool enables a building surface's effect to be finely controlled according to its extent of image-production interference. The new formal assemblies made possible by the pixel's limitless capacity to be numerically indexed to a range of explicit visual effects are then referenced in material matrices that position the architect in a pivotal role in implementing a new and highly interrogatory visual regime.

The ninth and final chapter of the book presents a series of speculative design investigations that adapt digital camera protocols associated with the reception of colour, brightness and shape to intervene in urban space in respective ways. Referring to the many situated webcams in Times Square, New York, the proposal applies adaptive techniques to direct the viewer's attention to the constructed nature of the globally transmitted images and their promotional presentation of an iconic city.

The presentation of the effects of deploying pixel grid geometry as a generative architectural tool is one of the research's intended outcomes; provision of a predictive means to apply them is another. These are the practical means by which the tools and techniques of architecture are realigned with the contemporary digital frame. However, this very realignment creates the imperative to reassess both the new disciplinary role and status of the image and the rapidly transitioning agency of the architect.

Notes

1 Walter Benjamin, 1936. *The work of art in the age of mechanical reproduction*. London: Penguin Books, p. 42.
2 Dziga Vertov, 1984. *Kino-eye: The writings of Dziga Vertov*. Berkeley, CA: University of California Press.
3 Benjamin, *The work of art in the age of mechanical reproduction*, p. 37.
4 Benjamin, *The work of art in the age of mechanical reproduction*, p. 15.
5 Graham Cairns, ed., 2016. *Visioning technologies: The architectures of sight*. Abingdon-on-Thames: Routledge.
6 Mario Carpo, *The alphabet and the algorithm*. Cambridge, MA: MIT Press, p. 43.
7 Carpo, *The alphabet and the algorithm*, p. 126.
8 Carpo, *The alphabet and the algorithm*, p. 125.
9 Carpo, *The alphabet and the algorithm*, p. 125.
10 Carpo, *The alphabet and the algorithm*, p. 43.

1 The problem of the image of the city: From perspectival to digital space

With the advent of linear perspective came a particular way of understanding space. Its application to the image produced a highly controlled viewing condition that deliberately directed the viewer's gaze according to the artist's intent. Linear perspective functioned as the dominant *modus operandi* of Western image-making from the Renaissance through to the advent of photography in 1826.[1] Other image-making techniques, with few exceptions, did little to contest its coercive visual and cognitive effects.

This chapter explores linear perspective and digital images in parallel, understood through diverse, yet interconnected, optics, geometry and technology frameworks. In particular, the comparison pivots on how the fragmentary and disjunctive modes of spatial representation led by the work of the Soviet filmmakers in the early 20th century, notably Sergei Eisenstein and Dziga Vertov, departed from linear perspective's singular narrative space. This new visual model would fundamentally shift future modes of urban representation and, by extension, initiate new conditions for architectural design. It is proposed that, when reworked and resituated within a contemporary digital image-making context, Vertov's adapted film techniques interrogate a similar relationship between politics and the city's form to that of their earlier counterparts. It is argued, that by being connected to the digital's unique formal and material assemblies, these strategies shift the image's role within the architectural discipline, and are accompanied by profound implications for form-making and the types of conditions and responses it can and might initiate.

Disruptive techniques of spatial representation

The montage technique used by 20th-century Soviet filmmakers exploited one of optics' most important procedural functions: saccadic scanning. As we now know, for the generation of a new optical scan path to take place, the saliency of the viewed object needs somehow to be disabled before the viewer's attention, and thus the scan path can shift.[2] Montage not only dismantles the 'planned route' of the eye in that instance, but, in a broader context, disrupts the cognitive 'learned' model that suppresses an intuitive,

DOI: 10.4324/9781003133872-3

non-learned response. Put simply, a perceptual shock can disrupt visual complacency when the content of the visual field remains uncontested, thus reintroducing a critical awareness to the viewing process.

For Eisenstein and Vertov, the innovative montage technique worked to achieve different ends, yet both filmmakers used it to disrupt the film's continuity for a specific reason. The use of a 'jump cut' not only ruptured spatial continuity for the observer but forced him or her to engage actively with content. Referring to Eisenstein's 'Montage of Attractions', Richard Koeck described this artist's technique as 'an aggressive, disruptive narrative strategy that should stimulate the sensual apparatus of the audience and encourage it to perceive a certain ideology ... a reality that is principally generated in the eyes of the beholder'.[3] In this instance, the visual disconnect's shock value literally disrupts learned response by intervening within the viewer's internal optical procedures. By forcing the eye to move forward to the next visual 'event', this montage 'jolt' dismantles any existing singular, continuous understanding of space and time. In cinematic montage, the viewer is 'free from the relational constraints of "space" and "time" since it does not intend to uphold the illusion of their continuity'.[4] In Vertov's case, the disruption of optical space, seen in his movie *Man with a Movie Camera*, meant that the city's architectural space was also disrupted. Montage as fragmentation and montage as a connection of fragments now became synonymous with modern life,[5] and modern life took place in the city's three-dimensional space that was no longer experienced as either a continuous or single visual space.

Despite the perceptual transformation that had taken place with Eisenstein and Vertov's radical visual language of montage, by the end of the 1930s this technique had been assimilated into the internal cognitive visual model and 'simply supported the telling of stories'.[6] By returning to simple narrative, film had lost its capacity to influence the conceptual understanding of time and space.[7] A new version of the visual 'shock' was needed to extend the duration of what Benjamin regarded as an 'absent-minded criticality' of urban space. This was to come with the advent of the digital image.[8]

The digital image is seemingly another descendant of the perspectival lineage, casting the viewer into a powerful singular spatial and visual narrative. 'Computed perspectives ... insert our disembodied viewing presences into modeled, fictional worlds ... our perceiving faculties are pried apart from our corporeal existence and sent to places where our bodies cannot follow.'[9] However, despite residing within a perspectival perceptual framework, profound compositional and geometric differences prevail. By its very nature, the digital image is discontinuous and fragmentary. Unlike the linear perspective image, an uninterrupted line between (x, y) coordinates, the digital image is an array of adjacent but discontinuous pixels. In the first instance, at its very material level, the digital image already embodies specific 'genetic' qualities that predispose it to the optical dismantling strategies of Eisenstein and Vertov. In the second, each pixel's discrete, individual nature means that the line is no longer the dominant organising principle of image-making. What were formerly two intersecting lines that converged at infinity in a linear perspective schema, instead become an array of self-contained pixels whose individual variations of colour and brightness properties determine adjacency and thus image content. Quite simply, this means that the image's affective, qualitative properties – namely colour and brightness – that derive from variable ambient urban conditions such as light, weather and various human transactions within this space are pre-eminent. By extension, this sets up equally unique conditions for translating the same affective properties into architectural form and, importantly, for developing new pathways for their inclusion and deployment within the city.

Singular or narrative spaces of representation

The 'symbolic' intent of linear perspective geometry

Brunelleschi's discovery of linear perspective in 1425 and the subsequent development of a range of perspective instruments, from armillary spheres through to Vignola and Durer's perspective machines, escalated the development of a new technique that was to transform both the representation and the form of the city.[10] The implementation of a rational, repeatable and, above all, highly transportable system meant that the city could now be considered and planned speculatively.[11,12] Works such as the Urbino Panels (second half of the 15th century) exemplify this, revealing, as Hubert Damisch observed, perspective's capacity to integrate ideal with historical form in a seamless, single image. '[The Baltimore Panel] … offers up a veritable display of ancient and modern architecture, something resembling a repository of monuments – the equivalent of a carefully preserved historic district, though one into which buildings have been introduced that must be qualified as "avant-garde".'[13]

However, the geometric constraints of this system and its gridded picture plane meant that, while space could now literally be conceived as infinite, its operability was limited in the same breath by restricting the observer to a fixed viewing position. The conception of perspective entailed the construction of a site where everything would be, in Serlio's terms, *a suo luogo* (inscribed in its place), dominated by a singular spatial principle that 'precludes us from thinking of bodies apart from the places they occupy'.[14] Referring to Panofsky, Damisch aligned the spatial array of elements within the Cartesian grid's field of view to the tightly held syntactic structure of language and its explicit philological hierarchies.

> In the art of painting the impact of perspective is not limited to the register of the imaginary; it not only facilitates the construction of

images, it assumes a role, a function that we may properly designate as symbolic. Perspective, I repeat, is not a code, but it has this in common with language, that in and by itself it institutes and constitutes itself under the auspices of a point, a factor analogous to the 'subject' or 'person' in language, always posited in relation to a 'here' or 'there', accruing all the possibilities for movement from one position to another that this entails.[15]

However, while Panofsky asserted that elements contained within the perspectivally ordered visual field assume a status or symbolic function according to their preassigned locations, just as do words in a sentence, he did not extend the analogy to speculate upon the outcome of reordering those viewpoints. This highly political act was to come with the work of the Soviet filmmakers in the early 20th century.

The perspectival city

Diverse applications of the perspective machine extended the design and construction of stage scenery directly into the form of the Renaissance city. 'The principles of symmetry, perspective, and intelligibility that were shaping the stage were also informing the layout of avenues, vistas, piazzas.'[16] Perspective machines were used by engineers, surveyors, artists and scenic designers, expanding linear perspective projection from a visual into a new formal language. However, to recall Panofsky, the translation of the stagecraft principles into urban form inevitably brought with it the assignation of highly organised and politically underscored viewpoints.

The transformation of early 17th-century Genoa literally into a stage by its architect, Peter Paul Rubens, became a projective organisational urban model for northern European noble patrons. Able to be viewed only from explicit, predetermined positions, the aristocratic Strada Nuova operated as a *scaena frons* (front of stage) for Genoese nobility and an aristocratic centre signifying wealth and social aggrandisement within the larger city.[17] Serlio's Vitruvian 'tragic' stage was here translated into a microcosm of the city's predominant social order, and its institutional framework seen through the lens of the linear perspective system's need to privilege a singular viewing space.

Genoa is only one of many examples of the translation of perspectival theatrical devices into formal architectural proposals. Others include the *tromp-l'oeil* gardens of Salamon de Caus, who used linear perspective as a technical tool to deal with discrete garden units and specific moments of privileged viewing, as described by Morgan: 'De Caus's emphasis on the viewing position of the spectator implies a relationship between garden design and perspective construction: both depend, to varying extents, on a single, defined viewing position for their full effect.'[18]

Gorse argued that these types of theatrical representations not only formed the visual stage model for absolutist regimes of the baroque era but operated as a microcosm of a larger urban spatial arrangement, deploying visual geometry to reinforce existing social mores and codes.

> The Strada Nuova represented the center of the aristocratic culture and politics, society and economy of seventeenth-century Genoa. For them, the Strada Nuova was Genoa in microcosm, the new patrician hub of the commonweal, the focal point of a classical urban stage, representing the old (and then new) nobility in all its scenographic splendor. But in its origins, the Strada Nuova was designed as a classical stage for the old nobility, a ceremonial mask for the absolutism of a corporate aristocracy that rose above the medieval communal center.[19]

The tendency towards ocular centricity in Western culture produced a visual condition that was increasingly non-reflexive and quantitative from the Middle Ages onwards. The introduction of the Renaissance instruments of vision only intensified this condition. The folded forms of the Baroque were the inevitable reaction to the constraint of an imposed viewing condition that attempted 'to reduce the multiplicity of visual spaces into … one coherent essence'.[20] Works such as Borromini's San Carlo alle Quattro Fontane in Rome, despite being symptomatic of the desire to seek 'differentiated ocular experiences',[21] nevertheless remained both bound by the formal constraints of an overarching geometry and tied to the embedded ambitions of its symbolic intent.

Photography as the bearer of truth

> Photographs are necessarily partial documents of the real, through which elements are selected or excluded, made visible or invisible, and are often subject to staging of one kind or another.[22]

The invention of photography in the mid-19th century raised constructed views of power and place made possible by linear perspective to a higher register. Discussing the emergence of early 19th-century photographic portraiture, Walter Benjamin wrote of 'a magical value, such as a painted picture can never again have for us'.[23] As the century progressed, the camera's highly imitative reproductive process came to invest the image increasingly with a perceived objective authenticity and truth.

As Matt Dyce noted, the shift from human to machine entailed a fundamental shift in the status of the photographic image. In a range of instances, such as the map's replacement by the aerial photograph, the photographic perspective view could now provide a more authentic documentation of reality than the human-made diagram through a paradoxical but significant inversion of the image-making procedure. Discussing William Drewry's 1889 account of the replacement of the map by the aerial photograph, he explained, 'we have the object or its plan to produce the perspective' whereas in photographic surveying 'we have the perspective to produce the plan'.[24] Moving from map to photograph, Drewry suggested, meant a loss of authorship and control over the view. However, as Dyce observed, while the limitation of human influence over image-making in the field seemingly guaranteed greater accuracy in aerial photographs, ironically, 'it was the implicitly human act of reading the image in the laboratory after its production that became the hallmark of objective science'.[25]

The proliferation of 'spirit photography' – obviously manipulated images of the supernatural and the dead that emerged at this time – was one of the more bizarre and somewhat ironic results of vast investment in photography's capacity to 'see the invisible and reveal truths beyond the powers of the human eye'.[26] The inconsistency of this practice with claims made about the photograph's mechanical objectivity only indicates the power of this new mechanical visualisation of the world that was even more compelling than linear perspective painting. By eliminating the observer's mediating presence, the camera's ability to supersede its human counterpart in recording time and space gave the powerful impression of improving upon vision. However, there was much at stake in this conflation of representation and reality. As Susan Sontag so aptly put it, 'A fake painting (one whose attribution is false) falsifies the history of art. A fake photograph (one which has been retouched or tampered with, or whose caption is false) falsifies reality.'[27] The alignment of photography with scientific data to preserve the truth and uniformity of a stable, seamless narrative of the world meant removing anything within the frame of the photograph that was inconsistent with verifiable fact. An essential part of this homogenous, stable and seamless narrative of the world therefore inevitably included architectural form.

Returning to the 19th-century beginnings of photography, we see the implementation of this approach in the detailed architectural views of Charles Marville. The images assert the built world as an incontestable physical truth produced by a seemingly invisible and unbiased hand. Marville's compelling shots of Baron Haussmann's architectural transformation of mid-19th-century Paris bear witness to a transition from unsanitised, dark alleys to clean light-filled avenues, while always concealing the deliberate perspectival framing of the space. Nigel Green described the visual authority achieved by these types of highly curated images as follows:

> whereas the frame in painting defines a space for representation to be layered or mapped over time, the photographic frame constitutes a 'cut' into an existing field of vision whereby composition neatly excludes peripheral information. It is the mechanical recording or 'indexicality' of the image facilitated by this 'cut' that underpinned photography's privileged claim to the representation of physical reality.[28]

14 *Constructed fields of vision*

By the turn of the 20th century, Atget's nostalgic views of Paris and its environs signalled the photograph's diversification into more qualitative, evocative trajectories, extending its function beyond the simple notion of objective visual 'truth'. Relying upon heavily manipulated techniques to evoke particular atmospheric effects of light and shadow,[29] Atget's use of the 19th-century albumen process was a deliberate choice over the new and more stable gelatin silver papers to achieve greater clarity, richness of detail and nuanced tones, as was his use of techniques such as vignetting to highlight and frame architectural subjects. Despite their divergent approaches and philosophies, techniques of photographic manipulation link his work to that of the Surrealists, principally Man Ray, in processes of 'dematerialization and spatial ambiguity',[30] and arguably, Atget's work resides partly in both singular and fragmented spaces of representation.

The same technological developments that permitted manipulation were accompanied by mechanical reproduction. The issue of multiple prints from one negative meant that a proliferation of images could reach a vast viewing audience. Walter Benjamin regarded this as a commodification of photography, which was 'more concerned with eventual saleability than with insight'.[31]

This type of ambition is only too clearly played out in state photographs of public housing in socialist Romania between 1950 and 1970. Juliana Maxim recounted how the imaging of urban space, fostered by new technology and its accompanying techniques, was singularly targeted to promoting socialist productivity.

> The rise of photography as the preferred means of representing architecture echoed the transformation of architecture itself, and, more specifically, the dramatic intensification of standardized, industrialized mass-housing construction in the late 1950s. Henceforth, the accelerated architectural production matched closely the state's accelerated capacity to produce and circulate images …. The new alliance between photography and architecture therefore corresponded to a deep change in the actual definition of architecture: modernized techniques of representation accompanied modernized techniques of production.[32]

Maxim argued that these powerful architectural portrayals drew upon techniques of spatial ambiguity established by the work of Man Ray and Vertov to achieve a 'new alliance between photography and architecture'.[33] However, it is an alliance that is not new at all. Indeed, there are certain differences in photographic style between these and the seemingly 'authentic' representations initiated by 19th-century scientific photography. Also, the sweeping iconic views of Haussman's Paris have now been replaced by fragmentary, scaleless images that reconcile the viewer to the endless banality of socialist housing landscapes. Yet, despite their apparent differences, they are all aligned with a singular, continuous spatial narrative. In the words of Nigel Green, these images neither admit the existence of a world beyond the space described by the image nor act as a mechanism for its critique. 'The canonical architectural photograph, like academic painting, defines itself in relation to the frame as a form of natural construct – a world that is visually coherent and complete and which functions independently of what is unseen beyond the frame.'[34] To rediscover this, we must return to the montage techniques associated with Vertov's moving image.

Fragmentary spaces of representation

Anamorphosis and the reversal of logic

> Perspective has become so completely integrated into our knowledge, at the most implicit or unconscious level, that today we must turn to another kind of knowledge, erudite knowledge, and embark on an anamnestic project designed to recover it from the technological oblivion into which it has been plunged by ideology.[35]

It is important to note that linear perspective's universal acceptance as a representational mechanism did not go unchallenged in the centuries that followed its discovery and pervasive implementation. Its interrogation as a singular, irrefutable space of viewing is evidenced as early as the 16th century in works such as Hans Holbein's *The Ambassadors*.[36] In a bid to restore agency to the viewer, Holbein used the anamorphic technique to probe issues of linear perspective's spatial control and the viewer's relationship to the surface of the painting.[37] A century later, manipulating the mathematics of Cigoli's linear perspective machine, two Minim monks, Jean-Francois Niceron and Emmanuel Maignan, again used anamorphosis to overturn both the rational integrity and reliability of linear perspective.

The emergence of multiple secondary images, seen in Maignan's 1640 fresco *San Francesco di Paola*, in the church of San Trinità in Rome, reinstates the subject's viewpoint from one of singularity to one where direct physical engagement with the picture plane offers a new type of engagement with the space of the image and the phenomenal space of reality. As the viewer passes along the linear trajectory of the picture plane, several micro-landscapes unfold. This fluctuating visual journey, in which the viewer successively occupies and vacates a series of viewpoints, serves as a constant reminder of the actual *space* of viewing and the *act* of viewing itself, in which, as Massey observed, 'Perspective thus becomes a property of man's movement and trajectory in physical space'.[38] Thrusting the viewer firmly into an active and autonomous experience of the image's spatiality, Maignan's anamorphic portrait undermines the linear perspective system's 'construct'. With the viewer no longer asked to 'see through' the picture plane into a projected and hypothetical, infinite space beyond the image,

16 *Constructed fields of vision*

but instead activating the experiential space in front of the picture plane, the theatre of linear perspective is undone.

> In fact, the anamorphic picture is the antithesis of the Albertian window. If the window provides an analogy for the centred Cartesian subject who surveys the world as picture, anamorphosis turns this illusion inside out, forcing the viewer to see perspectival space as a fiction of geometry and to see the pictorial surface as an object that stares back.[39]

By dividing perceptual agency, the dual operation of the anamorphic displacement demands a degree of interaction and autonomy.[40]

While Bryan Reynolds argued that anamorphic perspective enables social change through the simultaneous destabilisation of the dominant re-presentational model,[41] these anamorphic strategies nevertheless remain variations of the same geometric schema. In other words, although the radical fracturing of the singular perspectival space of the painting permitted scrutiny of its underpinning logic, it was delimited by the constraints of its geometry. As part of the Cartesian system and therefore ultimately subject to the same geometric dictates, anamorphosis was not the mechanism that could respond to the 'changing needs emerging through the evolutionary process' described by Damisch.[42] Instead, the opportunity to recover from 'the technological oblivion'[43] of linear perspective's association with ideology would come with the advent of the moving image.

The Vertovian image: Issues of critique, representation and form-making

Its limitations notwithstanding, anamorphosis introduced the idea of plural space, and with it, the notion of how this plurality might play out both architecturally and optically. Perhaps one of the best examples of this is Giovanni Battista Piranesi's mid-18th-century 'I Carceri' drawings. Foreshadowing the Soviet filmmakers of the early 20th century, Piranesi's 'cinematic montage'[44] technique uses the collision of saccadic scan paths to produce a visual jolt, thus disrupting the learned internal visual model. For Bois and Shepley, the importance of Piranesi's drawings is therefore that, as images, they profoundly disrupt the continuity of a singular spatial narrative and as architectural representations, their profound disconnect between plan and elevation shifts the status of the ground plan and 'its traditional domination over traditional space'.[45] So too did the photographic works of László Moholy-Nagy and Neues Sehen (The New Vision) at the Bauhaus in the 1920s and 1930s explore visually disruptive and abstracting techniques, such as the use of unusual viewpoints, extreme cropping and close-ups to recalibrate existing ways of seeing the city and the built environment in general. Simultaneously, in Russia, artists such as Alexander Rodchenko and El Lissitzky deployed similar techniques of disruption and fragmentation to represent the results of the political upheaval brought about by the Revolution. 'Photography was no longer seen as a tool of representation but as an opportunity for creation.'[46]

However, it was the extension of static image space into a temporal frame that was to reconstitute the image's political agency radically. Soviet filmmakers seized this opportunity to reintroduce critical function to a mechanism that was, as they saw it, overburdened and tied to the ideals of the privileged. Dziga Vertov's 1929 film *Man with a Movie Camera* took the deliberate disruption of the image's geometry and the fragmentation of its spatial narrative to a register beyond Piranesi. His unusual frame compositions, camera angles and montage exploited the camera's mobility and ability to manipulate time, record urban space and recreate the relationship between the viewer and the exterior world.[47] Like Eisenstein, Vertov's use of non-sequential filmic jump cuts[48] drew the viewer's attention to the deliberate dismantling of any traditional understanding or experience of the city by leading the viewer beyond the filmic frame.

Vertov's 'new fragmentary visual effect' that 'picked up on the question of the city and modern life'[49] had soon begun to inspire other users. Walter Ruttman's 1928 film *Berlin–Symphony of a Great City*, with its fragmented, conflated and juxtaposed spaces and times, stands in high contrast to the type of singular political narrative later seen in Leni Riefenstahl's epic *Triumph of the Will* (1935). Sergei Eisenstein also deployed a fragmentary style to reinforce dramatic effects and emotional content while remaining firmly within a narrative style. Composing what Cairns identified as 'a mutual set of interests emerging in both architecture and film in the early twentieth century',[50] Vertov's most significant distinguishing feature was his treatment of film as a documentary rather than a narrative medium. This set the ground for a new type of engagement with visual content that would completely recalibrate the image's relationship with architecture.

Three defining features qualify Vertov's work for Damisch's critical task of image retrieval.

- The replacement of the predetermined classical framing of the figure by the active man and the technological eye of the camera to produce a composite, fragmentary city image conforming to neither conventional semantics of film shots nor relationships that would advance a narrative.[51] Importantly, implicit within this new construct is an awareness of process 'outside' the frame of the camera itself and 'indexed by the movements of the frame and within the frame. It is awareness of "life" – of what always lies beyond the frame, discontinuous with what is framed'.[52] Unlike the unflinching, didactic narrative of a work such as Leni Riefenstahl's *Triumph of the Will*, whose framed content is directly connected to an external world, the conditions external to Vertov's film are discontinuous with its content.

They do not refer to any single narrative either inside or outside the frame, but rather exist despite it.
- The deliberate inclusion of jump cuts or aberrations to disrupt the film's continuity. These legible discontinuities prevent film content, and in this case, the city image, from becoming 'normalised' or taken for granted, by intervening directly within the viewer's perceptual process and rupturing the tendency to privilege the learned visual pathway.
- The deliberate multiplication of viewpoints in the film restores agency to the viewer. Using deliberate visual references to both the camera operator and the camera itself means that the scope of viewing exceeds that of either a traditional narrative or the director's single vision. This technique transforms not only the viewer from a passive consumer of content into an active participant, but the image into a vehicle for social critique rather than ideology. Furthermore, for Walter Benjamin, the new emergent dialectic between politics and aesthetics that had arisen with the advent of the moving image and the capacity to reach a mass audience fulfilled the critical, political function of art 'by following a new law'.[53] It would also set the ground for a new approach to form-making.

Filmic space/architectural space

Vertov's radical departure from traditional cinematography modes engendered equally radical departures from the conception of architectural form. Rather than dwelling upon a catalogue of the many correspondences between post-Vertovian filmmaking and architecture, this discussion instead focuses on notable examples of disjunctive cinematic techniques transposed and incorporated into architectural form.

Perhaps a good place to begin is with Scott McQuire's insight into the expansive and, above all, disruptive creative field opened for architectural production by film's dynamic medium.

> Defined in terms of the orchestration of mobile and dynamic fields of vision, 'film' remains not only useful but essential to understanding the new conditions of transparency and opacity, of seeing and being seen, that continue to influence contemporary architecture. From this perspective, film and architecture are both implicated in the production of a new sense of social space born at the junction of increasingly 'open' architectural structures and mobile fields of vision. This is the unstable terrain that today grounds architecture in the digital urban milieu.[54]

Central to the notion of dynamism and instability, and among examples that precede the recent prolific deployment of digital video technologies, is the work of Diller and Scofidio. Their collection of hybrid media-object spaces,[55] such as The Shed (2019), draw upon transparency and surveillance themes to point to the same consciousness of a world beyond the camera frame demonstrated by Vertov. So too, does Jean Nouvel employ the notion of the jump cut in the sequencing of architectural space to introduce a visual jolt to the observer through a radical shift in the scale of adjacent spaces? Nouvel's Culture and Congress Centre in Lucerne manages the sequence of interior spaces as 'the architectural equivalent of a cut that jumps from one location, space or room, to the next'.[56] However, there is no more explicit example of spatial disruption applied to architectural space than Bernard Tschumi's *Manhattan Transcripts*. Tschumi's architectural event–space theory represents the architectural experience according to space, event and movement using plan, photography and the diagram respectively, where each frame expresses fragmentation and deconstruction.[57]

We see a further and more recent analogy with filmmaking in Mike Figgis' film *Timecode*, in which the viewing platform or screen is divided into four simultaneous and related but different sequences of events. Aylish Wood argued that visual fragmentation has real-world consequences:

> [Interfaces] ... reconfigure our relationships with the world by enabling us to inhabit it differently, and technological interfaces can be taken as articulations of a multiplicity of habitations. A striking facet of digital interfaces inscribed by competing elements is the level to which the image is fragmented rather than continuous .... The competing elements of interfaces offer a different mode of experience and perception, one in which agency can be gained through the process of making sense of the fragmented images.[58]

However, by extension, these consequences are also material and can be seen in the multiple conflicting activities overlaid in the single transparent space of Rem Koolhaas's CCTV building with its 'sites of multiple conflicting activities'.[59] In fact, it is precisely by producing the phenomenon of 'distributed attention' and rupturing the visual experience of the single filmic space that a new type of urban materiality can arise.

Vertov in the digital image: Envisioning the contemporary city

The increasing pervasiveness of digital technology throughout the modern city means that it is no longer seen from a single vantage point but understood instead through a series of snapshots supported by a network of distributed platforms. One of these, public urban webcam technology, provides viewers with a city image that is both fragmented and always changing. To recall Vertov, by continually shifting its frame of visual reference, this new mode of distributed attention breaks with the formula of visual narrative building, establishing a visual environment in which meaning is forever deferred. With the physical space of the city literally dematerialising through the effects of ever-encroaching and consuming technology, urban space becomes unimageable because of its radical dispersal, or at least in need of a new mode of representation that makes sense of its de-centredness.[60]

The webcam introduces new viewing conditions of an unprecedented scale and facilitates the itinerant Internet user's freedom to browse any global city's image at will. Its zoom capabilities also initiate new possibilities for how architecture might respond to the discontinuities and scalar shifts that constitute the new imaging, not just of a single city, but of all cities linked by the digital network's distributed gaze. At once disjunctive and yet highly connected, this digital topology also dictates unique formal and material assemblies that respond to a highly diverse, dynamic and yet unstable visual context. As Wood noted, 'these interfaces establish the ground from which it is possible to think about the materiality of digital imagery.'[61]

Another clear alignment with Vertovian visual recalibration strategies is the anamorphic operation of digital webcam technology acting in combination with digital geometry. Echoing Vertov, Susan Sontag reiterated the need for visual discontinuity to provoke the viewer's critical awareness by drawing attention to the visual field's constructed artifice. 'But photographic seeing has to be constantly renewed with new shocks, whether of subject matter or technique, so as to produce the impression of violating ordinary vision.'[62] Corresponding to the oblique views generated by linear perspective's previously described anamorphic variant, the public webcam allows the viewer to rotate the camera lens remotely to capture a wide field of view or to 'zoom' in on or magnify an object. Its action is also highly disjunctive. Furthermore, the pixel, the atomic unit of the digital image, is discontinuous and fragmentary by its very nature and actively contributes to the dismantling of a narrative space of viewing. Because the digital image is an array of adjacent but discontinuous pixels already predisposed to arrangement by grouping, it follows that, at a material level, conditions of discontinuity and fragmentation required to produce a jolting effect are therefore intrinsic to it.

As a final comparative point, the digital image takes the notion of multiplied Vertovian viewpoints to another level altogether. Its intrinsic geometry, its transmissibility within a distributed network and the viewing technology's physical action all foster the composite images with multiple authorships that grant new agency, as Martin Hand observed.

> Digitization radically changes the possibilities of reproduction and circulation as the image is detached from its primary material vehicle, altering its status (it can be deleted), who can view it (it can be networked) and how it can be interpreted (it can be simultaneously received and altered).[63]

The problem of the image of the city 21

Yet this condition also potentially informs a new type of architecture. In describing how *Timecode*'s split-screen prefigured the distributed gaze of the webcam network, Wood argued that the multiplication of the film's viewpoints is not only transformative for the viewer, but, even more importantly, generative.

> *Timecode*'s distribution of the viewer's gaze has the potential to be generative rather than dispersive, since it opens the viewing interface to a diversity of possible viewing positions. It is in negotiating these diverse viewing positions that a viewer's agency begins to become apparent.[64]

In a similar vein, the same 'diversity of possible viewing positions' offered by the webcam network is also generative in that it can avail architecture of multiple simultaneous viewpoints along with enhanced agency for the Internet viewer.

The image's repetitive geometric base unit, the pixel and its capacity to assemble into grouped, larger collective forms, also have significant implications for the types of formal conditions that these forms might instigate. By foregrounding qualitative properties of colour and brightness and replacing the linear (x, y) coordinates as the dominant organising principle of image-making, digital geometry shifts the criteria by which content is assembled. This condition similarly reorganises the ways that potentially determine the physical fabric of the city. Most importantly, unlike analogue representation, the intrinsic numerical basis of the qualitative image properties resident in its base unit, the pixel, establishes a new type of indexical relationship between the image and the perceptual, atmospheric effects of the city's material surfaces. Moreover, distinct from analogue procedures, the digital image's indexicality with the city is further influenced by the variability introduced by its multiple authors.

> Digital technologies inevitably break the indexical chain that, in the mechanical age, linked the matrix to its imprint. Digital photographs are no longer the indexical imprint of light onto a surface; digitally manufactured objects are no longer the indexical imprint of a mold pressed into a metal plate: and digital variability may equally cut loose the indexical link that, under the old authorial paradigm, tied design notations to their material result in an object.[65]

The privileging of different image features through the operation of digital geometry not only subjects the viewer to new perceptual conditions but opens up new ways in which the city's material form might engage with these conditions. In Benjaminian terms, these ways follow the 'new law',[66] not of a singular, but a fragmented, 'filmic' space.

The qualitative image and affective space

> Perhaps one of the surest things that can be said of both affect and its theorization is that they will exceed. Always exceed the context of their emergence, as the excess of ongoing process.[67]

A corollary of dismantling singular representational narrative is the dismantling of the known experiential field and the production of affect. Affect is an outcome of Vertov's jolt technique; in visual terms it is unsettling, a response to the removal of the learned receptive pathways where the subject is disoriented and unable to exert a controlled or expected reaction. Gregg and Seigworth described this phenomenon as both complex and omnipresent 'the name we give to those forces – visceral forces beneath, alongside, or generally *other than* conscious knowing, vital forces insisting beyond emotion – that can serve to drive us toward movement, toward thought and extension'.[68]

Here we are concerned with two principal areas of affect. The first, described by Marc Hansen,[69] relates to physical placement in space and deals with the body's capacity for extension beyond its known boundaries, particularly in relation to the computer screen. The second relates to 'generally non-Cartesian traditions in philosophy',[70] evidenced by the work of Brian Massumi. Massumi's work[71] explores affect in areas relating to the human visual system (HVS) optical cues of colour, brightness and shape, and examines human perceptual responses to spatial contexts according to contextual variations within these qualitative visual properties.

The relevance of Marc Hansen's work to the trajectory of this discussion concerns the experiential conditions of affect associated with the use of digital imaging technology and the effects of the webcam's zoom function upon the viewer. The camera's anamorphic pathway through virtual space is aligned with Hansen's notion of an 'affective virtuality',[72] where 'you experience a gradually mounting feeling of incredible strangeness'.[73] Hansen draws upon Robert Lazzarini's anamorphic sculpture *Skulls* (which in turn relates directly to Holbein's anamorphic reference within the painting *The Ambassadors*) to describe and investigate the effects of spatial disorientation invoked by the irresolvable topology of a digital landscape. The viewer's inability to resolve spatial orientation in relation to a digitally generated point of origin, 'the weird logic and topology of the computer',[74] coupled with its limitless variability, releases the viewer from the traditional expectations and experience associated with unambiguous linear perspective space while unleashing a volume of unexplored, new spatial and formal conditions.

The other type of affective response is found in the work of Brian Massumi, which explores the many ways in which the individual perceptual differences between the HVS cues of colour, brightness[75] and shape exceed their generally understood meanings. Drawing upon scenarios in which

The problem of the image of the city 23

perceptual inconsistencies produce an affective and complex outcome within the observer, Massumi argued that it is not possible to extract 'a simplicity from a complexity of experience'.[76] His essay *Too Blue* argues that colour cannot be quantified, its complex properties always resisting its reduction to a single idea:

> The remembered color exceeds the testable meaning of the word ... Between 'blue' used as the trigger for the production of memory, and 'blue' used to test the identity of that memory, something extra has slipped in, which the color-word, as the common property of the experimenter and the subject, does not designate.[77]

Brightness too, a correlate of colour and an equally uncontrollable phenomenon, is presented not as an undesirable visual aberration, but instead as a 'confound', where 'a measurable degree of brightness is an independent *variable*'.[78] Massumi argues against reductive approaches to vision that can only work to normalise the visual spectrum. 'The "anomalies" of vision can't be brushed aside for the simple reason that they are what is *actually* being seen.'[79] Drawing upon scientific research, he concluded that the perceptual processes of shape apprehension are 'visual chaos' in which the object has 'a vague, surfacelike field of objectlike or formlike tendency'.[80] For Massumi, broadening the understanding of the visual spectrum's complexity and an openness to ambiguity are therefore implicit factors in accessing 'the whole universe of affective potential'.[81]

The types of visual ambiguities that Massumi made explicit are also inherent to digital imaging. Because the image's base unit, the pixel, assigns numerical values to the HVS perceptual properties of colour and brightness (and shape, by the association of pixel groupings) on a two-dimensional grid, it follows that conditions of variability and ambiguity relating to these properties are automatically translated numerically as image values. The ambiguity Massumi foregrounded when he wrote of colour and brightness as having 'indistinct'[82] boundaries thus becomes image data and, ultimately, image content. This also means that the digital image has the potential to be highly affective, because it is not tied to a normative visual experience.

With the urban visual field presented according to qualitative visual properties that are readily translatable into data, a new approach to designing its physical surfaces becomes possible. An indexical relationship between the image and the city's viewed surface means that form can affect numerical values within the image. However, for the result to be affective, in the sense that it is '*other than* conscious knowing',[83] the inclusion of visual ambiguity within the material surface of the city needs to be something other than the dictates of the architect's hand. If affect is produced by releasing the image from the constraints of any singular representation of the city and about multiplying the ambiguity and complexity of urban conditions, then it is the capacity of these surfaces to disrupt the singular, visual narrative that will provide it with an appropriate context. The capacity to index the physical surface to qualitative, atmospheric properties of the image and in turn to the vagaries of the HVS, is thus key to any strategy that seeks to interrupt a predetermined visual narrative of the city. In this respect, both the numerical basis of the pixel and the anamorphic capacity of webcam technology ensure that the conditions for implementing such strategies are present and available.

Vertov's call to invest the urban observer with more agency is not only a call to the individual Internet user but the architect: 'with the transition from mechanical to digital technologies, and from identical to variable reproductions, a recast of architectural agency will also be inevitable'.[84] With the Internet user now a potential producer of image content by virtue of the accessibility of digital code, the architecture that might respond to this task is one that resides within and co-opts a high-exposure networked environment witnessed by an unlimited audience. If the following statement is true of the digital image's new status within the public domain, then the same issues are indeed worthy of consideration by the architect: 'the visualization of everything raises questions about who establishes the rules and conventions of vision and to what extent institutional, corporate and state power is increasingly manifest through the management of visual culture.'[85] To engage with the architecture of the city is also now to engage with the relationship between its built surfaces, the cameras that preside over them and the immanent presence of civic ownership. In this new operational frame, a profoundly different toolset is at work. As the base operational unit of the image and its technological procedures, the manufacture and operation of the pixel is the master key to all processes relating to the perception and the assembly of the form within the webcam's visual field.

Chapter 2 explores the unique viewing conditions initiated by the digital image and its authors, identifying key aspects of the image-making process that challenge the traditional relationship between viewer and represented space.

Notes

1 Zoï Kapoula et al., 2009. Eye movements and pictorial space perception: Studies of paintings from Francis Bacon and Piero della Francesca. *Cognitive Semiotics*, 5 (Fall 2009), pp. 103–121.
2 Laurent Itti and Christopher Koch, 2001. Computational modelling of visual attention. *Nature Reviews Neuroscience*, 2 (3), pp. 194–203.
3 Richard Koeck, 2013. *Cine-scapes: Cinematic spaces in architecture and cities.* Abingdon-on-Thames: Routledge, p. 77.
4 Koeck, *Cine-scapes*, p. 72.
5 Jonathan Beller, 2006. *The cinematic mode of production: Attention economy and the society of the spectacle.* Lebanon, NH: University Press of New England.

6 Graham Cairns, ed., 2013. *The architecture of the screen: Essays in cinematographic space*. Bristol: Intellect Books, p. 3.
7 Cairns, *The architecture of the screen*, p. 3.
8 Charles Rice, 2007. Critical post-critical: problems of effect, experience and immersion. In: J. Rendell, J. Hill, M. Dorrian and M. Fraser, eds. *Critical architecture*. Abingdon-on-Thames: Routledge., p. 267.
9 William J. Mitchell, 1992. *The reconfigured eye. Visual truth in the post-photographic era*. Cambridge, MA: MIT Press, p. 134.
10 Martin Kemp, 1990. *The science of art: Optical themes in western art from Brunelleschi to Seurat*. New Haven, CT: Yale University Press.
11 Erwin Panofsky and Christopher Wood, 1991. *Perspective as symbolic form*. Brooklyn, NY: Zone Books.
12 Daniel Cardoso Llach, 2015. *Builders of the vision: Software and the imagination of design* (1st ed.). Abingdon-on-Thames: Routledge.
13 Hubert Damisch, 1994. *The origin of perspective*. Cambridge, MA: MIT Press, pp. 244–245.
14 Damisch, *The origin of perspective*, p. 267.
15 Damisch, *The origin of perspective*, p. 53.
16 Peter Womack, 2008. The comical scene: Perspective and civility on the Renaissance stage. *Representations*, 101, p. 45.
17 George L. Gorse, 1997. A classical stage for the old nobility: The Strada Nuova and sixteenth-century Genoa. *The Art Bulletin*, 79, pp. 301–326.
18 Luke Morgan, 2005. The early modern 'trompe-l'oeil' garden. *Garden history*, pp. 286–293.
19 Gorse, A classical stage for the old nobility, p. 326.
20 Martin Jay, 1988. Scopic regimes of modernity. In: H. Foster, ed. *Vision and visuality*. Seattle: Bay Press, p. 17.
21 Jay, Scopic regimes of modernity, p. 20.
22 Martin Hand, 2012. *Ubiquitous photography*. Cambridge: Polity Press, p. 46.
23 Walter Benjamin, 1979. A small history of photography. *One-way street and other writings*. Brooklyn, NY: Verso, p. 243.
24 Matt Dyce, 2013. Canada between the photograph and the map: Aerial photography, geographical vision and the state. *Journal of Historical Geography*, 39, p. 75.
25 Dyce, Canada between the photograph and the map, p. 81.
26 Louis Kaplan, 2003. Where the paranoid meets the paranormal: Speculations on spirit photography. *Art Journal*, 62, p. 19.
27 Susan Sontag, 1977. *On photography*. London: Penguin Books, p. 86.
28 Nigel Green, 2016. The transformative interface. In: G. Cairns, ed. *Visioning technologies: The architectures of sight*. Abingdon-on-Thames: Routledge, p. 76.
29 Vladimir Rizov, 2021. Eugène Atget and documentary photography of the city. *Theory, Culture & Society*, 38 (3), pp. 141–163.
30 John Fuller, 1976. Atget and Man Ray in the context of surrealism. *Art Journal*, 36 (2), pp. 130–138.
31 Benjamin, A small history of photography, p. 255.
32 Juliana Maxim, 2011. Developing socialism: The photographic condition of architecture in Romania, 1958–1970. *Visual Resources*, 27, p. 157.
33 Maxim, Developing socialism, p. 157.
34 Green, The transformative interface, p. 77.
35 Damisch, *The origin of perspective*, p. 52.
36 Damisch, *The origin of perspective*, p. 55.
37 Nat Chard, 2003. Positioning and the picture plane. *The Journal of Architecture*, 8, pp. 211–220.

26 *Constructed fields of vision*

38 Lyle Massey, 2007. *Picturing space, displacing bodies: Anamorphosis in early modern theories of perspective*. University Park, PA: Penn State Press, p. 109.
39 Massey, *Picturing space, displacing bodies*, p. 68.
40 Jen Boyle, 2010. *Anamorphosis in early modern literature: Mediation and affect* (1st ed.). Abingdon-on-Thames: Routledge.
41 Bryan Reynolds, 2006. *Transversal enterprises in the drama of Shakespeare and his contemporaries*. New York, NY: Palgrave Macmillan.
42 Damisch, *The origin of perspective*, p. 53.
43 Damisch, *The origin of perspective*, p. 52.
44 Sergei Eisenstein, 1977. Piranesi, or the fluidity of forms. *Oppositions*, 11, 103.
45 Yve-Alain Bois and John Shepley, 1984. A picturesque stroll around 'Clara-Clara'. *October*, p. 52.
46 Valeria Carullo, 2016. The great publicist of modern building. In: G. Cairns, ed. *Visioning technologies: The architectures of sight*. Abingdon-on-Thames: Routledge, p. 89.
47 Malcolm Turvey, 1999. Can the camera see? Mimesis in 'Man with a Movie Camera'. *October*, pp. 25–50.
48 David Bordwell, Thompson, K., and Ashton, J. 1997. *Film art: An introduction*. New York, NY: McGraw-Hill. Bordwell et al. describe the jump cut as a technique used to deploy temporal dislocations to remove traditional notions of narrative.
49 Cairns, *The architecture of the screen*, p. 69.
50 Cairns, *The architecture of the screen*, p. 69.
51 Anna Lawton, 1978. Rhythmic montage in the films of Dziga Vertov: A poetic use of the language of cinema. *Pacific Coast Philology*, pp. 44–50.
52 Thomas Sheehan, 2003. Wittgenstein and Vertov: Aspectuality and anarchy. *Discourse*, 24, pp. 97–98.
53 Walter Benjamin, 1936. *The work of art in the age of mechanical reproduction*, Penguin Books, p. 37.
54 Scott McQuire, 2016. Intersecting frames: Film + architecture. In: G. Cairns, ed. *Visioning technologies: The architectures of sight*. Abingdon-on-Thames: Routledge, p. 153.
55 Cairns, *The architecture of the screen*.
56 Cairns, *The architecture of the screen*, p. 39.
57 Cairns, *The architecture of the screen*.
58 Aylish Wood, 2008. Encounters at the interface: Distributed attention and digital embodiments. *Quarterly Review of Film and Video*, 25, p. 223.
59 Cairns, *The architecture of the screen*, p. 70.
60 Christine Boyer, 1996. *CyberCities: Visual perception in the age of electronic communication*. New York, NY: Princeton Architectural Press.
61 Wood, Encounters at the interface, p. 222.
62 Sontag, *On photography*, p. 99.
63 Hand, *Ubiquitous photography*, p. 41.
64 Wood, Encounters at the interface, p. 225.
65 Mario Carpo, 2011. *The alphabet and the algorithm*, MIT Press, p. 43.
66 Benjamin, *The work of art in the age of mechanical reproduction*, p. 37.
67 Gregory Seigworth and Melissa Gregg, 2010. An inventory of shimmers. In: G. Seigworth and M. Gregg, eds. *The affect theory reader*. Durham, NC: Duke University Press, p. 5.
68 Seigworth and Gregg, An inventory of shimmers, p. 1.
69 Marc Hansen, 2004. *New philosophy for new media*. Cambridge, MA: MIT Press.
70 Seigworth and Gregg, An inventory of shimmers, p. 6.

71 Brian Massumi, 2002. *Parables for the virtual: Movement, affect, sensation.* Durham, NC: Duke University Press.
72 Hansen, *New philosophy for new media*, p. 223.
73 Hansen, *New philosophy for new media*, p. 198.
74 Hansen, *New philosophy for new media*, p. 202.
75 In general terms, brightness is the perceptual luminance effect of a source or an object upon an observer. It is an absolute quantity that only depends on the RGB values of the given image. Contrast is the perceptual colour separation between two different colours and is a relative quantity that depends upon the object's background. In this chapter, the term 'brightness' is used directly in relation to the perceptual effects of luminance upon an observer, while 'luminosity' is used in scientific contexts where it is a quantifiable wavelength emitted from a light source (Ferreira, T. and Rasband, W., 2011. *The ImageJ User Guide*. National Institutes of Health, USA).
76 Massumi, *Parables for the virtual: Movement, affect, sensation*, p. 20.
77 Massumi, *Parables for the virtual: Movement, affect, sensation*, p. 210.
78 Massumi, *Parables for the virtual: Movement, affect, sensation*, p. 163.
79 Massumi, *Parables for the virtual: Movement, affect, sensation*, p. 162.
80 Massumi, *Parables for the virtual: Movement, affect, sensation*, p. 146.
81 Massumi, *Parables for the virtual: Movement, affect, sensation*, p. 43.
82 Massumi, *Parables for the virtual: Movement, affect, sensation*, p. 163.
83 Seigworth and Gregg, An inventory of shimmers, p. 1.
84 Carpo, *The alphabet and the algorithm*, p. 44.
85 Hand, *Ubiquitous photography*, p. 27.

2 The pixel's visual territory

> We usually like to think in positive terms about how various parts of systems interact. But to do that, we must first have good ideas about which aspects of a system do not interact ... In other words, we have to understand insulations before we can comprehend interactions.[1]

From analogue to digital

Image formation has been and remains an imperfect process. There is no unique way to infer a scene from its representation. As a solution to this problem, we either gather more data or 'make assumptions about the world',[2] and, generally speaking, these two strategies continue to underpin the principles of image-making. This chapter discusses the correspondence between digital image geometry and earlier image-making techniques, specifically linear perspective painting. It reveals how the new viewing conditions associated with the digital image, unique aspects of its manufacture and structure radically challenge the traditional viewing relationship.

In 1425, Brunelleschi's invention of the linear perspective technique enabled the visible world to be understood according to a new system of points, lines and planes that retain their character under projection. Previously, artists had employed a version of the linear perspective technique known as 'herringbone perspective',[3] in which all lines converge on a vertical axis that runs down the central spine of the painting. However, this technique offered no sense of spatial continuity between the viewer and the picture plane or 'transparent' surface through which the viewer's gaze was directed. Instead, linear perspective projection provided a highly accessible formula for converting three-dimensional form into its two-dimensional counterpart. Furthermore, the technologies of vision that had evolved from their inception in the early Renaissance now provided a highly controlled relationship between the viewer and the image plane.

By contrast, the recent advent of digital technology has meant that the imaging process now undergoes an additional transformation to the one brought about by linear perspective projective geometry post-Renaissance.

DOI: 10.4324/9781003133872-4

Unlike the analogue image, whose medium is physically fixed and does not evolve temporally, the digital image operates within a fluid spatio-temporal context. In this new scenario, the imaging technology is a camera and the image 'plane' a computer screen on which the image can be viewed and adjusted over Internet protocol (IP) networks. Each camera has an IP address and is connected directly to a local area network (LAN) or the Internet, using either a couple charged device (CCD) or complementary metal-oxide-semiconductor (CMOS) image sensor to convert image data into an electronic signal. These data are then transmitted to the host computer.

Furthermore, in the same way that the many elaborate examples of Renaissance and Baroque painting sought to impose a religious metaphor of optical dynamics upon the viewer by using projective geometry techniques, so do the processes of digital image manufacture affect the presentation of urban space. Imaging procedures such as smoothing or averaging, 'noise' removal or filtering, edge detection and contrast enhancement all reflect explicit decisions to ensure control over image quality and content. However, unlike analogous processes in which both the medium and the technology ensured a finite 'snapshot' of space and time, the digital image's structure, and its exposure to a network system, extends the rights of intervention beyond that of a single author, as WJT Mitchell observed:

> The act of publication is an act of closure. You can modify a printed score or text by hand, but this process produces a new (if unoriginal) work, not a redefinition of the existing finished work ... But there is no corresponding act of closure for an image file.[4]

The consequences of this for future ways we engage with the image are twofold. In the first instance, the image's author can accomplish modification (or manipulation) before its release into the public domain. At this point, the image is the original author's property, much in the same way as a painting or a photograph is the artist or photographer's property and therefore subject to the same processes and influences. However, it is also worth noting that at this stage, the image has numerous other hidden authorships embedded within both the software and the hardware that precede any manipulation the artist might undertake. These can result from computer autonomy, the product of the machine set in motion implementing an algorithmic progression, which can give rise to 'glitches' or inadvertent aberrations. Alternatively, they can be the result of deliberate human choice. In the latter case, this can result in an image reflecting imposed normative processes, such as fewer aberrations or 'undesirable' artefacts that might interfere with visibility.

In the second, once the image is launched into the public domain, it is exposed to third-party intervention, or to put it simply, it is public property.

In this case, the operating system forestalls the author's capacity to maintain control over the imaging process by virtue of its public location and open structure. Therefore, once in the public domain it has collective authorship, and succeeding authorships supersede earlier authorships, preventing it from being normalised or stable and thereby establishing its uniqueness.

Unique modes of digital assembly

Photography's fundamental concept has been about light imprinting an image at a specific juncture in space and time. Digital imaging breaks the customary prescription by giving imagemakers authority not only to determine place and time but to control space and time. This is possible because images are formed into a binary numerical code that is electronically stored and available for future retrieval.[5]

The discontinuous digital line

During digital image formation, an integer value is assigned to a pixel to specify tone or colour. A whole image is constructed by assigning colour values to all pixels in the picture-plane grid. At close scale, digital image elements' internal structure, comprising points, lines and planes, is very different from their analogue counterparts. While an analogue element is related to physical quantities, such as the process of translating a video signal into electronic pulses, 'digital' refers to the interpretation of data by a device as binary units, in the form of zeros and ones, to undertake functions and store it in the same format. Precisely speaking, this can be characterised as either degree of continuity or discreteness. Digital geometry comprises discrete sets of numbers or integers combined in grid formation to represent the exact location and time of image or object luminosity in either two- or three-dimensional space.[6] In other words, the digital process is a subset of the measurable Euclidean system in which an object is replaced by a discrete set of its own points on a rectangular grid containing an orthogonal array of pixels or voxels (a voxel is a 'volume pixel' or the smallest distinguishable box-shaped part of a three-dimensional image).[7] The smallest unit within this system, the pixel embeds distinguishing characteristics that distinguish it from the structure, and therefore operation, of linear perspective geometry.

One example concerns the conceptualisation of the line and its trajectory. In linear perspective geometry, parallel lines intersect at the point of infinity rather than abiding by the Euclidean proposition that they never intersect. However, although reliant upon the same perceptual principle, paradoxically, digital lines can cross without intersecting because they are composed of pixel sequences that intersect in segments. There is no common pixel at the intersection point. Put simply, while

The pixel's visual territory 31

these two geometries are perceptually alike, they are structurally radically dissimilar, and it is precisely this structural dissimilarity that describes the digital image's many new representational opportunities.

Qualitative content is connected data

Other properties of connectivity, differentiation and reproducibility, also contribute to the unique perceptual conditions associated with the digital image. Again, they have clear consequences for its role as a representational device.

A point or pixel in the digital plane, as a geometric descriptor, has integer coordinates only. Since a line, whether Euclidean or non-Euclidean, essentially consists of points, its digital representation is a sequence of points whose coordinates can only be two integers, rather than the projective Cartesian coordinates (x, y, z). Therefore, the dissimilarity between a real point and a digital point lies in their coordinate constraints,[8] although the rapid sequence of images generated by contemporary imaging technology does extend the image beyond the x, y digital plane into a third z or temporal plane. **This feature means that the numeric structure of digital geometry can assign precise, layered data to its base compositional element, the pixel, to form a dynamic, time-based data unit.** Importantly, this also means that qualitative image properties such as colour and brightness (luminosity) are assigned to the image at the very forefront of the image-making process, rather than applied retrospectively (and selectively), as they would be in analogue representation.

The discrete point sets or arrays that constitute a digital geometry structure are patterns of elements with specific and well-defined relations. The topological description of these digital patterns is concerned with connections rather than exact distances and angles. Digital connectivity then becomes the determinant of the types of relationships that the pixel can have within the context of any binary image, which has only two possible values for each pixel. These values usually represent colour properties: black and white, although any two colours can be used. In colour pictures, triples of scalar values such as red, blue and green or hue, saturation and intensity represent pixels' values.

The variable element within this connectivity pattern is the number of edges aligned in various combinations with neighbouring pixels. In digital imaging, connectivity has three levels of complexity and operates according to proximity and grey levels' ability to satisfy pre-determined similarity types. Conditions of '4-connectedness', where pixels are connected through edge only, '6-connectedness', where they are connected through a hexagonal format and '8-connectedness', where they are connected through both edge and vertex neighbours, are all highly predictable geometric compositional behaviours that are also highly controllable and editable.

Constructed fields of vision

The predictability of pixel relationships

The opportunity for intervention presented by the connective properties of digital geometry is further reinforced by the definable or finite set of characteristics that determine image assembly. The principle of *'explicit naming'*[9] of groups of elements allows properties to be attributed so that external processes can reference them efficiently. This means that the structure of the digital image is highly accessible precisely because it is identifiable. Conversely, non-digital images do not possess any type of identity; the colour, shape and size of analogue images such as photographs and paintings are continuously ordered, and their limits vague, indeterminate and therefore not finitely differentiated. Unlike their digital counterparts, unambiguous type membership cannot be established between the internal picture components.[10]

Digital images have structural constraints that dictate their mode of assembly and which also make the act of third-party intervention readily accessible and traceable. One of these is the feature that determines continuity. Because pixel sizes are finite and those sizes corresponding to pixel fractions do not exist within the array's scheme of sizes, separations occur between the size-types that the display can generate. The presence of these separations means that each digital 'set' is readily identifiable and unambiguous because it is both finite and discontinuous.

The number of shapes generated by pixel displays is also finite. All of the shapes that a pixel display can generate are analysable into values on a Cartesian coordinate system, and comprise a finite number of positive integer values corresponding to the number of pixels on the screen. The display can therefore generate only a finite number of shape types. The number of colours that digital geometry can instantiate is also finite, because it is limited by its correspondence with the number of binary-code possibilities.[11]

However, perhaps one of the most striking examples of the digital image's capacity to support multiple authorships and interventions involves its reproductive procedure – converting the analogue signal into digital form. The conversion of spatial data into a stream of numbers entails two procedures: sampling (discretisation) and quantisation. In the same way that pixel fractions do not exist within a pixel array's scheme of sizes, giving rise to information gaps, converting the analogue signal into digital form relies upon approximation or algorithmic guesswork to overcome missing data. This occurs because in the discretisation stage the space of the signals is partitioned into classes of equivalence. Subsequently, the following quantisation procedure replaces those signals with a representation of the corresponding equivalence class, in which values from a finite set merely approximate the representative signal values. In addition to this, when the scale of the image is increased, known as the interpolation process, sample points are taken from the original data array, and the values of the unknown pixels in the projected larger array are effectively produced through programmed guesswork.

Ultimately, the digital's refusal to be controlled by any one author and, by extension, normalised, sets it apart from other pictorial production processes. The predictability of the finite numerical values of pixel geometry and the data array's open structure, reliant upon an automated algorithmic procedure, shift the image into a new arena. Here, the image's collective ownership and its alterability open it to diverse applications and generative procedures. In so doing, they establish a new indexical relationship between the image and the surfaces it represents.

Digital geometry's intersection with optical science

A working definition of realism could now be the following: What is realistic is whatever the viewer will accept as such – whatever convinces the viewer enough to suspend disbelief.[12]

Perceptual behaviours

There have been many attempts to define the operation of human perception. The science of optics emerged in the 16th century as part of the Renaissance determination to return to science's Greek origins. This complete science of vision encompassed the nature and behaviour of light and the anatomy and functioning of the human eye. Perception was regarded as a discrete human act activated by a sensory impression.

Recent scientific advances in this area redefine previous optical theories, instead favouring an approach that promotes a direct and active relationship with an object or figure. In previous theories, active optical properties were attributed to objects themselves, much like the Renaissance 'eye beams' where an object possessed inherent optical properties. 'It has been customary to say that perception is something more than sensory impression, that perception is *of an object*, that it corresponds to a stimulating object.'[13] However, Helmholz's reaction-time experiments in the mid-19th century opened up a new empirical approach to understanding human perceptual processes and the 'possibilities of measuring human *decision times*'.[14]

While many perceptual theories have proliferated in the last century, two principal yet contrasting approaches to human vision dominate current scientific discourse.[15] The first of these is a 'top-down' theory, based upon Helmholz's classical constructivist–inferential approach. It was developed by Edwin Boring,[16] whose work distinguished between 'core' and 'context' responses, and elaborated by Rock and Palmer[17] and Gregory.[18] This theory is the forerunner of current constructivist thinking. It claims that perceptual processes are indirect and, depending upon the viewer's expectations and previous knowledge, act in conjunction with information from the stimulus itself. Because this type of visual processing uses contextual information for pattern recognition, it is also connected to the Gestalt psychologists' approach to visual organisation (Wertheimer,[19] Köhler[20] and Kanizsa[21]).

The second dominant perceptual theory is 'bottom-up' or data-driven processing, in which perception commences with the stimulus itself rather than being reliant upon either context or memory. This 'ecological' theory is mainly associated with Gibson's work, *The Ecological Approach to Visual Perception*,[22] arguing that processing occurs only in one direction from the retina to the visual cortex. Each successive stage in the visual pathway carries out an ever more complex analysis of the input.

There have been successive attempts to reconcile these opposing theories based upon their respective advantages and shortcomings, but ultimately current thinking is integrative, merging the two ideas.[23] Norman[24] proposed a cogent argument for a binary ventral and dorsal system, wherein:

> the ventral system performs those functions that supporters of the empiricist/constructivist position claim to be the essence of visual perception, while the dorsal system performs those functions that Gibson and his followers hold to be of central importance in seeing the world.[25]

While taking both theories into account, the discussion of human optics focuses mainly on the ventral system, as Norman identified, which constantly compares the recognition and identification of visual input with existing, stored representations. This is because the ventral system processes are more relevant to the investigation of a condition in which the viewer is either remote or not physically active, such as being seated in front of a computer screen. On this basis, it is assumed that our perception of an object or figure remains constant despite changes in other conditions that might affect sensory impressions relating to this perception. In other words, under certain circumstances, the brain corrects and overrides the initial retinal image perception, correcting it in accordance with stored sensory data. This means that rather than being seen simply as a function of the sense organs, perception is understood as an integrative brain function. Following this theory, contextual conditions relating to a viewed object or figure (such as those that trigger memory) can override the actual physical apparatus that imprints an image upon the retina. As a consequence, this places great emphasis upon context in digital image production.

Drawing directly upon the seminal work of Edwin Boring,[26] the sensory data contributing to perception can be categorized as 'core' or 'context'. Core means any fundamental sensory excitation that initiates perception and connects it directly to the perceived object (i.e. retinal excitation), whereas context refers to the brain's acquired properties specific to a perception event and causes the core information to be modified. Further to this, Kanizsa distinguished the functions of perception as 'seeing' versus 'thinking'.[27] In this scenario, thinking leads to the conception of a spatiotemporal phenomenon based on visual data, while seeing is more immediate and does not require conscious mental effort. However, perhaps the most obviously analogous theory to digital image structure is that of Livingstone identifying three separate brain-processing systems in the core process.[28] One system appears to process information concerning shape perception, a second processes colour information and a third information about movement, location and spatial organisation. According to this theory, contextual properties are associated with colour, brightness and shape clues about the perceived object, and the viewer's past experience exclusively determines all. Consequently, any reduction of context will reduce perception, while an increase of context will increase the perceptual correspondence to the object.

When context takes precedence over the retinal imprint or core perception, phenomena commonly described as visual illusions, ambiguities or inconsistencies also come into play. Perceptual conditions that precipitate this are the size, colour, brightness (luminosity) and shape of both the figure or object and, importantly, its context.[29] The contextual conditions relating to the occurrence of these types of illusory visual phenomena and the identification of digital geometric properties that enhance them are the subject of the remainder of the chapter.

The digital mediation of colour, brightness and shape

> All real recording media, including photographic film, are limited in their range and resolutions ... This means that a recorded image is always filtered in some way.[30]

Technological disruption

The representation process involves a perceptual adjustment by the viewing subject in relation to the object or figure, which an instrument of vision has mediated. The instrument or device has transformed over time from the analogous mechanisms of the Renaissance, which allowed the artist to convert mathematical information into a two-dimensional representation on a physical surface, to the photographic camera, which produced a finely detailed, unbroken sequence of tonal and hue gradations on an emulsion-coated surface. One of many emerging contemporary instruments of vision, the digital webcam produces images encoded by subdividing the picture plane into a finite Cartesian pixel grid and assigning finite intensity values to points (pixels) on this grid. The resulting array is then transmitted electronically to either displays or printed images. Unlike photographs, the fine details in the digital image are approximated to the grid, and the continuous tonal gradients are divided into discrete steps.[31]

Image production operates between the simulated medium and the physical medium. In the simulated medium, the artist or designer extracts information from the natural world to mimic its effects, and the viewer perceives the translation of these effects in the physical medium. However, the similarity between analogue and digital processes ends here. The simulated digital medium has profoundly different implications for the optical reception because it is time-based, which means that the image's visual context is continually changing. Importantly, this means that the digital image, by way of its very mode of production, actively inhibits the eye's tendency to stabilise the image and resolve ambiguity. 'The main function of perception is to decode the transient retinal image in order to achieve constancy: the perception of the external world in terms of its stable and intrinsic characteristics.'[32] In other words, the digital viewing mechanism activates our tendency to allow context to override core retinal imprint. As Barbara Gillam's extensive work in this area reveals, this has further implications for the effects of visual phenomena, such as visual illusions, which are effectively instances of the same optical 'suppression' process. 'Illusions do not result from the movements of the eye; experiments show that the illusions, usually of full magnitude, emerge when a figure is exposed too briefly for the eye to scan it.'[33]

This phenomenon is clearly evidenced by the continually shifting gaze of the many urban webcam sites distributed internationally. One such example is the privately owned Times Square webcam in New York,[34] whose rapid pan-tilt-zoom (PTZ) function delivers repeated instances of camera glitches that are too fleeting for the eye to translate, but which nevertheless are highly disruptive to the visual continuity of conventional footage.

The erroneous visual content becomes incorporated into the event's perception as a powerful, yet momentary and often unseen, transition from 'normal' to aberrant visual content. Intentional or not, this feature introduces a potentially disruptive measure to digital image propagation that disables its capacity to operate as either a stable or 'faithful' index of the city.

Digital colour: Unique translations of digital technology

Colour, one of the principal components of perception, is highly dependent upon context. However, past sensory colour data's immediate presence can also override the retinal imprint and substitute the remembered colour. Edwin Boring gave specific examples of this occurrence in film:

> Twenty years ago the technicolor motion pictures were using only two component hues to make colors that should have been trichromatic. One color was put on each side of the film, and the film had only two sides. It was the blues that were cheated. The colors used were a slightly bluish red and a slightly bluish green, which will mix to give good reds

and greens, poor yellows and very poor blues. What happens is that, under certain circumstances the brain corrects the perception that depends initially upon the size of the retinal image, corrects it in accordance with other sensory data that indicate the distance from which the retinal image is projected.[35]

The ability to control an image's colour and brightness is a huge benefit in image-making because these qualitative factors determine the visibility of a scene's components. For example, in the dynamic red, green and blue (RGB) model used on computer screens, greater intensity of combined individual colour produces greater brightness and therefore greater visibility, while the reverse scenario operates in the subtractive or cyan, magenta, yellow and key (CMYK) model upon which printing and photography are based. In this case, combined colour produces black and therefore diminished brightness. This means that the arrangement and proximity of individual picture components have different implications according to whichever model is used, because certain types of colour adjacencies can produce profoundly different effects upon an object's visibility.

An example of how colour adjacency affects an object's visibility is the phenomenon of successive and simultaneous contrast, in which adjacent and interspersed colours influence a surface's colour appearance. Staring at one of two complementary colours will cause its complement to appear when attention is moved to a neutral ground. For example, staring at red and then focusing on a neutral grey background will cause green to appear.[36] Artists using traditional painting techniques commonly exploit this illusory phenomenon. However, digital technology's ability to manipulate the scale, plus its dynamic temporal operation, strengthen its effect in the following way. The zoom trajectory of the webcam and the ease with which it can shift between colour channel transmission modes (from full colour – RGB – to mono or black and white) mean that the occurrence of a single visual phenomenon frequently occupies the entire screen while the image shifts between colour modes. Consequently, the overriding effect of such visual phenomena can be easily and deliberately introduced into digital transmission systems through the platform's highly accessible structure.

The geometric disposition of the digital image enhances the potency of visual phenomena associated with colour adjacency. This is because its clarity of structure (distinct edges), and the uniform distribution of internal chroma across the pixel, seen when the camera's zoom trajectory is activated, strengthens the relationship between individual pixels' colour effects at close scale.[37]

Unlike painting and photography, in which a close-scale view produces a continuous and more blurred gradation of tone in the picture's elements,[38] the digital image is not limited to the constraint of an 'ideal' viewing position, generating instead ambiguous visual effects throughout a range of viewing distances.

The profoundly different and complex contextual responses engendered by the new colour conditions of the digital present an equally broad range of conditions to anyone who engages with urban representation. They require technology and its supporting software developers to acquire a new awareness of the image's internal dynamic properties. They also ask the same of architects, one of whose important roles is to manage the relationship between the city and its representation. With the digital image now adaptable to the colour and visibility of ever-changing contexts and scales and determined by any number of successive authors during its lifetime, the architect can establish a new mode of exchange between the image's qualitative aspects and their physical counterparts.

Contrast perception, luminosity and the contextual advantages of pixel geometry

Human perception of the contrast of a scene – unlike the perception of shape and colour, which are both heavily driven by context – is largely dependent on the biological procedures of human optics. Perceptual ambiguities of contrast denote certain survival-related biological aspects of vision that enhance our understanding of form.

Lateral inhibition is an optical effect that works inversely to secure a clearer perception of an object. Neighbouring visual neurons respond to a lesser degree if they are simultaneously activated rather than if an individual neuron is activated. In other words, the fewer neighbouring neurons stimulated, the more strongly a neuron responds. This process can be understood in biological terms; the HVS's capacity to respond to a contour's edges is vastly increased because neurons respond to the edge of a stimulus more strongly than to the middle.[39] Examples of this are the Hermann–Hering grid illusion, in which dark illusory spots are perceived at the intersections of horizontal and vertical white bars viewed against a dark background,[40] and Mach bands. In the latter condition, light distribution at a shadow's edge produces bands which mimic the actual pattern of illumination and appear to curve inward or gradate, whereas each is, in fact, a solid colour.[41] Neighbours inhibit these illusions' 'edge' neurons on one side only (the side away from the edge), while neurons stimulated from the middle of a surface are inhibited by the neighbouring neurons on all sides.

All of this has powerful parallels with the digital imaging model's grid matrix, in which the connectivity, and therefore effectiveness, of pixel elements within the data array structure depends upon the number of edges that align in various combinations with neighbouring pixels. In terms of luminosity or brightness, any computer transformation algorithm of a captured image makes neighbouring pixels, or pixels that are alike within a digital image, inhibit each other, which means that difference or 'edge' is strengthened and clearer.[42] By extension, it means that any illusory effect produced by these edge conditions is similarly strengthened.

The pixel's visual territory 39

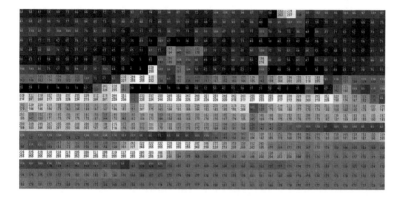

Figure 2.1 Image of Bondi Beach, Australia, generated in PixelMath software. The image shows the distinct edges and the RGB value of each pixel. (Original image source: Google Earth 7.1 (2013), Bondi Beach, altitude 1.31 kms)

Google Earth's zoom capability unveils exactly these parallels between the digital imaging model's grid matrix and the lateral inhibition perceptual ambiguities of the human eye. Figure 2.1, processed through the open-source program PixelMath, shows the numerical assignation of colour values to each pixel. The similarity between the appearance of curvature in the gradation of the clearly defined edges of the individual pixels and the optical phenomenon of Mach bands is obvious. Furthermore, effects such as these emerge at many different scales according to the camera's zoom trajectory and the viewer's engagement with the technology.

So too does the innate structure of the digital image lend itself to occurrences of visual brightness phenomena, in which the core HVS response is once again suspended in favour of context. While they cannot be eliminated from automatic image transmission, unintentional occurrences of diffraction aberrations that profoundly elevate an image's brightness can nevertheless be encouraged. As further examples of the city's abstract, qualitative properties, their inclusion in the canon of digital urban representation only exacerbates the dismantling of any promotional urban view.

Therefore, we see that the digital image's structure endows it with a far greater capacity for qualitative adjustment than analogue modes of image production. At its most basic level, the digital image's geometric arrangement predisposes it to the occurrence of many visual phenomena. At the same time, its technology makes their observation possible at a close scale, and therefore heightens the effect. The ability to identify and control image content, and therefore techniques of representation in an ongoing timeframe, was and is a visual resource unavailable to painters. Most importantly, it is the ability to perceive, know and manage these dynamic

Form perception and the inherent imperatives of pixel geometry

The phenomenal effects of digital colour override the core retinal imprint within both physical virtual contexts, as do several depth-perception cues used for shape identification. The identification of shape or form is the dominant part of the perceptual system, taking precedence over the perception of colour and motion.

Gestalt theory's principles operate similarly to that of optical illusion. Brain operation overrides the perception of the individual components of a figure or object and instead views its parts as a whole. This process of grouping is a stabilising and normative device, probably connected originally to survival. It belongs to our tendency to contextualise this object or figure in terms of a remembered expectation.[43] Specific types of Gestalt grouping principles, such as notions of proximity and similarity associated with the shape or form of objects, operate by transforming the individual parts of an object into the perception of a single entity.[44] However, the functions of Gestalt organisational principles vary greatly between digital and analogue media.

Artists have long grouped pictorial elements in two-dimensional representation according to Gestalt properties of similarity or proximity. This is a strategy used to direct and influence the viewer's gaze, and also acts in conjunction with illusory depth cues such as perspective and contrast. The combination of similarity and proximity has an extremely potent effect upon the viewer, as evidenced by the many painterly masterpieces of the Renaissance and the Baroque in which Gestalt principles of grouping intentionally direct the viewer's gaze to key aspects of composition. The overall 'gestalt' of Paolo Uccello's *The Battle of San Romano* relies upon the salient figures' orientation in the foreground towards one central point. Uccello achieves this through the effect of linear perspective technique acting in combination with Gestalt organisational principles of similarity.[45]

The basic functional unit of digital geometry, the pixel, also favours combinatorial arrangements that connect individual pixel elements into compositional image groups or patterns. Unlike the essential continuous line element of analogue painting or the photograph's uninterrupted tonal gradation, these types of groupings coincide naturally with particular powerful Gestalt groupings of individual elements. Pixel groups naturally align with Gestalt principles, thereby strengthening object perception, because they occur in exclusively finite and mathematical increments defined by their properties of similarity. Furthermore, the interpolation process, in which information is gathered from each neighbouring pixel, determines the propagation of individual elements, meaning that these create mutually detailed contexts based on similarity and proximity of form, colour, contrast and brightness. By extension, a pixel is also interpreted by the prevailing geometry as visual noise and therefore ignored if it has a value that is incongruent with its neighbours in a particular context,[46] thus strengthening the tendency for the viewer to perceive only visible groupings.

Digital geometry, therefore, tends to privilege compelling formal associations of colour, contrast and brightness that are invisible in analogous image-making processes. Moreover, according to Gestalt principles, the digital camera's zoom operation to a close scale makes the alignment of pixels more prominent, producing figural cohesion and strengthening. Conversely, enlargement or a close-up view of the analogue image has a weakening effect, producing new visual information in the irregular and illegible form of tonal gradients, which yield a fuzzier and grainier picture.[47] In this regard, the viewer is compelled to investigate different digital image scales to achieve new and highly phenomenal or 'overriding' experiences of the scene at a close scale, while the analogue viewer is not. The unexplored potency of digital geometry thus resides with its extension of the image's optical range and scale. The continual unveiling of its undisclosed geometries across a temporal frame presents new opportunities to exploit its secrets.

Representation and the pixel's 'symbolic form'

> In the last analysis the sole purpose of 'symbolic forms', their sole product, is just this: *the conquest of the world as its representation*.[48]

Many authors

From the ancients' finite cosmos to the infinitely extendable space of the Renaissance, the contemporary worldview has long influenced the relationship between the viewer and spatial context. By extension, the specific geometric principles and unique viewing conditions associated with it have also influenced its representation.

Any notion of infinite or continuous space was absent in the antique image of space. 'Rather, the totality of the world always remained something radically discontinuous ... bodies are not absorbed into a homogeneous and infinite system of dimensional relationships, but rather are the juxtaposed contents of a finite vessel.'[49] Restricted to a herringbone technique in which the lines of projection converged on a vertical axis at the centre of the picture rather than on a central vanishing point, antique perspective offered no sense of spatial continuity between the viewer and the picture plane. The illusory space of the new perspectival world, however, was infinitely extendable.

> Homogeneous space is never given space, but space produced by construction ... In a sense, perspective transforms psychophysiological space into mathematical space. It negates the differences between front and back, between right and left, between bodies and intervening space ('empty' space), so that the sum of all the parts of space and all its contents are absorbed into a single 'quantum continuum'.[50]

The collapsing of 'psychophysiological' or perceived space required the painting's surface to have a quality of transparency, achieved through both the erasure of the medium of paint and the perception of the artist's hand. Furthermore, with erasure came other political opportunities. Seen in many religious works, such as Andrea Pozzo's 1694 perspective ceiling *The Transmission of the Divine Spirit*, the act of seeing through and beyond the picture plane provided the Church with the means to foster the notion of infinite space, and with it, a single indisputable 'truth'. The intention of this single-point perspective masterpiece was declared by Pozzo himself in the preface to his treatise, *Perspectiva pictorum et architectorum*, to 'draw all the lines to that true POINT, the Glory of GOD', who 'sends forth a ray of light into the heart of Ignatius, which is then transmitted by him to the most distant regions of the four parts of the world'.[51]

Automation further extended the possibilities engendered by illusory space. The *camera obscura*, photography, film and television's perfection of the linear perspective technique all mirrored the natural world while increasingly removing the human agent from the task of reproduction. Now 'more concerned with saleability than with insight',[52] the image was no longer the product of an individual but of many authors. However, if the photographic image's reproducibility extended the authorship beyond a single creator, then the automation of the digital image dispenses with it altogether. 'A flat, isotropic platform where the traditional divide between sender and receiver, or author and audience, is fading.'[53]

In the initial stages of image-making, the digital image is subject to multiple anonymous authorships present in the vast range of decisions embedded during the formative stages of both software and hardware, as Mario Carpo observed: 'this technical state of permanent interactive variability offers unlimited possibilities for aggregating the judgement of many, as theoretically anyone can edit and add to any digital object at will.'[54] Although humans initially author computers and computer-imaging programs and participate in relinquishing an artwork's sole authorship, the image-making process's subsequent automation does not require human intervention. On the one hand, this endows programs with a high degree of autonomy. On the other, digital technology, and more specifically, digital processing, employs erasure or effacement as part of its process. Thus, despite the involvement of human programmers in image pre-production, their collective efforts ultimately erase individual members of the programming class.[55] This twofold process of image 'pre-production' does not have a counterpart in painting. The decision-making process is a discrete procedure, in terms of both authorship and final publication. Similarly, in photography and film, while the pre-production processes can include multiple interventions, there is a final act of publication beyond which alteration does not occur.

Significantly, the automation of the digital image and the erasure of single authorship are accompanied by a reversal of authorial concealment seen in earlier linear perspective painting. Digital publication can never be an act of closure because the image metadata's numeric structure provides a clear trace of its historical intervention and the provenance of the hardware used. These features offer new agency to a distributed collective of anonymous authors, and do the same for designers whose role it is to mediate between the image and urban form. Therefore, it is no longer a singularly manufactured view that describes the city, but the anonymously authored representations of the digital platform that offer it up for consideration. 'To embrace digital authorship in full, however, designers will need to rise to the challenge of a new, digitally negotiated, partial indeterminacy in the process of making form.'[56]

The technical underpinnings of navigating a design pathway between the digital and indeterminacy are the subject of the following chapter.

Notes

1 Marvin Minsky, 1988. *Society of mind.* New York, NY: Simon and Schuster, p. 319.
2 Vishvjit S. Nalwa, 1994. *A guided tour of computer vision.* Boston, MA: Addison-Wesley, p. 4.
3 Hubert Damisch, 1994, *The origin of perspective.* Cambridge, MA: MIT Press.
4 William J. Mitchell, 1992. *The reconfigured eye: Visual truth in in the post-photographic era.* Cambridge, MA: MIT Press, p. 51.
5 Robert Hirsch, 2008. *Seizing the light.* New York, NY: McGraw-Hill, p. 470.
6 Nalwa, *A guided tour of computer vision.*
7 Reinhard Klette and Azriel Rosenfeld, 2004. *Digital geometry: Geometric methods for digital picture analysis.* Boston, MA: Elsevier.
8 Partha Bhowmick, 2009. Evolution of geometric figures from the Euclidean to the digital era. *Proceedings of the First International Conference on Intelligent Human Computer Interaction,* pp. 19–36.
9 D. Marr and H. K. Nishihara, 1978. Representation and recognition of the spatial organization of three-dimensional shapes. *Proceedings of the Royal Society of London. Series B. Biological Sciences,* 200, p. 276.
10 John Zeimbekis, 2012. Digital pictures, sampling, and vagueness: The ontology of digital pictures. *The Journal of Aesthetics and Art Criticism,* 70, pp. 43–53.
11 Zeimbekis, Digital pictures, sampling, and vagueness.
12 Edwin Blake, 1990. The natural flow of perspective: Reformulating perspective projection for computer animation. *Leonardo,* 23 (4), p. 403.
13 Edwin Boring, 1946. The perception of objects. *American Journal of Physics,* 14 (2), p. 99.
14 Ian E. Gordon, 2004. *Theories of Visual Perception* (1st ed.). Hove: Psychology Press, p. 4.

15 Saul McLeod, 2007. Visual perception theory. *Simply Psychology* [online]. Available from: http://www.simplypsychology.org/perception-theories.html [Accessed 17/02/2015].
16 Boring, The perception of objects.
17 Irvin Rock and Stephen Palmer, 1990. The legacy of Gestalt psychology. *Scientific American*, 263 (6), pp. 84–91.
18 Richard L. Gregory, 1997. Knowledge in perception and illusion. *Philosophical Transactions of the Royal Society B*, 352 (1358).
19 Michael Wertheimer, 2012. *On perceived motion and figural organization*. Cambridge, MA: MIT Press.
20 Wolfgang Köhler, 1967. Gestalt psychology. *Psychologische Forschung*, 31 (1), pp. XVIII–XXX.
21 Gaetano Kanizsa, 1979. *Organization in vision: Essays on Gestalt perception*. New York, NY: Praeger Publishers.
22 James Gibson, 1979. *The ecological approach to visual perception*. Boston, MA: Houghton Mifflin.
23 Vicki Bruce, Patrick Green and Mark Georgeson, 2003. *Visual perception: Physiology, psychology and ecology*. Hove: Psychology Press, p. 417.
24 Joel Norman, 2002. Two visual systems and two theories of perception: An attempt to reconcile the constructivist and ecological approaches. *Behavioral and Brain Sciences*, 25, pp. 73–96.
25 Gordon, *Theories of visual perception*, p. 180.
26 Boring, The perception of objects.
27 Kanizsa, *Organization in vision*.
28 Margaret S. Livingstone, 1988. Art, illusion and the visual system. *Scientific American*, 258, pp. 78–85.
29 Boring, The perception of objects.
    Kanizsa, *Organization in vision*.
30 Mitchell, *The reconfigured eye*, p. 114.
31 Mitchell, *The reconfigured eye*.
32 Barbara Gillam, 1980. Geometrical illusions. *Scientific American*, 242, p. 108.
33 Gillam, Geometrical illusions, p. 102.
34 This webcam is available at: http://www.earthcam.com/usa/newyork/timessquare/?cam=tsrobo3
35 Boring, The perception of objects.
    Kanizsa, *Organization in vision*, p. 99.
36 Brian Evans, 1990. Temporal coherence with digital color. *Leonardo*, 23 (6), pp. 43–44.
37 Developed by the University of Washington, PixelMath allows the user to access and manipulate an image's actual pixel values numerically. The software is available at http://pixels.cs.washington.edu/PixelMath/pmdownload/request.php
38 Neo-Impressionist artists developed a technique in which small distinct points of primary colour give the impression of a broad range of secondary and intermediate colours.
39 Richard Gregory, 1997. *Eye and brain: The psychology of seeing*. New York, NY: Princeton University Press, p. 55.
40 Nigel P. Davies and Antony B. Morland, 2002. The Hermann-Hering grid illusion demonstrates disruption of lateral inhibition processing in diabetes mellitus. *British Journal of Ophthalmology*, 86, pp. 203–208.
41 Frederick A. Kingdom, 2014. Mach bands explained by response normalization. *Frontiers in human neuroscience*, 8, p. 843.
42 Mitchell, *The reconfigured eye*.
43 Boring, The perception of objects, p. 107.

44 Richard D. Zakia, 2013. *Perception and imaging: Photography – A way of seeing*. New York, NY: Taylor & Francis.
45 Ian Verstegen, 2010. A classification of perceptual corrections of perspective distortions in Renaissance painting. *Perception*, 39, pp. 677–694.
46 Mitchell, *The reconfigured eye*.
47 Mitchell, *The reconfigured eye*.
48 Ernst Cassirer, 1968. *The philosophy of symbolic forms* (trans. Ralph Manheim), Yale University Press, p. 383.
49 Erwin Panofsky and Christopher Wood, 1991. *Perspective as symbolic form*. Brooklyn, NY: Zone Books, p. 44.
50 Panofsky and Wood, *Perspective as symbolic form*, p. 30.
51 Martin Kemp, 1990. *The science of art: Optical themes in western art from Brunelleschi to Seurat*. New Haven, CT: Yale University Press, p. 139.
52 Walter Benjamin, 1979. A small history of photography. *One-way street and other writings*. Brooklyn, NY: Verso, p. 255
53 Mario Carpo, 2011. *The alphabet and the algorithm*. Cambridge, MA: MIT Press, p. 113.
54 Mario Carpo, 2017. *The second digital turn: Design beyond intelligence*. Cambridge, MA: MIT Press.
55 Jay D. Bolter and Richard A. Grusin, 1999. *Remediation: Understanding new media*. Cambridge, MA: MIT Press.
56 Carpo, *The alphabet and the algorithm*, p. 127.

3 Seeing through digital image-making technology

Colour's transformation

Regarded by contemporary design practice as a supplement to the line, colour has always been relegated to a secondary role in the image. The advent of the digital has only reinforced this tendency, with the proprietary interests of technology manufacturers and the promotional ambitions associated with site ownership reflecting colour's continuing entrapment by what Jonathan Crary described as 'forms of power that depended on the abstraction and formalization of vision'.[1]

The dominance of line over colour in pictorial representation has a long history. For Aristotle, visual clarity was of the highest value, a preference that persisted in the aesthetic thought of Alberti, Thomas Aquinas and the luminaries of the High Middle Ages. Consequently, the line was regarded as a more appropriate vehicle for truthful representation than colour.[2] The reflections of Renaissance artists such as Leonardo da Vinci further reinforced this view. Unable to resolve his colour observations into a coherent theory, da Vinci instead advanced light and shade as the primary visual components of representation.[3] Leonardo's use of the *sfumato* technique, which subordinated colour to tone, tied him to Aristotelian scales of colour value and contributed to his increasing confusion, as Martin Kemp noted.

> The problem with light and colour was that the phenomena – even for Leonardo – proved to be particularly intransigent whenever he tried to effect a three-fold union between the observed effects, Aristotelian science and the painter's practice. This intransigence became more rather than less of a problem as his understanding of colour science gained in sophistication.[4]

The inability to resolve this issue differentiates Leonardo from his Italian predecessors. It also foreshadows colour's new mode of expression in the work of Turner and the Impressionists, and its central role in the generation of De Stijl form. The difference is that the Quattrocento painters attempted

DOI: 10.4324/9781003133872-5

to represent objects as they knew them to be, whereas Leonardo sought to represent objects' optical effects.[5] In other words, by presenting the world perceptually rather than conceptually, and using colour effects to establish a new interactive relationship between the artist and his subject, Leonardo, and others after him, was able to unleash colour's affective capabilities.

Gage's essay broadly divides Western colour theory – from antiquity to the present – into two distinct phases, pivoting on Newton's work.[6] Until the 17th century, the concern was with colour's objective status and its organisation into a coherent relationship system. By contrast, post-Newtonian approaches to colour, seen in works such as Goethe's *Farbenlehre*, were preoccupied with understanding colour's mediation by mechanisms of vision and their effect upon the viewer. The increasing emphasis upon the subjective aspects of vision as an effect of developing visual technology is dealt with in depth in Jonathan Crary's *Techniques of the observer*.[7] Revealing how 19th-century experimentation completely transformed the notion of vision, Crary argued that the earlier *camera obscura* model, which subordinated vision to a 'truthful' image of the world, was overthrown by a perception-based model. 'The body that had been a neutral or invisible term in vision was now the thickness from which knowledge of the observer was obtained.'[8] The role of passive observer had been converted into that of an autonomous producer, able to adapt to new functions of the body and different modes of social intercourse that were evolving out of experimentation and innovation and demanding new articulations of languages and forms. The response can be seen clearly in the works of Goethe and Turner, especially the latter, in which 'irrevocable loss of a fixed source of light' and 'the dissolution of a cone of light rays' testify to the breakdown of a model that had, until then, separated the observer from the site of optical experience.[9] Underpinned by Leonardo's much earlier experimental *sfumato* techniques, Turner's work paved the way for new articulations of painting, and, ultimately, its emergence in the architectural discourse of the Modernist period.

Colour as form

In a parallel world of architectural representation, Leon Battista Alberti continued the Aristotelian tradition of regarding colour as a property of an object's surface rather than a perceptual phenomenon. His 1435 treatise, *De pictura*, discouraged artists from either enjoying or recording the contextual environmental effects of colour.[10] Architectural form, seen in the notion of the *città ideale* in works such as the Urbino, Baltimore and Berlin panels and the works of later Baroque and Rococo artists, was presented in the neutral tones of its own composite natural materials. Colour continued to provide a blank canvas against which brightly clad figures were thrown into sharp contrast.

However, Quatremère de Quincy's 1832 discovery and subsequent publication of ancient polychrome statuary, in conjunction with the ensuing widespread polychromy debate,[11] reversed the tradition of colour suppression seen in previous representations of classical architecture. Arguing that colour had been applied ubiquitously to ancient temples and buildings for aesthetic and status-based reasons, de Quincy proposed that the 'colourless' architecture of the 19th century would have appeared not only unusual to the ancients but impoverished.[12]

Nevertheless, de Quincy's revelations did little to shift colour away from its marginal, decorative role. 'Gradually colour became accepted, but often on the periphery of mainstream artistic practice – regarded at best as an interesting oddity.'[13] It was not until JMW Turner's work that a heightened awareness of the role of colour in painting began to emerge. Locating the experience of vision within the body as a perceptual phenomenon that produced 'chromatic' rather than 'formal' events,[14] Turner's paintings began to reverse the longstanding hierarchy of line and colour. In his later works, colour's release from coherent form liberated it from its former association with worldly objects. Importantly, it also freed its affective properties, as did the works of the Impressionists. In their quest to re-establish colour as a primary organising element of representation, this group of artists completely rejected its association with solid objects,[15] thus freeing it from any association with inherent symbolism.

The convergence of art movements that took place at the beginning of the 20th century produced painting that was exclusively non-figural. As Eugene Elliott noted, 'it was, of course, in the pursuit of non-representational painting that the possibilities of composition by color contrast could be explored most freely, liberated from the object.'[16] Colour was understood to provide access to an inner reality, with its properties able to convey complex everyday experience.[17] The advent of Modernism and abstract painting extended these notions in artists such as Wassily Kandinsky, who believed that colour could directly and immediately influence the observer without acquired memory or experience.

By the time of Van Doesburg's 1923 De Stijl manifestos and the establishment of the Bauhaus, colour had been established as the primary mechanism linking space and time. 'The new architecture permits colour organically as a direct means of expressing its relationships within space and time. Without colour these relationships are not real, but *invisible*.'[18] For the Bauhaus practitioners, by converging art and life in the tectonic, colour had become the means of remaking the everyday. This notion gave rise to various attempts at establishing an operable colour 'doctrine' within the Bauhaus, with Itten and Kandinsky investigating the creation of a 'scheme of equivalents' between 'basic' colours and 'basic' forms.[19] However, attempts at standardisation undermined the very objective of the Bauhaus artists: the release of colour's affect.

By attempting to establish an objective basis for the application of colour, the Bauhaus artists were binding it to an idealised model rather than allowing its properties of chroma, contrast and brightness to unfold as part of a natural context. As a result, all perceptual inconsistencies were regarded as a reflection of uncertainty, instability and a departure from the normalised model, reviving, yet again, colour's history of marginalisation. This can be seen in a plastic formal translation in the work of architect Gerrit Rietveld, who regarded colour as necessary only if the physical organisation of a space did not demonstrate the appropriate characteristics.[20] 'I see in every direct application of the compositions of Mondrian to architecture the danger of a rapid shift to decorative prettiness, and this precisely by virtue of the very analytical beginnings of De Stijl.'[21]

Rietveld used colour in his Schröder House to demarcate physical space in the same way that Mondrian used it to compose his paintings' relational content. Citing Van der Leck, a De Stijl writer of the time, Yves-Alain Bois revealed how those in the Bauhaus saw this as a triumphant moment of artistic unison, due to the 'flatness' of both the painting's planar surface and the architectural elevation combining into the 'zero degree of their art ... because its means of expression have been purified'.[22] Van der Leck saw this as the erasure of linear perspective representation; interchangeable in art and architecture, the flat plane now carried the entire responsibility of presenting and re-presenting a spatial continuum.

> The description of time and space by the means of perspective has been abandoned: it is henceforth up to the flat plane to transmit the continuity of space .... Painting is today architectural because in itself and by its own means it serves the same concept – the space and the plane – as architecture, and thus expresses 'the same thing' but in a different way.[23]

Paradoxically, both Braque's and Picasso's attempts to dissociate literal surface from depicted surface using either coloured or non-coloured planes, a technique extensively explored by Mondrian, meant that the observer was denied any autonomous engagement with the work. Referring to Mondrian's *New York City I*, Bois argued that by contesting the painting's material identity and its 'geometric cohesion', the artist wanted to establish an opaque surface that was optically impenetrable, one in which the affective qualities of colour were erased. 'It is as though in New York Mondrian wanted to travel in reverse along the path that had led, in Mantegna's epoch five centuries earlier, to that piercing – that annihilation – of the painting's plane.'[24] By quantifying and 'purifying' colour, the Bauhaus artists had unwittingly produced the very reverse of their original intention.

50 Constructed fields of vision

The digital manipulation of colour

Proprietary colour

The historical relegation of colour to secondary status continues in the digital image. With mediating technology now able to offer a vast range of colour nuances, its production tends to be inflected towards the proprietary interests of the camera and software manufacturers.

The specification of colour in digital image-making devices is notated according to the idea of a 'colour space' representing the human perception[25] of the visible electromagnetic spectrum.[26] Colour can be assigned to an object in different ways. Tkalcic and Tasic proposed dividing colour spaces into three distinct categories distinguished by their respective relationships to the HVS and their device dependency. These are HVS colour spaces, principally phenomenal spaces motivated by the conditions of the HVS, such as the device-dependent RGB colour space; application-specific colour spaces, also device-dependent, including spaces taken from television (TV) systems, photosystems and printing systems (CMYK); and device-independent Commission International de l'Éclairage (CIE) colour spaces,[27] using 'tristimulus values',[28] proposed in 1931.

The RGB colour space tends to organise colours according to hue, saturation and brightness, based upon human perception. Unlike physical quantities such as intensity and luminance, these perceptual quantities cannot be measured. 'The temporal structure of the sub-pixel values varies wildly between different types of displays and can have a great effect on the eye's perception of the display.'[29] The RGB trichromatic theory, based on the work of Maxwell, Young and Helmholtz, identifies three types of photoreceptors, approximately sensitive to the red, green and blue regions of the spectrum. The 'additive' mixing of colours occurring on self-luminous displays means that light spectra of the three light beams combine, wavelength for wavelength, to compose the spectrum of the final colour: black is the least bright colour and white is the brightest colour.[30]

Furthermore, the RGB or additive colour model correlates with receptor cells in the human eye that respond preferentially to red, blue and green wavelengths of light. For three monochromatic sources with the same radiant power, green will appear the brightest, red will appear less bright and blue will be the darkest.[31] The privileging of green by both the eye and autofocus systems not only means that other colours are defocused, leading to chromatic aberrations, but reinforces the effect of other perceptual issues, such as the eye's poor acuity for colour relative to luminance.[32] In response to this shortcoming, Livingstone[33] has shown that movement or stereopsis in combination with colour can enhance an object's visibility. So, while compensations for diminished acuity can always be made in the pursuit of enhanced colour, the specific properties of the HVS acting in combination with the RGB colour space administered by digital technology have profound implications for image content.

The addition of a particular mapping function between a colour model and a colour space produces a defining gamut or footprint within that space, and is specified by the software producer. Proprietary processes are often under-researched and exclusively product-driven, as Barneva and Brimkov revealed:

> The industry usually requires [laboratories] to produce software in very short periods of time without serious research. Unfortunately, in many cases this leads to lowering the quality in terms of time and memory efficiency of the developed algorithms and of the accuracy and reliability of the obtained solutions.[34]

A further variant of the RGB colour space, the standard RGB (sRGB) colour space, was created cooperatively by the Hewlett-Packard and Microsoft corporations for Internet use.[35] The Adobe RGB colour space is yet another. The following examples illustrate just a few ways in which software, in conjunction with proprietary hardware, operate to control and delimit the experience of colour.

Adobe Creative Suite's Photoshop software is a powerful image processing tool that allows the user to manipulate all aspects of the image's internal architecture, namely, the shape of content, luminance or brightness, colour and basic pixel geometry. As part of the software package, and to reduce the occurrence of so-called 'aberrant' colour combinations, Adobe introduced secondary software, Kuler, to guide the user through over a million predetermined colour schemes. These can then be exported directly to other Adobe family members. (Kuler is only one of many freeware applications that make stable colour solutions available to designers. ColorSchemer Studio[36] identifies colour harmonies for the web (RGB) or print (CMYK), creating palettes from photos using over a million pre-existing colour schemes.) The colour schemes are based on thematic 'harmonious' assumptions made by Adobe to achieve a particular response to either a location or a product. However, the software compliances that produce the predictable colour behaviour demanded by hardware manufacturers are often based upon outdated and highly prescriptive theories of colour, which need revision.[37] Thus, in the same way that the Bauhaus' attempts at standardisation prevented the release of colour's affective potential, so do the prescriptive, normalising protocols embedded in digital image production diminish both its representational agency and atmospheric impact.

Colour by guesswork

The detection of embedded colour production protocols is more complicated than it first appears. The processes associated with image reception and transmission, or the image 'pipeline', are highly deterministic precisely because they are hidden. Certain assumptions are made to bridge the gap between the image-making source (the camera), the image renderer (the computer screen) and the viewer. One of these, sub-sampling, is a filtering process that exploits the reduced human capacity for colour acuity relative to luminance, discarding chroma samples at the video decoder to achieve higher speed and more efficiency. The missing samples are then 'guessed' or approximated by an interpolation algorithm in a demosaicing process.[38,39,40] A key component of this process, the CCD or CMOS sensor, contains grids of pixels used as light-sensing devices for image interpretation. The grid's hundreds of individual pixels are arranged in horizontal and vertical directions over the sensor area, with a colour filter array (CFA) located above the pixel sensors to capture colour information for conversion to a full-colour image. The most common array is the Bayer CFA, with a pattern of 50% green, 25% red and 25% blue, based on the greater optical capacity of the human eye to resolve green light. The Bayer array is only one of many possible CFA distributions, but is regarded as the optimal arrangement of three colours on a square grid.[41] The CFA's location above the image sensor allows only one colour measurement at each pixel: red, blue or green. However, image reconstruction requires three colours per pixel to output an image. Therefore, to achieve a high-resolution image, the other two colours must be estimated using a demosaicing algorithm to complete the interpolation process.[42] Of the many interpolation algorithms used, the simplest is nearest-neighbour interpolation, which replicates an adjacent pixel of the same colour channel. In contrast, bilinear interpolation computes the red value of a non-red pixel as the average of the two or four adjacent red pixels, and similarly for blue and green.

The problem with these pipeline processes is not only that they are hidden, but that they do not disclose the history of the image's data processes. Therefore, it is reasonable to speculate that the intention behind the highly automated process of image production is to ensure the image's colour aligns with the promotional interests of site ownership. This also applies to features of image-making hardware, such as the CFA, whose composition is geared primarily towards generating maximum brightness and clarity and eliminating any artefacts.

This raises the issue of how to find alternative ways to represent the city's many qualitative variables and its 'complexity of experience'[43] using a digital network that continues to mediate the colour of real objects. With the ambition of forestalling the inherent colour assumptions and constraints of proprietary software and hardware, the following part of this chapter explores aspects of digital technology that open new possibilities for architecture's re-engagement with colour.

New digital opportunities

Non-proprietary colour and open-source code

> If architects today wanted to prove themselves equal to the new technologies ... they would make the software themselves, they would get back inside the machine. Penetrate the machine, explode it from the inside, dismantle the system to appropriate it.[44]

The source code of open-source software is free to users and developers alike. Its associated collaborative communities offer development support and mean that future enhancements are not dependent on the decisions of a single organisation. Open-source code enables colour's release from some of the constraining aspects of proprietary software. Many open-source software programs avail themselves of the open-source GNU/Linux code to avoid the numerous image 'enhancement' decisions embedded within it. For example, GIMP[45] is a freely distributed expandable and extendable program that allows the user to undertake image manipulation at all levels of complexity, including photo retouching, image composition and image authoring. Others, such as Color Blender[46] and Pipette,[47] operate exclusively to override any default hardware colour choices, allowing the user to access the image's internal colour geometries, thus controlling the predictive assemblies of multiple colour palettes.

However, the hidden choices embedded in the more inaccessible regions of the image processing pipeline pose the greatest obstacle to disclosure of the secrets of the image-making process. To date, proprietary software manufacturers have discouraged intervention because the colour interpolation process, being tied to product copyright, is automated. 'In practice, it is extremely rare to have access to any history of the processes to which image data has been subject, so no systematic approach to enhancement is possible.'[48] However, another cross-platform image-processing program, Raw Therapee,[49] intervenes at the beginning of this process, allowing 'raw' or untampered files to be read by the computer. This program gives the user advanced control over the colour interpolation procedure, enabling the use of various algorithms rather than being subject to the camera's built-in code.

While the specificity of open-source software makes it a universally useful imaging tool for architecture, its operational framework is often shared with other disciplines. An example of this is the tracking and mapping of disease progression or remission, commonly referred to as diagnostic imaging. This software genre demands a high degree of accuracy, producing a reality index specifically configured to the delivery of raw images that avoid

54 Constructed fields of vision

deliberately introduced figural ambiguities, such as enhancement. An example is ImageJ, open-source Java-script software that allows custom acquisition, analysis and processing plug-ins to be developed using an internal editor and Java compiler.[50] The specific problem set addressed by diagnostic imaging is temporal-based analysis, or put simply, the observation of change over time. The conditions identified by progressions of colour, brightness (luminosity) or density in a disease analysis context are easily transposable to a context of constantly shifting urban space. Importantly, the digital translation of these properties into data components – particularly colour, because of its highly qualitative nature – releases their potential to underpin a new mode of urban representation.

Exploiting CFAs

The CFA's role in the interpolation process is crucial to the determination of colour within the image.[51] The process's highly automated nature, in which two missing colours at each pixel must be estimated using an algorithm, places it at the generative centre of image content. Simultaneously, it raises questions about its uncontested structure and the impact of variations of this structure. The numerous CFA pattern arrangements that could outperform the traditional Bayer CFA pattern remain invisible to the camera user and unexplored. Before Lukac and Plataniotis published their seminal examination of 10 patterns, only the Bayer pattern had ever been the subject of investigation: 'there is no known work addressing the performance issues for other CFA's [sic] ... in such a comprehensive and systematic way.'[52] In the absence of any 'perfect' CFA, Lukac and Plataniotis' investigation of 10 variants of the RGB CFA proposed a new hierarchy of CFA contributions to the sensor pipeline that can profoundly influence its performance. John Savard presented further variations of the pixel distribution of these patterns,[53] proposing unprecedented combinations involving pixel breakdowns into secondary RGB colours, some of which extend pixel geometry beyond its traditional square into hexagonal or round forms. Savard and Li[54] revealed that while these shapes do, in fact, enhance the interpolation process, their incorporation into standard hardware remains delimited by the latter's display capability.

To some extent, the manufacture of digital colour offers a counter to Mario Carpo's contention that 'architects that by choice or by necessity intervene in someone else's digital design environments are to some extent only secondary authors – end users and not designers'.[55] Digital technology's open-source software and hardware variants can forestall the deliberate exclusion of an extensive and uncurated range of urban colour and its artefacts by destabilising attempts to align urban representation with deterministic codes or proprietary concerns. However, colour is just one of the factors that contribute to the restoration of disciplinary agency.

The remainder of this chapter presents further alternative representational environments that can be accessed by exploring opportunities associated with the camera's appropriation of HVS brightness and shape cues and the release of the city's qualitative properties.

The digital perception of brightness

> Like single-point perspective, clearly directional lighting limits the capacity of the viewer to interpret the image freely by moving around it.[56]

While our perception of shape relies heavily upon context, our perception of the brightness and contrast of a scene is principally related to two independent and opposing factors: optical glare and spatial contrast.[57] Intraocular veiling glare reduces the range of luminance on the retina,[58] while the effect of simultaneous contrast works directly against it to increase perceived differences. In other words, the positive effect of contrast cancels out the negative effects of glare.[59] Also, as if to reinforce this feature, the retinal cell does not respond to uniform light across the field of vision; instead, it is highly stimulated by edges and responds most powerfully to a white object in a black field.[60] Therefore, our understanding of either black or white is based on a comparison of the range of intensities in a scene rather than on the notion of the darkness or lightness of any individual element within it.[61] Furthermore, the HVS's colour receptor mechanism is organised in what Jameson and Hurvich described as a 'parallel processing' format, in which three independent physiological pathways 'report' on white or black, yellow or blue and green or red.[62] In this hue-coding system, three pigments activate three kinds of cell systems. In one kind, the black or white type, the three inputs have exactly the same effect on the cell and do not differentiate according to wavelength. This is the cell that codes luminance, or brightness, the range from black through grey to white.

Shifting the register: The pictorial application of brightness

Unlike traditional pictorial representation, which is limited to a low contrast range, the HVS system can cope with a vast range of luminous intensities. Image-makers have always had to find ways to compensate for this discrepancy. In pre-Renaissance representation, artists used only uniform illumination to render scenes and could not overcome painting's low dynamic range. However, from the 15th century, technical innovations such as oil paint replacing egg tempera and canvas replacing wooden picture panels introduced transparency and translucency into the artist's repertoire of techniques. These devices elevated a painting's dynamic range, or range of luminance, through local spatial manipulation. The switch to canvas from wooden painting panels also reversed the tonal gradient of the image's ground, and meant that artists could create a composition that established brightness as the central visual point of the painting. This liberated landscape from the subordinate role it had previously played, paving the way for the more sophisticated alignments of painting's dynamic range and the HVS that came with the *chiaroscuro*[63] technique.

However, it was Leonardo da Vinci's use of the *sfumato*[64] technique that comprehensively subordinated painting's colour to its tonal value. His preoccupation with optics meant that subjects were affected by changes in contextual luminosity, and hues were toned down to respond to changes in light, resulting in black and white dominating over colour. 'Objects no longer have a basic color but become a field for a subtle play of varied colors.'[65] The *chiaroscuro* technique therefore not only signified the separation of light from colour[66] but the extension of painting's dynamic range using new mechanical techniques. Developed further in the Baroque period by artists such as De La Tour, von Honthorst and Rembrandt, the manipulation of the material medium and the struggle to capture a high dynamic range scene in low-range reflective paint meant that light could occupy as little as one-eighth of the picture surface. Throughout this period, between 1590 and 1725, *chiaroscuro* techniques were developed to contextualise much larger scenes. In Giovanni Fumiani's 1680–1704 ceiling fresco of *Il Martirio di San Pantaleon*, an elevation in the fresco's overall luminance register signifies the division of the two spheres of heaven and earth. Fumiani's highly articulated classical structures stand in sharp contrast to the 'unknowable' contours of the celestial realm, which is flooded with brightness. Il Correggio's *Assumption of the Virgin* (1526–1530) utilises a similar shift in the painting's tonal gradient in a bid to elevate its dynamic range to a level that exceeds the luminance legibility of the HVS (Figure 3.1).

In contrast to smaller works, in which the darkest part of the painting's dynamic range is black and outside the HVS's capacity to distinguish form, the overall ratio of darkness to light in these large frescoes is adjusted so that even the darkest areas of the painting remain visible. Suppressing the work's figural content by favouring its affective properties was therefore an unprecedented strategy that allowed both perceptual mechanisms of the HVS – spatial contrast and optical glare – to be addressed simultaneously. It also found its way into architectural manipulations of fenestration and interior lighting, intended to extend and enhance a building's spatial qualities. The use of interior materials such as marble or stucco in contrasting dark and light colours, or alternatively in uniform colour, in churches such as Sant'Andrea della Valle in Rome, was intended to give the feeling of increased space[67] and to mimic the illegible brightness of heaven.

The deliberate incorporation of optical glare into representations of the city through the manipulation of dynamic range came to be understood as merging the heavenly and earthly through the joint operation of colour and light. This continued through to the 19th century in JMW Turner's works, in which the deliberate inclusion of optical glare artefacts offered an

Digital image-making technology 57

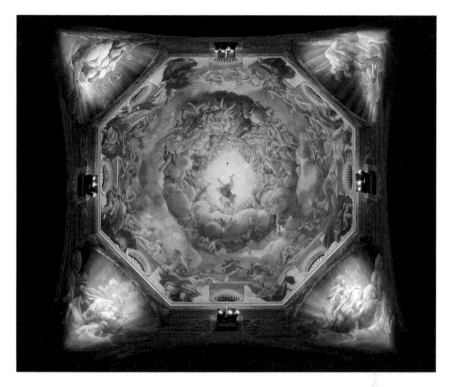

Figure 3.1 Antonio da Correggio, *Assumption of the Virgin*, 1526–1530.
Source: Wikimedia Commons. Photographer: Livioandronico 2013.

enhanced viewing experience. The Impressionist artists' use of short brushstrokes of pure unmixed colour was similarly intended to produce an intense colour vibration effect, using an optical mixture to supersede the traditional mix of colour pigments in the palette.[68] Here the two dominant HVS perceptual mechanisms affecting the reception of contrast and brightness – spatial contrast and optical glare – operate in a united attempt to bring painting's dynamic range in alignment with the HVS.

> Contrast effects are effects of spatial interactions and spatial interactions imply a dependence on spatial dimensions. If these dimensions are sufficiently small, as in the separately painted and differently coloured dots of a pointillist painting, then contrast gives way to spatial mixture. If one stands at a sufficient distance from a painting such as Seurat's *Grand Jatte*, the size of the individual pigment dots is so small and the grain of adjacent image elements on the retina is so fine that they are not resolved as separate elements but rather blend as in a superimposed light mixture.[69]

Monet's *Rouen Cathedral* series exhibits a technique that exploits the latent additive light properties of the material paint medium in a way only seen in the mechanism of contemporary digital cameras. Monet's masterly use of paint works against the medium's limitations so that the eye responds as if the individual points of the painting had been superimposed as if in an additive mix of light.[70] While this technique allowed content to be addressed in a completely new way, such that the formal clarity or *disegno* of the image was subordinated to the eye's optical performance, the perceptual effects of contrast and brightness were nevertheless dependent upon the distance from which the work was viewed. Notably, despite the advances in brightness-related techniques, the observer remained subject to the physical dictates of traditional pictorial representation.

Eliminating the uncontrollable: Brightness as an artefact

With the advent of photography and its capacity to deliver a higher reproductive accuracy index, any luminosity exceeding certain specific perceptual limits became regarded as unwanted glare. The attempt to return the image to scientific principles that could produce an exact 'replica' of a real-time scene also demanded the 'cleansing' of the image's more obvious aberrant properties, effectively reversing earlier artists' approaches to spatial contrast and brightness. Because negatives are designed to capture all the information in a scene, replicating reality became more feasible, particularly when undertaken in conjunction with retrospective technical editing and enhancement. In this context, excessive brightness came to be regarded as an aberration or an undesirable artefact. McCann and Rizzi defined glare as 'an uncontrolled spread of an image-dependent fraction of scene luminance caused by unwanted scattered light in the camera and in the eye'.[71] The desire to eliminate glare led to the development of a new process called high dynamic range (HDR), in which three or more photographic exposures are superimposed at different exposures to manage any extreme difference between low and high levels of brightness,[72] while spatial contrast became highly controllable and unambiguous through local spatial manipulation. The desire to replicate reality through the camera mechanism ultimately superseded the pursuit of optical effects through the medium of paint. In so doing, representation also became less concerned with the experiential effect of the synthesis of colour and light's interaction with the eye and more preoccupied with representation of a scene's 'truth'. This led to the erasure of any image property that might diminish an exact reproduction of a scene or inhibit its legibility.

While painting and photography have continued to operate as parallel modes of representation, the camera-generated image has resisted the incorporation of colour and brightness-related ambiguity. With the exception of more recent contemporary approaches to image manipulation that actively explore the structural principles associated with digital image manufacture, such as the work of Thomas Ruff, the perceptual aspects of the image, and certainly its brightness, remain tightly controlled and geared to optimise HVS perception. However, to recall Brian Massumi's observation, the anomalies of vision nevertheless remain part of the whole visual spectrum and are 'what is *actually* being seen',[73] and it is these anomalies that remain unpredictable and uncontrollable.

Fraunhofer diffraction as a productive aberration

Of the numerous artefacts to be avoided in the current pursuit of image perfection, the most threatening are the products of spatial contrast and optical glare: chromatic aberration and lens flare or diffraction.[74] Fraunhofer diffraction occurs when the luminance range of scattered light falling on the camera's image sensor exceeds its measurement capability,[75] because camera response functions are tuned to perform in low contrast, uniformly illuminated scenes specifically designed to avoid optical overload or 'glare spread function'.[76]

To maintain the image's integrity, camera manufacturers tend to avoid diffraction at all costs, with contemporary digital camera lenses explicitly designed to minimise production of diffraction. In such a context, the output of the distributed digital camera network controlled by proprietary authorities has thus become a highly controlled and normalised product, avoiding anything other than an ideal presentation of the city. Therefore, today's webcam image only incorporates high levels of brightness when there is a desire to present the city as an exciting tourist venue and thus brightness becomes associated with the more dynamic aspects of city life.

However, certain aspects of the camera's function, acting in conjunction with the behaviour of light, are elusive and unable to be eliminated. The fact that light passes through the camera lens exposes the image to all the effects and potential aberrations of the external physical world. The most significant of these are the countless permutations of Fraunhofer diffraction brought about by shifts in light over 24 hours, or for that matter, through seasonal changes that cannot be compensated for in advance.[77] Therefore, in the same way that the Impressionist painters exploited the additive colour model's effects to address the perceptual effects of colour in painting, so is the formal clarity or *disegno* of certain digitally produced RGB images subordinated to optics. Furthermore, because the perceptual effects of brightness and contrast in this environment can vary according to the distance from which the work is viewed, the camera's zoom mechanism enhances the intensity of the diffracted digital image's perceptual effect. In other words, 'unwanted' optical diffraction effects, facilitated by the camera's zoom mechanism, can release new and hitherto ignored properties of the city. In the same way that Turner's departure from traditional approaches to colour, light and form extended the mechanical properties of the paint medium beyond the physical dictates of tradition to unleash the city's affective properties, so does the digital camera's vulnerability to the unregulated occurrence of so-called 'aberrant' digital image exceed its commonly accepted acuity threshold. In so doing, it offers further untapped opportunities for the release of the city's qualitative properties.

Digital image legibility: Shape

> There remain certain classes of problems that appear to be fundamentally beyond the capacity of the digital computer. In fact, the very problems that are most difficult for computers to address, such as extraction of spatial structure from a visual scene, especially in the presence of attached shadows, cast shadows, specular reflections, occlusions, and perspective distortions, as well as the problems of navigation in a natural environment, defined by irregular and fragmented forms, and so on, are problems that are routinely handled by biological vision systems, even those of simpler animals.[78]

The human perception of shape

The HVS's explicit purpose is to exploit the perceived distribution of light to construct mental representations of natural scenes. These can, in turn, be reinterpreted and represented in pictorial form.[79] This system's biological functioning has sparked much debate about a disparity between the 'real' object and its internal optical counterpart and the key procedural aspects involved in the chain of perception. These differences have significant implications for understanding visual strategies employed in apprehending the physical world, and importantly, for how third-party representation mechanisms continue to reinterpret such strategies.

The continuing incorporation of HVS tactics as perceptual strategies within mechanical visioning devices has meant that the distinction between reality and representation is fast becoming imperceptible. Historically, pictorial representations have relied upon known optical devices, such as linear perspective, to consciously manipulate the viewer's reception of the image; the discrepancy between reality and its representation was an accepted fact. By contrast, the increased sophistication and extended viewing field of distributed digital networks and the incorporation of HVS tactics in viewing technology have collapsed any discrepancy between artifice and reality. The image has now literally 'become' reality. The introduction of the ubiquitous high-definition webcam has also meant that the formal properties of the urban landscape are now conflated with their image, as Julian Hochberg observed:

> While depth information can be powerful in near space ... and while parallax from limited bodily action can be significant for about 50 feet [15 metres], after that the real world need not be that different from a

Digital image-making technology 61

flat picture screen, and whatever discrepancies and viewpoint-based distortions arise with pictures or other surrogates can simply be disregarded or dismissed.[80]

Additionally, the webcam image is dynamic, tracing reality across a constantly evolving frame that collapses even further any perceptible difference between the city and its representation. Considering this, the HVS's tendency to privilege the perception of shape over colour and brightness is pivotal. This is because webcam technology's adaptation of HVS strategies, particularly the salient shape perception, exposes it to exploitation through precisely those perceptual cues. By extension, if exploitation is understood as the act of drawing attention to the distinction between the conceived image and its real counterpart, then surely one of its possible implementations falls to the architect, whose interventions might be designed to draw attention to the conflation of real and virtual space.

The human visual system and scan path theory

Eye movements are thus an action by which the observer 'enters', 'inhabits' the painting.[81]

Noton and Stark's theory[82] of visual pattern perception and the correlation between external and internal 'remembered' patterns is commonly accepted. The theory proposes that the HVS records the external world as a series of patterns, represented in memory as a network of memory traces. It assumes that learning to recognise a pattern involves the construction of an internal representation of the pattern, and that recognising it is the process of finding its counterpart in the internal memory. During the process of recognition, the matching of the pattern with its internal representation is driven by the latter, directing sequential attention to the individual features of the pattern through a series of saccadic eye movements.[83] Feature detection is not uniform in this process, varying from detailed and precise perception in the retina's foveal centre, which has the highest concentration of photoreceptors, to coarse perception in the peripheral regions.

The theory also proposes that, although the internal representation of an object is 'a piecemeal affair',[84] visual perception is based upon 'a bag of tricks'.[85] Among these is a directive to gather visual information controlling a search-path sequence of eye movements – the scan path. The scan path theory[86] proposes that when an image is encoded, the associated eye movements are stored in memory as a spatial model.[87] This theory asserts that the internal cognitive model of what we 'see' not only controls our vision but drives a scan path sequence of rapid eye movements and fixations, integral to the memories upon which recognition is based. It also reveals that these movements are idiosyncratic to the subject and to the picture. (This is based on Yarbus's[88] theory that

62   Constructed fields of vision

the scan path depends on the task.[89]) Therefore, because the internal cognitive model or 'schema' rather than the external world drives the scan path, the viewer's initial apprehension of the object dominates the effect of any subsequent viewing.

> Largely derived from low-resolution peripheral information ... The schema guides [sic] the order in which information is input and provides [sic] an overriding plan or map which may influence and be influenced by perceptual encounters with the immediate environment occurring within a glance.[90]

Although more recent developments of this theory have outlined its limitations,[91,92] it has nevertheless identified an operational platform from which automatic digital image-processing strategies can be extrapolated according to various compositional relationships between objects and their resulting saliency.

The division of the HVS into a bifold system of low-resolution peripheral vision and high-resolution foveal vision means that two types of processes are constantly in operation and, in a sense, in competition. In what can be described as a 'coarse-to-fine' procedure, the first process, executed by the full retinal vision, employs the scanning mechanism in a random information-gathering process across a wide visual field to detect relevant regions.[93] This initial scanning process is the primitive form of the cognitive spatial model preceding the second, more detailed foveal process and controls the sequence of visual tracking.[94]

Described as 'more primitive than form recognition',[95] the pre-processing or 'fast-track' function is able to influence behaviour rapidly, based on the coarse pattern, without waiting for the exact details to arrive.[96] It also includes the ability to discriminate an object's surface texture before recognising its spatial connectedness. In what Noton and Stark identified as a 'serial hierarchical' procedure rather than an instantaneous one geared to establish true recognition, this process nevertheless relies upon an initial Gestalt-like apprehension of an object's 'primitive unity'[97] to establish it as a discrete entity. Given that the initial viewing of an object drives the internal cognitive model, this early perceptual stage is critical to the perceptual pathway. Furthermore, drawing first upon an object's affective, qualitative properties gives these properties agency. As Melcher and Cavanagh noted, 'it is the coarse information that plays the predominant role. In fact, these coarse pictorial cues in art and in visual perception information can affect our responses even to stimuli that we do not really see.'[98] More recently, while acknowledging the complexity of the relationship between visual imagery and perception, Gurtner et al. confirmed the predominance of nonlinear systems, stating that 'spatial and temporal gaze behavior during visual imagery depend on the semantic content of the mental image'.[99]

Digital image-making technology 63

In representational terms, the internal cognitive model's dominance opens up two distinct pathways by which the artist can influence the viewer: either the unconscious coarse pathway or the slower, more detailed foveal pathway. Among the strategies historically used to exploit the coarse visual pathway are those developed by artists such as Rembrandt, whose technique of 'textural agency' employed the selective variation of image detail to guide the observer's eye.[100] Based on extensive tests, DiPaola et al. concluded that the strategy's influence occurred on at least two levels: the first belonging to the coarse, low-level perceptual pathway directing the viewer's gaze, and the second belonging to the higher-level, detailed pathway influencing the viewer's appraisal of the artist's skill.[101] Melcher and Cavanagh[102] also revealed how Cubist and Impressionist artists exploited the internal cognitive model of the HVS to reconstruct scenes suggested by a pattern. Picasso, Severini and Miró all employed distortion to evoke facial recognition to draw upon the brain's 'holistic' visual processing, which is based on a Gestalt-like pattern instead of more detailed attributes. Melcher and Cavanagh proposed that by deliberately associating a shape with a coarse, low-level and affective stimulus, a preference for that shape occurs. By extension, the privileging of the coarse visual pathway by these artists, particularly Monet, Degas and Renoir, accounts for their overwhelming popularity with the untrained public.

Conversely, the slower, more detailed pathway associated with foveal processing relies upon a range of object features contributing to perceptual saliency in varying strengths.[103] In a serial 'bottom-up' procedure, feature contrast primarily directs the attentional scan path rather than an object's absolute local feature strength. In other words, an object's saliency is contextual, and cannot be established without the benefit of its surrounding environment. Renaissance artists exploited this phenomenon by using the linear perspective technique to establish the spatial relationships between individual image elements to provide a narrative structure and influence the observer's perceptual behaviour. In contrast to the highly associative and emotional coarse-level perception of shape, in this case, the higher-level, detailed foveal end of the perceptual chain produces a more stable and controlled understanding of pictorial space. Perceptual saliency also relies upon an object's angles or sharp curves at this end of the visual chain. In the scan path, viewers' fixations are clustered around particular shape properties in a 'winner-take-all' network,[104] establishing a repetitive cycle such that dominant perceptual properties attract attention to then converge upon the next most salient location, and so on. Kapoula et al.'s[105] extensive study of Piero della Francesca's *Annunciation* in the *Polyptych of St. Anthony* (1467–1469) supports this idea, showing that the saccades of multiple subjects were driven first by the painting's perspective structure (Figure 3.2).[106]

After an initial inspection, the gaze trajectories move from the background towards the foreground figures, following the ideal diagonal line forward from the vanishing point, rather than performing the perceptual

64 *Constructed fields of vision*

Figure 3.2. Piero della Francesca, *Annunciation (St Anthony)*, 1460–1470.
(Image source: Wikimedia Commons)

itinerary according to the biblical narrative. Most research subjects used in Kapoula et al.'s case study acknowledged the importance of the basic tenets of perspective geometry: the central axis as the marker of spatial depth and the vanishing point carrier. In this case, the perspective exploits the natural optical saliency of angles and sharp curves to reinforce the architectural elements, and the narrative, in turn, 'hangs' upon them. The study shows that all saccadic eye fixations were directed spontaneously to the central perspective area and subsequently to various architectural features within the painting. The subjects did not proceed according to the painting's narrative order. Instead, their first fixations explored the perspective structure, moving initially towards the background and then towards the foreground.

This is highly significant for historical instances of urban representation because it reveals that observer gaze is driven by architectural information rather than narrative per se, and further demonstrates the potency of information presented according to a particular geometry to elicit uniform viewer behaviour.

Further to this theory, tests undertaken by Quiroga and Pedreira[107] reinforce the notion of the gaze trajectory's connection to the spatial

Digital image-making technology 65

organisation and perceptual saliency of image elements, because in even more abstract conditions, the gaze is still attracted to an area of sharper resolution. Most of Mariano Molina's contemporary painting, *Center of gaze* (2011), is deliberately blurred, and all subjects' saccades were attracted to the defined centre of the image. The blurred peripheral area gives the image an almost perspectival quality as it diminishes to a vanishing point in the centre, where the sharper definition and angles of the elements contribute to greater saliency.

Saliency and the advantages of webcam technology

> Some others [workers in visual perception] ... assume that visual perception is based on a 'bag of tricks'.[108]

The advent of film and the moving image introduced an additional feature to image legibility, with the saccadic scan path playing a significant role in developing particular filmic strategies. Scanning, or saccadic motion, is central to the perceptual pathway because it provides information about a scene and establishes an internal cognitive model that serves as a basis for the viewer's planned perceptual actions. The way a scene is viewed is highly dependent, not only upon object salience, but upon the enactment of this model in the form of 'the viewer's goals beyond the next fixation'.[109] Analogously, in film, this means that the integration of successive shots can be guided by configuration and landmark salience and narrative-based expectations. By mimicking saccadic action, the technique of non-overlapping 'cuts' reinforces the film's narrative. 'Filmmakers tend to avoid substantial overlap, which can produce disturbing jump cuts (unwanted motion between salient objects or features, which must then be cured by cutaways, which are brief nonoverlapping inserted views).'[110] However, filmmakers such as Eisenstein and Vertov reversed this strategy, deliberately introducing jump cuts produced by overlap and apparent motion between salient objects or features ('bad cuts') to produce a visual jolt, possibly to slow the viewer's comprehension of a scene.

Contemporary image-makers have continued to appropriate scan path trajectories to mimic the HVS to maximise image saliency and produce a minimal discrepancy between robotic and human vision. The webcam's image sensor uses various architectures to convert the analogue electrical light charge into a digital value, and all these processes involve the encoding, decompression and subdivision of information into sequences of scan lines or raster scans.[111] The procedure of ordering pixels by rows is a highly strategic process whose direction and vertical retrace action are controlled by a pre-determined algorithm programmed to prioritise the production of a seamless moving image. Notably, many variations of this scan-order code also enable the process to isolate and prioritise image regions of specific interest,[112] further attesting to this procedure's capacity to lend itself to the interests of producing a stable and highly curated image. The optimisation of camera vision also means that tasks that might have been cumbersome or impossible are now readily achievable. The implementation of ubiquitous image-making networks, combined with camera technology developments, allows the city to be understood as an 'ideal' tourist venue without blemish either in real or virtual terms.

The sophistication of urban webcam technology and the raster scan's capacity to deliver comprehensive and detailed visual information about a scene extend surveillance into hitherto unprecedented public spaces where any incipient threatening event or terrorist act can be readily identified. In these instances, the webcam's sensitivity patterns are extrapolations of the HVS saliency factors relating directly to coarse or low-resolution peripheral vision, and therefore operate according to the same criteria. In the same way that an object's salience is highly dependent upon its context, so is the detection of anomalous motion patterns based upon any merging or splitting of groups, as well as upon interactions within these groups.[113] In the imaging process, these activities would normally be detected through the selective application of a scan pattern to yield maximum information. Conversely, at the other end of the perceptual pathway, the extrapolation of the foveal high-resolution scanning process is used in more quantitative applications, such as cartography and index maps, where traffic flows are assessed by scan paths based on the appropriated visual cues of size, number, texture and rate of change.[114] Again, these trajectories are implemented within the camera's procedural pathways according to their optimal productive capacity, and do not always reflect a neutral agenda: '[webcam] viewers must be wary that maps, photographs, and webcams, particularly in combination, can present a purposefully selective, highly rhetorical landscape narrative.'[115]

The zoom function, a feature of the camera mechanism, interacts with the HVS's perceptual mechanism in a unique way to maximise the camera's generative potential and its tracing accuracy. During the scanning process, which needs to generate additional attentional scan paths continually, the saliency of the viewed object needs to be somehow disabled before the viewer's attention, and thus the scan path, can shift.[116] In a viewer-operated camera system such as a webcam, the manoeuvrability of the zoom lens physically enhances the disabling of the most recent salient location in favour of the next, and in so doing, is able to exploit the generative potential of HVS perceptual pathways. The multiplication of viewing trajectories fostered by this instrument operates such as a series of movie cuts, which collectively contribute to continuity and narrative structure by replicating saccadic eye movements' central task to extract information from a scene.

> Attentive glances not only parse objects, they (and movie cuts) bring new parts of the world into view; and objects not only serve to relate

their parts to each other, they serve as landmarks in relating successive views of the world to each other.[117]

With the navigation of the image now in the control of the viewer, the webcam's PTZ mechanism contributes actively to image continuity. In this new scenario, the notion of the Vertovian 'jump cut' can no longer be deployed to rupture the viewer's spatial continuity through the foregrounding of the medium and its technology. Instead, by mimicking saccadic action, the webcam zoom function enacts the viewer's 'planned perceptual actions'.[118] This, in turn, serves to reinforce rather than disrupt visual narrative based upon a pre-established internal cognitive model derived from the Gestalt or coarse visual pathway. In this respect, the ability to draw attention to any deliberate narrative construct is linked to disrupting the viewer's presumption of a smooth self-directed image based on planned perceptual actions. However, the very presumption of planned perceptual action offers further opportunity to influence perceptual cues and behaviours, which resides in the numerical procedures and assembly of the digital image itself.

The productive inclusion of digital artefacts

> The main function of perception is to decode the transient retinal image in order to achieve constancy: the perception of the external world in terms of its stable and intrinsic characteristics.[119]

Digital cameras focus incoming light onto a light-sensitive, solid-state sensor comprising a rectangular array of equidistant discrete light-sensing elements or photo-sites. Each photo-site then becomes electrically charged in direct proportion to the amount of light that strikes it over a given period.[120] Two main types of image sensor architectures, CCD and CMOS, are used for image processing. While both methods utilise a scanning process to convert the analogue electrical charge into digital bytes of data, the CCD sensor has 10 times more light sensitivity than the CMOS sensor, which has more inadequate dynamic response.[121]

The CCD sensor uses one of two methods to display a video image on an electronic screen: either 2:1 interlaced scanning or progressive scanning.[122] In interlaced scanning, each row of pixels is scanned in a particular order and orientation using a scan path. This technique, commonly used by commercial webcams, uses two fields to create a frame: one that contains the odd and the other the even lines of the image.[123] This allows a higher scanning rate within a given bandwidth to reduce flickering and to allow motion to be portrayed more naturally. It also produces a visual 'combing' artefact when a video is displayed on anything other than traditional CRT-based screens and must be converted to the progressive mode or deinterlaced before being viewed on LCD or plasma screens.

68 Constructed fields of vision

Interlaced scanning is just one of many image-making techniques that exploit the HVS at its most fundamental level of operation: the translation of the external world into a series of stable and recognisable images.[124] Its capacity to do so is only challenged by its tendency to produce visual artefacts. However, with the rapid delivery of multiple images into the public domain and the exposure of the image-making platform to proprietary and promotional agendas, opportunities to contest these controlling strategies also arise. Works by contemporary artists such as Anna Elise Johnson deliberately draw upon the 'combing' artefact inherent within the interlacing technique to reveal how antithetical conditions of disruption and ambiguity are introduced by directly targeting the processing function that enhances speed and image quality. Instead of reconstituting the two parts of the same divided video signal into one enhanced image, Johnson's work *Camp David, November 15, 1986, Reagan/Thatcher* (2011) deliberately combines two separate images in a bid to comment on its political content. This intentionally non-traditional technique is used in another process known as lenticular interlacing, wherein the optical artefact forms the image. The introduction of tactics that disrupt conventional image saliency thus extends the appropriation of the HVS into a new affective realm by drawing upon the qualitative perceptual attributes of the coarse perception pathway. Importantly, the refusal to conflate the notion of image transmission with image enhancement instead draws a distinction between the real and the virtual, and in the case of the urban webcam, between the real and the virtual city.

The next chapter introduces further strategic responses to the situated nature of extensive global webcam networks. These explore and initiate similar diversionary tactics to contest and disrupt standardised and authorised image production.

Notes

1 Jonathan Crary, 1992. *Techniques of the observer: On vision and modernity in the nineteenth century.* Cambridge, MA: MIT Press, p. 150.
2 Moshe Barasch, 1998. *Modern theories of art, 2: From Impressionism to Kandinsky.* New York, NY: New York University Press.
3 John Gage, 1990. Color in Western art: An issue? *The Art Bulletin,* 72, pp. 518–541.
4 Martin Kemp, 1990. *The science of art: Optical themes in western art from Brunelleschi to Seurat.* New Haven, CT: Yale University Press, p. 267.
5 James Ackerman, 1994. *Distance points: Essays in theory and Renaissance art and architecture.* Cambridge, MA: MIT Press.
6 Gage, Color in Western art: An issue?
7 Crary, *Techniques of the observer.*
8 Crary, *Techniques of the observer,* p. 150.
9 Crary, *Techniques of the observer,* p. 138.
10 Ackerman, *Distance points.*

11 David Van Zanten, Architectural Polychromy: Life in Architecture. In: R.D. Middleton, ed. *The Beaux-Arts and Nineteenth-Century French Architecture*, London: Thames and Hudson, pp. 197–215.
12 Antoine Quatremere De Quincy, 1832. *Dictionnaire historique d'architecture: Comprenant dans son plan les notions historiques, descriptives, archéologiques … De cet art. Tome 1*, Le Clère et Cie Paris.
13 Edouard Papet, 2012. Permanent colour. The revival of polychrome sculpture in late 19th century France. *Apollo Magazine*, CLXXVl (601).
14 Crary, 1992. *Techniques of the observer: On vision and modernity in the nineteenth century*.
15 Barasch, *Modern theories of art*, p. 57.
16 E. C. Elliott, 1960. Some recent conceptions of color theory. *Journal of Aesthetics and Art Criticism*, 18 (4), p. 497.
17 Barasch, *Modem Theories of Art*, p. 325.
18 Theo Van Doesberg, 1924. Towards a plastic architecture. *De Stijl*, 12 (6/7), p. 80.
19 John Gage, 1982. Colour at the Bauhaus. *AA Files*, (2), p. 51.
20 T. M. Brown, 1965. Rietveld's egocentric vision. *Journal of the Society of Architectural Historians*, 24 (4), pp. 292–296.
21 Gerrit Rietveld, 1955. Mondrian en het nieuwe bouwen. *Bouwkundig Weekblad*, 73 (11), p. 128.
22 Bart Van der Leck, 1917. De plaats van het moderne schilderen in de architectuur. *De Stijl*, 1, pp. 6–7.
23 Van der Leck, 1917. De plaats van het moderne schilderen in de architectuur.
24 Yve-Alain Bois and A. Reiter-McIntosh, 1988. Piet Mondrian, 'New York City'. *Critical Inquiry*, 14 (2), p. 270.
25 The HVS measures a section of the electromagnetic spectrum between 300 and 830 nm.
26 M. Tkalcic and J. F. Tasic, 2003. Colour spaces: Perceptual, historical and applicational background. *The IEEE Region 8 EUROCON 2003. Computer as a Tool*, p. 301.
27 Tkalcic and Tasic, Colour spaces: Perceptual, historical and applicational background.
28 CIE standardised the XYZ values as tristimulus values that can describe any colour that an average human observer can perceive.
29 Charles Poynton, 2012. *Digital video and HD: Algorithms and interfaces*. San Francisco, CA: Morgan Kaufmann Publishers, p. 2.
30 Steven L. Tanimoto, 2012. *An interdisciplinary introduction to image processing: Pixels, numbers, and programs*. Cambridge, MA: MIT Press.
31 Poynton, *Digital video and HD*.
32 Poynton, 2012. *Digital video and HD*.
33 M. S. Livingstone, 1988. Art, illusion and the visual system. *Scientific American*, 258, pp. 78–85.
34 R. P. Barneva and Valentin Brimkov, 2009. Digital geometry and its applications to medical imaging. In: J. M. R. S. Tavares and R. N. Jorge, eds. *Advances in computational vision and medical image processing*. Dordrecht: Springer, p. 79.
35 Yun-Qing Shi and Huifang Sun, 2017. *Image and Video Compression for Multimedia Engineering: Fundamentals, Algorithms, and Standards, Second Edition*, CRC Press.
36 ColorSchemer, no date. Available from: https://www.apponic.com/developer/colorschemer-11646/ [Accessed 23/10/2021].
37 Zena O'Connor, 2010. Colour harmony revisited. *Color Research & Application*, 35 (4), p. 272.

38 Poynton, 2012. *Digital video and HD: Algorithms and Interfaces*.
39 Nadia Saleh, 2010. Demosaicing of true color images using adaptive interpolation algorithms. *Journal of Education and Science*, 23 (1), pp. 64–83.
40 Yue Lu and M. Vetterli, 2009. Optimal color filter array design: Quantitative conditions and an efficient search procedure. *Digital Photography V*, 7250, p. 725009.
41 Alleysson, David, Sabine Süsstrunk, and Jeremy Hérault, Jeremy, 2002. Color demosaicing by estimating luminance and opponent chromatic signals in the Fourier domain. *Proceedings of Society for Imaging Science and Technology, 10th Color Imaging Conference*, 10, pp. 331–336.
42 Alleysson et al., Color demosaicing by estimating luminance and opponent chromatic signals in the Fourier domain; Ramanath, Rajeev, Wesley Snyder, Griff Bilbro, and William Sander, 2002. Demosaicking methods for Bayer color arrays. *Journal of Electronic Imaging*, 11 (3), pp. 306–315.
43 Brian Massumi, 2002. *Parables for the virtual: Movement, affect, sensation*. Durham, NC: Duke University Press, p. 209.
44 Sylvère Lotringer and Paul Virilio, 2005. *The accident of art*. New York, NY: Semiotext (e) Foreign Agents, p. 74.
45 An acronym for GNU Image Manipulation Program. The software is available at: http://www.gimp.org/
46 Color Blender software is available at: https://meyerweb.com/eric/tools/color-blend/#:::hex
47 Pipette software is available at: http://www.charcoaldesign.co.uk/pipette
48 Poynton, *Digital video and HD*, p. 383.
49 Raw Therapee software is available at: http://www.rawtherapee.com/
50 ImageJ software is available at: http://rsb.info.nih.gov/ij/
51 Rastislav Lukac and Konstantinos N. Plataniotis, 2005. Color filter arrays: Design and performance analysis. *IEEE Transactions on Consumer Electronics*, 51 (4), pp. 1260–1267.
52 Lukac and Plataniotis, Color filter arrays, p. 1260
53 John Savard, 2009. Color filter array designs. Available from: http://quadibloc.com/other/cfaint.htm [Accessed 06/06/2009].
54 Xiangjian He and Jianmin Li, 2007. Linear interpolation for image conversion between square structure and hexagonal structure. In *PAMM: Proceedings in Applied Mathematics and Mechanics*, 7 (1), pp. 1011001–1011002. Berlin: WILEY-VCH Verlag.
55 Mario Carpo, 2011. *The alphabet and the algorithm*. Cambridge, MA: MIT Press, p. 126.
56 John Gage, 2013. *Shadowy figures*. Available from: https://wengam.com/PDFs/john_gage_light_from_shadow.pdf [Accessed 13/04/2013].
57 John McCann, 2007. Art, science, and appearance in HDR. *Journal of the Society for Information Display*, 15 (9), pp. 709–719.
58 John McCann, and Alessandro Rizzi, 2009. Retinal HDR images: Intraocular glare and object size. *Journal of the Society for Information Display*, 17(11), pp. 913–920.
59 John McCann and Alessandro Rizzi, 2007. Camera and visual veiling glare in HDR images. *Journal of the Society for Information Display*, 15 (9), pp. 721–730.
60 McCann, Art, science, and appearance in HDR.
61 Frédo Durand and Julie Dorsey, 2002. Fast bilateral filtering for the display of high-dynamic-range images. *ACM Transactions on Graphics*, 21 (3), pp. 257–266.

62 Dorothea Jameson and Leo M. Hurvich, 1975. From contrast to assimilation: In art and in the eye. *Leonardo*, 8 (2), p. 128.
63 Claire J. Farago, 1991. Leonardo's color and chiaroscuro reconsidered: The visual force of painted images. *The Art Bulletin*, 73 (1), pp. 63–88. *Chiaroscuro* is a technique in which the focus of the painting is illuminated, as if in a spotlight, while the surrounding field is dark and monochromatic.
64 Alexander Nagel, 1993. Leonardo and sfumato. *RES: Anthropology and Aesthetics*, 24 (1), pp. 7–20. *Sfumato* uses a subtle gradation of tone to obscure sharp edges and create a synergy between lights and shadows, increasing according to the distance away from the central viewing point of the painting.
65 Ackerman, *Distance points*, p. 168.
66 Maria João Durão, 2008. Sketching the Ariadne's Thread for alchemical linkages to painting. *Fabrikart*, 8, p. 113.
67 Robert Venturi, Martino Stierli, and David Bruce Brownlee, 1977 (2nd ed.), *Complexity and contradiction in architecture*. London: Architectural Press.
68 Anais Atencia, Vincent Boyer, and Jean-Jacques Bourdin, 2008. From detail to global view, an impressionist approach. In *2008 IEEE International Conference on Signal Image Technology and Internet Based Systems*, pp. 366–374.
69 Jameson and Hurvich, From contrast to assimilation, p. 129.
70 Jameson and Hurvich, From contrast to assimilation.
71 John J. McCann and Alessandro Rizzi, 2007. Spatial comparisons: The antidote to veiling glare limitations in image capture and display. *Proc. IMQA*.
72 Danielle Torcellini, 2010. Painting and photographing the sunlight. A comparison between old-school and avant-garde techniques. *Proc. CREATE*, pp. 353–358.
73 Massumi, *Parables for the virtual*, p. 162.
74 Cambridge in colour, no date. Digital camera diffraction, part 2. Available from: https://www.cambridgeincolour.com/tutorials/diffraction-photography-2.htm [Accessed 06/06/2009].
75 McCann, Art, science, and appearance in HDR.
76 McCann and Rizzi, Spatial comparisons.
77 McCann and Rizzi, Spatial comparisons.
78 Steven M. Lehar, 2003. *The world in your head a gestalt view of the mechanism of conscious experience*. Mahwah, NJ: Lawrence Erlbaum Associates, p. 60.
79 Virginio Cantoni, Stefano Levialdi, and Bertrand Zavidovique, 2011. *3 C vision: Cues, context and channels*. Waltham, MA: Elsevier.
80 Julian Hochberg, 2007. Looking ahead (one glance at a time). In: M. A. Peterson, B. Gillam and H.A. Sedgwick, eds. *In the mind's eye: Julian Hochberg on the perception of pictures, films, and the world*. New York, NY: Oxford University Press, p. 402.
81 Zoï Kapoula, Qing Yang, Marine Vernet, and Maria-Pia Bucci, 2009. Eye movements and pictorial space perception: studies of paintings from Francis Bacon and Piero della Francesca. *Cognitive Semiotics*, 5 (Fall), p. 105.
82 David Noton and Lawrence Stark, 1971. Eye movements and visual perception. *Scientific American*, 224 (6), pp. 34–43.
83 David Noton, 1970. A theory of visual pattern perception. *IEEE Transactions on Systems Science and Cybernetics*, 6 (4), pp. 349–357.
84 Noton and Stark, Eye movements and visual perception, p. 38.
85 Bela Julesz, 1991. Early vision and focal attention. *Reviews of Modern Physics*, 63 (3), p. 767.
86 Noton and Stark, Eye movements and visual perception.

Constructed fields of vision

87 Katherine Anne Humphrey, 2010. *Eye movements and scanpaths in the perception of real-world scenes*. Thesis (PhD). University of Nottingham.
88 Alfred L. Yarbus, 1967. Eye movements during perception of complex objects. In: Alfred L. Yarbus, ed. *Eye movements and vision* (pp. 171–211). Boston, MA: Springer.
89 Cantoni, Levialdi, and Zavidovique, *3 C vision: Cues, context and channels*.
90 Barbara Gillam, 2007. *Hochberg: A perceptual psychologist*. In: M. A. Peterson, B. Gillam and H.A. Sedgwick, eds. *In the mind's eye: Julian Hochberg on the perception of pictures, films, and the world*. New York, NY: Oxford University Press, p. 431.
91 Humphrey, 2010. *Eye movements and scanpaths in the perception of real-world scenes*. Humphrey, citing Groner et al. (1984) and Mannan (1996) and Ruddock and Wooding (1996), argued that the limitations of this theory are that it is top-down and does not take into account bottom-up influences, such as low-level visual saliency or the variability in scanpaths across viewings by the single and multiple observers.
92 Schütz, Alexander, Doris Braun, and Karl Gegenfurtner, 2011. Eye movements and perception: A selective review. *Journal of Vision*, 11(5):9, pp. 1–30.
93 Cantoni, Levialdi, and Zavidovique, *3 C vision: Cues, context and channels*, p. 3.
94 Gillam, *Hochberg: A perceptual psychologist*, p. 431.
95 Julesz, Early vision and focal attention, p. 44.
96 David Melcher and Patrick Cavanagh, 2011. Pictorial cues in art and in visual perception. In: F. Bacci and D. Melcher, eds. *Art and the Senses*. New York, NY: Oxford University Press, p. 364.
97 Noton and Stark, Eye movements and visual perception, p. 36.
98 Melcher and Cavanagh, Pictorial cues in art and in visual perception, pp. 264–265.
99 Lilla Gurtner, Matthias Hartmann, and Fred W. Mast, 2021. Eye movements during visual imagery and perception show spatial correspondence but have unique temporal signatures. *Cognition*, 210, pp. 104597–104610.
100 Steve DiPaola, Caitlin Riebe, and James T. Enns, 2010. Rembrandt's textural agency: A shared perspective in visual art and science. *Leonardo*, 43 (2), pp. 145–151.
101 DiPaola et al., Rembrandt's textural agency, p. 145.
102 Noton and Stark, Eye movements and visual perception.
103 Laurent Itti and Christof Koch, 2001. Computational modelling of visual attention. *Nature Reviews Neuroscience*, 2 (3), pp. 194–203.
104 Itti and Koch, Computational modelling of visual attention, p. 6.
105 Kapoula et al., Eye movements and pictorial space perception.
106 These authors refer specifically to Piero della Francesca's *Annunciation* because this artist wrote a practical treatise for painters on perspective drawing.
107 Quian Quiroga and Carlos Pedreira, 2011. How do we see art: An eye-tracker study. *Frontiers in Human Neuroscience*, 5 (98).
108 Julesz, Early vision and focal attention, p. 767.
109 Hochberg, *Looking ahead (one glance at a time)*, p. 406.
110 Hochberg, *Looking ahead (one glance at a time)*, p. 407.
111 James D. Foley, Foley Dan Van, Andries Van Dam, Steven K. Feiner, John F. Hughes, Edward Angel, and J. Hughes, 1996. *Computer graphics: Principles and practice*. Hoboken, NJ: Addison-Wesley Professional; Herman Kruegle, 2007. *CCTV surveillance: Analog and digital video practices and technology*. Amsterdam: Elsevier Butterworth Heinemann.
112 Cantoni, Levialdi, and Zavidovique, *3 C vision: Cues, context and channels*.

113 Kruegle, *CCTV surveillance: Analog and digital video practices and technology*, p. 110.
114 Mark Monmonier, 2000. Webcams, interactive index maps, and our brave new world's brave new globe. *Cartographic Perspectives*, 0 (37), pp. 51–64.
115 Monmonier, Webcams, interactive index maps, and our brave new world's brave new globe, p. 57.
116 Itti and Koch, Computational modelling of visual attention, p. 9.
117 Hochberg, *Looking ahead (one glance at a time)*, pp. 404–405.
118 Hochberg, *Looking ahead (one glance at a time)*, p. 400.
119 Barbara Gillam, 1980. Geometrical illusions. *Scientific American*, 242, p. 108.
120 National Instruments, 2006. *Anatomy of a camera*. Available from: https://www.ni.com/en-au/innovations/white-papers/06/anatomy-of-a-camera.html [Accessed 27/12/2021].
121 Diffraction, 2021. *CCD versus CMOS: Which is better?* Ottawa, Canada: Diffraction. Available from: https://diffractionlimited.com/ccd-versus-cmos-which-is-better/feature-image/. The human eye can see objects under a light condition of 1 x Lux, but the CCD sensor operates at 0.1–3 x Lux.
122 Progressive-scan cameras operate by transferring an entire frame from the image sensor in a single action without performing any line-interlacing. National Instruments, 2006. *Anatomy of a camera*. Available from: https://www.ni.com/en-au/innovations/white-papers/06/anatomy-of-a-camera.html [Accessed 27/12/2021].
123 AXIS Communications. 2021. Technical guide to network video. Available from: http://www.axis.com/products/video/camera/progressive_scan.htm [Accessed 29/06/2021].
124 Gillam, Geometrical illusions.

4 The new agency of distributed digital networks

Digital anamorphosis and the virtual picture plane

An analog input (the original photograph) undergoes a process of digital distortion that yields an analog output (the close-up). If we are to understand the impact of this complex transformation, we must deprivilege our modalities of understanding enough to allow the digital middle to matter.[1]

Pre-digital anamorphic techniques

The interrogation and manipulation of linear perspective's geometric underpinnings manifested in anamorphic techniques corresponding to a similar range of spectator viewpoints to those initiated by the contemporary webcam network. Both have profound consequences for viewer engagement. Early versions of linear perspective techniques include what Jurgis Baltrušaitis described as either 'accelerated' or 'decelerated' perspective.[2] The two types of geometric distortions, operating perpendicular to the picture plane, were used to exploit linear perspective geometry by either increasing or decreasing the depth perception. Accelerated perspective was commonly used to construct 16th-century stage sets to counteract the theatre's spatial limitations, by contracting the sidewalls and raising the horizon to increase the illusion of distance. Conversely, decelerated perspective acted as a 'brake' on the vanishing point to make objects appear closer than they are by increasing the dimensions of distant elements. This illusory device is deployed in Michelangelo's *Last Judgement* in the Sistine Chapel, Rome, where the three horizontal rows in the painting become progressively larger towards the ceiling (Figure 4.1). The intention behind both of these types of anamorphic projection was to preserve an alignment with the linear perspectival representation of real space, rather than to contest it, and was thus complicit in this technique's overarching objective to collapse real with represented form.

However, Hans Holbein, Jean-François Niceron and Emmanuel Maignan employed another type of anamorphic technique that directly

DOI: 10.4324/9781003133872-6

New agency of distributed digital networks 75

Figure 4.1 Michelangelo Buonarotti, *The Last Supper* (1536–1541).
Source: Wikimedia Commons.

contested the linear perspective schema. The technique worked by forming an alternative, secondary image or images from an oblique viewing point to the picture plane, to either reinforce or subvert the primary image's content. As does the contemporary aerial Google Earth view, this new anamorphic technique directly opposed the assumption that the viewer is perpendicular to the viewing frame, and had the express purpose of cleaving apart linear perspective's conflation of real and represented form. In the case of Maignan's *San Francesco di Paola* in Trinità dei Monti in Rome, the superimposition of the distance point (a fundamental tenet of linear perspective construction) upon the principal point profoundly altered the traditional linear perspective viewing schema. This viewing scenario forced the viewer to assume a position of extreme proximity to the picture plane's physical surface to view the primary image correctly. As they passed along the picture's surface, several sub-images unfolded. This conflation of viewer and image was so profound that in Niceron's anamorphic grids, the diagrammatic viewing figure was completely erased from the diagram altogether, instead being supplanted by the actual viewer, as Lyle Massey recorded: 'When Niceron constructs his anamorphic grids ... the distance point figure disappears. That is, a figure no longer is used to represent the viewer because it has been altogether replaced by the viewer.'[3]

This second type of anamorphic technique operates in two ways. The first is concerned with opening a new representational dialogue that casts doubt upon the integrity of the perspective system by revealing 'the inherent deceivability of sight'.[4] The fact that Niceron's anamorphic technique was derived from linear perspective theory and geometry exposed the precarity of the latter's resilience and integrity. Secondly, and importantly, the anamorphic technique served as the mechanism by which the body is put back into motion: the viewer's physical repositioning shifted the image's agency back into an experiential realm.

The affective anamorphic network

Acting as a surrogate for the body by launching it into hitherto inaccessible locations of proximity to the city, the webcam network presents multiple views of the urban landscape often associated with site owners' proprietary interests. However, the camera can allow the viewer to engage with the city in ways that overcome these types of inscribed agendas.

In *New Philosophy for New Media*, Mark Hansen referred to 'our coupling with the computer' as a new form of 'embodied perception' in which the digital transformation of the analogue world has both perceptual and experiential consequences entirely specific to digital topography.[5] Hansen illustrated his point using Robert Lazzarini's *skulls*, a sculptural installation composed of four skulls, drawing upon the precedent of anamorphic content in Holbein's *The Ambassadors* to reveal fundamental distinctions between the products of perspectival and digital geometries. Hansen asserted that the viewer's failure to be able to assume a 'correct' viewing position to resolve the distorted view of each skull points to a domain of digital geometry whose topology or 'territory' remains largely uncharted, thus initiating a new type of affective response in the viewer. By extension, the global webcam network only heightens this experience because the sheer multiplication of viewpoints correspondingly increases the number of anamorphic views. In addition to this, by separating the viewer from the 'real' content of the image, the webcam's zoom mechanism – acting as the viewer's optical surrogate – shifts the experiential mode of viewing into an even more extreme and potentially affective state of embodied perceptual experience. Rather than relying upon their own perception, here the viewer uses the surrogate projectively to navigate and identify the city's form.

> To the extent that our perspectival grasp of the image is short-circuited, we do not experience the image in the space between it and our eye (as in normal geometric perspective); and to the extent that we are thus 'placed' into the space of the image (though without being able to enter into it), our visual faculties are rendered useless and we experience a shift to an alternate mode of perception rooted in our bodily faculty of proprioception. We could say then that Lazzarini's work functions by 'catalyzing' an affective process of embodied form-giving, a process that creates 'place' within our bodies.[6]

In the same way that *skulls* points to a new mode of engagement with the artefact by raising the consciousness of our engagement with digital topology, so does the webcam network present an alternative and unprecedented experiential engagement with the image through engagement with the operation of a digital optical mechanism. 'It deploys the anamorphing of form as the opening of a whole new domain.'[7]

Digital anamorphic techniques

The contemporary webcam network's fixed pivot point limits the viewer to a position that is not always without political intent; as Mark Monmonier noted, '[the webcam] ... can present a purposefully selective, highly rhetorical landscape narrative.'[8] However, many developing aspects of this viewing mechanism circumvent this operational constraint. Recent advances in technology assign mechanical control devices to the viewer, thereby eliminating the presence of an overriding central organisation. An example of this is the PTZ action of the camera, totally controlled and updated by the user rather than by a central server.[9] The PTZ function extends the camera's representational capacity because the 'ideal' utopian city view no longer presides over the received image's type or angle.

Both the accelerated and decelerated modes of anamorphic perspective have correlates in the webcam's zoom mechanism that are associated with more democratising aspects of technological development. Depending upon an individual camera's magnification factor, the zoom device allows the viewer to undertake a trajectory towards the object that can exceed the image's resolution, thus releasing them from the possibility of achieving any single 'ideal' viewing position. Like earlier anamorphic projections of this kind, the assumption is that the viewer is perpendicular to the picture plane. However, here the analogy breaks down because, unlike these earlier viewing conditions, the viewing trajectory is entirely user-operated. At the close-up extremity of the zoom tool, the resolving capacity of the camera lens, unlike the naked eye, cannot compensate for the extent of the accelerated trajectory. At this point, the internal architecture of the image generated by the camera begins to override the representation, and the portrayal of the 'ideal' city breaks down in favour of the image's interior pixel architecture. At this extreme point of proximity, the mediated city literally takes on the form of the pixel. So, what was formerly a device that successfully exploited the geometry of linear perspective to conflate representation with reality here works against this ambition, where its capacity to reveal new close-scale viewpoints instead restores the distinction between the represented and the physical city.

The other type of anamorphic technique that forms an alternative, secondary image or images from an oblique viewing point to the picture plane also finds a contemporary counterpart in the webcam's PTZ mechanism. Like earlier versions of this technique, the webcam action contravenes the traditional assumption that the viewer is perpendicular to the viewing frame. The proliferation of the webcam network and the multiplication of viewpoints mean that, paradoxically, a primary viewpoint does not exist. Instead of a single privileged vantage point that presents the 'ideal' image of the city, perspective camera views work together to compose a collective 'imagescape', where all views are primary yet contain secondary oblique landscapes. Furthermore, as Leonard Shlain observed, while on the one hand, the experience of represented volumetric space is flattened by the camera image, on the other, this compression also conceals numerous alternative views, once again multiplied by the many webcam sites. 'Spatial representations also merge at high speeds. As space is compressed, multiple views of objects are possible from a single perspective because planes and volumes become one.'[10] Much in the same way that Maignan's San Trinità fresco concealed within the principal anamorphic image several micro-landscapes that were only visible at specific viewpoints, so too is there a reciprocity between an array of webcam views of the same location and the various 'micro-scenes' that emerge from the different views achievable at this location. Rather than one single 'correct' anamorphic viewpoint from which, such as Holbein's anamorphic skull, resolution is achieved by a shift to a 'perfect' location that destabilises the overarching perspective schema, here the anamorphic condition works to contribute collectively to the promotion of site ownership through multiple camera locations.

An example of this is the Times Square webcam network, owned by Earthcam, a United States (US) company that works in partnership with other first-world corporations such as Microsoft, Kodak and Coca Cola, to name a few, to provide 'webcam technology and managed services consisting of live streaming video, time-lapse cameras and 360° reality capture for corporate clients and government agencies in major cities around the world'.[11] Promoted by Earthcam for tourism purposes, the Times Square network consists of several PTZ user-operated webcams that deliver simultaneous streaming video footage from several locations in this vicinity. In this precinct, the 'ideal' presentations of these simultaneously captured views (except the Google Earth view, which is not live) are only achievable in conjunction with each other's existence, or in other words, the images are symbiotic. Additionally, the vertical Google Earth view of this location, acting in conjunction with the webcam views, provides even more visual information unavailable from the other camera positions. So, while earlier versions of this particular anamorphic technique cast doubt upon the integrity of the perspectival system by establishing a single alternative oblique viewpoint, here instead, multiple 'ideal' presentations of the city contribute to the final image rather than contest it, which is perhaps because all camera locations reflect the site owners' promotional ambitions.

Unlike its forebears, this oblique version of the anamorphic technique does not exploit its own geometrical constraints to scrutinise established geometries and modes of image production. It nonetheless initiates a corresponding affective response of the type identified by Marc Hansen. In the same way that Holbein's *Ambassadors* generates a condition of disorientation and self-reflection in the viewer through the forced assumption of an oblique viewing point, so does the capacity to navigate the city using the digital webcam image initiate a similarly affective condition. It achieves this by repositioning the viewer in a highly accelerated way within the urban landscape, as Keith Broadfoot pointed out.

> When the spectator does see the skull, he sees the skull facing towards the place where he was standing in front of the painting. At the moment the spectator sees the image of the skull, there is the retrospective realisation that this image of death was 'always-already' looking at the spectator without the spectator being able to see it.[12]

The webcam's ability to offer multiple, rapid oblique views of the same urban space means that it is a simple matter to assume a new viewpoint that explains its oblique counterpart. This instigates in the viewer a sense of self-determined engagement with the landscape, only questioned by the operation of a potentially disturbing spatial and temporal condition. Depending upon the camera's pivot and with two computer screens operating simultaneously, the viewer is literally able to observe themselves in the act of viewing. Thus, just as the deleted viewing figure in Niceron's anamorphic diagram is replaced by the actual viewer (the result of superimposing the distance point upon the principal point), so does the webcam introduce the actual viewer into the field of representation by using the image-making device 'against itself' to produce an entirely disorienting and affective experience.

The digital webcam network offers the possibility of questioning the mode and intent of representation through the operation of anamorphic techniques that work differently from those of their earlier counterparts. As

Hubert Damisch observed, the representational capacity of linear perspective geometry has exhausted the constraint of its own instrumentalisation favouring new modes of operation that require new conditions and modes of representation and viewing.

> Such an observation should be sufficient to render suspect any assimilation of *perspectiva artificialis* to an instrument that has been incrementally perfected over time until finally, no longer responding to changing needs emerging through the evolutionary process, it must be replaced by another one better adapted to those needs.[13]

Therefore, in conjunction with the urban viewing instrument, it remains for the designer to find ways to exploit the new capacities of the webcam's reinterpretation of the anamorphic technique. It also falls to the designer to restore anamophosis's critical potential so that urban form does more than simply uphold the existing relationships between power and place associated with the surveillant mode of representation. It is now a design task to define 'what, in painting, are the conditions prerequisite to the making of statements (or: that might help us think, in terms of painting what such conditions would be)'.[14]

However, any contemporary reinstatement of anamorphosis's critical potential needs to consider a different spatial context from that of its 17th-century counterpart. It is, therefore, the webcam image's dynamic property that facilitates the release of the image's adversarial capacity. This is discussed in the following section, which locates the webcam's generative status within the context of the moving image. The discussion also defines the new conditions of urban imaging and formal generation that can emerge from the webcam's capacity to respond to an expanded temporal frame.

The expanded image

The distributed network and the multiplication of viewpoints

> Many military technologies have gone from classified to omnipresent, from expensive to free, and from centralized to distributed, downloadable on our desktops anywhere on earth with access to the Internet.[15]

Deleuze and Guattari's 'rhizomic' model finds material form in the structure and operation of the contemporary webcam network, where each intersecting point is required to connect to every other intersecting point in an open structure, and where the number of connections always exceeds the number of paths that can actually be monitored.[16] The shutting down of one pathway in this type of model automatically reveals an alternative option. In its abstracted form, its behaviour is theoretically capable of multiple, ubiquitous encounters with obstruction that systematically give rise to a range of 'resistances', and thus new growth paths.

As William Bogard argued, with these sorts of opportunities for network intervention becoming available, the digital webcam calls into question traditional notions of surveillance and, more generally, the role of image-making within the public realm.

> Digital media today allow an unprecedented level of scrutiny of the powerful by the powerless, rulers by the ruled, the rich and famous by the 'common people'. There has never been another time when the means of surveillance have been so widely distributed in the general population, by the very powers that depend upon them for control.[17]

Traditional panoptic power, best understood in the Bentham and Foucault models, is very different from that initiated by a digital network. Like the digital network, the panoptic model is ubiquitous, relying for its potency on a collective, reciprocal surveillance schema in which the prison is at once both surveillant and surveilled.[18] However, the 'de-territorialised' webcam network instigates a new type of urban surveillance: whereas traditional panoptic power operates through indeterminacy by avoiding visibility, the webcam operates through direct, resistant practices such as file sharing, spam and identity theft.[19]

The webcam network's rhizomic structure means that any attempt to block or control the flow of information only results in the generation of yet another new pathway and the establishment of a new viewing subject that contests obstruction. 'The most important dimension of immaterial production from the point of view of surveillance is the production of a subject.'[20] The ongoing generation and proliferation of alternative viewpoints is thus one of the capacities of this type of structure, or as Deleuze and Guattari would describe it, 'assemblage', which 'is a multiplicity composed of other assemblages that are also multiplicities that together form a functional, ever-changing ensemble'.[21] This not only means that any exclusionary strategies of data control are unlikely to succeed, but, more importantly, initiates a new type of surveillance that is both reflexive and performative. By being liberated from time and location constraints and instigating a reflexive dualism of observer and observed, digital media confer a new active agency upon the populace. The function of transforming 'overseers' into 'viewers',[22] instigated by webcam technology, again returns how the city is perceived and experienced to the moving image.

Just as Vertov and Eisenstein used montage to shift the viewer's understanding and perception of the city from that of a single, continuous spatial narrative, so do new modes of urban navigation and perception transform the experience of public space. The viewer's engagement with a device that can traverse the urban landscape in an unprecedented way amplifies experience. For example, 'television's system of instantaneous electronic transmission, and its ability to switch viewpoints and locations at a moment's notice, calls the notion of a continuous urban fabric into question',[23] positioning technology and the image in a highly instrumental role concerning the formal consequences arising from this new type of engagement with public space.

However, with the reversal of hierarchical observation and the multiplication of subjectivities or Deleuzian 'hybrid subjects'[24] instigated by the network camera system, comes a fragmentation. For Deleuze, the shift to virtual modes of surveillance is tightly tied to the architecture of the digital system itself, in that the virtual counterpart of the individual is a fragmented 'replicant' or 'dividual' whose internal elements can be freely recomposed.[25] The notion of dismantling the singular subject, first presented to the established world of cinematic tradition by Vertov's film, is now extended to a global scale by the functionality of the rhizomic network system, in which the formation of new digital pathways is both infinite and constantly developing. Furthermore, based upon a composite of multiple vantage points captured over time, the contemporary notion of the city releases the individual into a new concept of place. The 'ageographic'[26] representation of the world offered by the webcam is, according to John Macarthur, 'a nowhere, imaginary place'.[27] The webcam network's extensive capability as a representational tool in this newly elevated realm hitherto remains largely unexploited. However, what emerges here is an unprecedented opportunity for the viewer to activate the right to explore and delineate the new 'aesthetic of above'. 'Altitude and viewing angle dictate an entirely distinctive visual regime: as details disappear and scale becomes relative, we witness the transformation of a familiar, human-sized and human-centred view into something altogether different.'[28] As Macarthur pointed out, while modern painting – in a departure from the tradition that had governed painting since Alberti – transposed the relation of pictorial depths into a relation of surfaces, then so too does the aerial vantage point transpose the variation of landscape contours into a relation of patterns and textures awaiting release.

Traces of public space ownership are visible in both the type and distribution of textural patterns in the representations produced from the new aerial viewpoints. It is not surprising, then, that Google Earth views of politically sensitive zones are heavily edited and pixellated below a certain elevation, as one example of many possible kinds.[29] The images produce a particular type of pattern, recognisable by its association with a particular activity type and located in a particular place. Conversely, zones of less political interest are neither pixellated at corresponding elevations nor traceable through any particular pattern type. The patterns emerging at specific elevations also bear witness to the impact of the history of different political regimes and cultural mores upon individual land ownership. Their diversity at corresponding aerial elevations in different locations sets up an indexical relationship between the vertical representation of space and the materiality nature and scale of its content, played out in a correspondence between the landscape's physical occupation and the magnification index of the camera.

Laura Kurgan described the images generated in pervasive time-lapse recording of the planet by US satellite imaging systems such as Landsat as 'something more disorienting, an "emptiness and abstraction" that resists sovereign control and opens itself to other sorts of interpretation'.[30] Drawing upon the work of Thomas Nagel and Svetlana Alpers, Kurgan, such as Macarthur, attributed the affective property of these images to the fact that aerial perspective is 'the view from nowhere', and also one without a subject, unlike the effect of being 'safely' located within the linear perspective grid, 'which is viewed from somewhere – the point of view of the subject who both constructs and is constructed by that view'.[31] However, the aerial image's amenability to common access leads to a forensic unravelling of its sometimes questionable historical deployment. Referring to their 'authorless' origin, Kurgan's discussion of their many inclusions in evidence relating to political scenarios unveils the true extent of this amenability. This author's work on the scale and levels of pixel data within the satellite image also reveals how intensity and contrast can be indexed to situated events. In images of mass war graves in Kosovo in 1999, each pixel represents 10 square metres. Each has an address expressed in longitude and latitude that corresponds with a unique location. Each reveals the heat value of that place at the time the image was captured.

Concluding that 'there is no such thing as neutral data', Kurgan described images of this genre as 'para-empirical' in the sense that this type of technology operates 'alongside the world' to open up representation to the plurality and ambiguity of space rather than to act as a singular, stable index of reality.[32]

The 'guerilla' tactics of urban groups such as the New York-based Institute of Applied Autonomy present an alternative example of how the same aerial platform might engage the viewer in the production of a new type of landscape pattern. The group's i-See program is a web-based application[33] that maps the locations of closed-circuit television (CCTV) cameras in urban environments to provide the user with an Internet-free route to a destination. The mapped routes reveal a strong correlation between areas with the highest incidence of cameras and politically, morally or economically sensitive property, whose 'stability' is theoretically maintained by camera vigilance. Accordingly, by avoiding detection and reversing the idea of personal visibility, the individual i-See user can subvert the original surveillant intention of the camera network. The selection of a 'path of least resistance' against acknowledged ownership means that unorthodox routes across the urban landscape progressively become associated with particular activity types or programs. The consequences of this are potentially profound. As the inhabitation of these spaces associated

84 Constructed fields of vision

with non-conforming citizens evolves, the image-making platform gradually becomes linked to the city's material evolution in ways that reflect engagement with the visioning system.

In this respect, the network system's open structure fundamentally alters the agency of the image by fostering a redistributed, more diverse ownership of public space. These assembled patterns of the new urban imagescape, composed of both horizontal and vertical viewpoints, are now emerging indices and agents of the redistributed ownership of civic space. The i-See program is one significant example of how the distributed camera network can potentially affect the composition of civic space. By opening the city's elevated viewpoint to the Internet user, this system directly affects how the image can influence both the form and the occupation of urban space.

An expanded temporal frame

> Space is no longer an emptiness to be filled with things. It is no longer static, waiting to be organised by perspective. It is a generative moving medium, having its own powers and forces that become manifest and vary in relation to our movements in an expanded field of cultural and ecological relations.[34]

The cinematic montage's advent extended the image's temporal frame beyond a single, fixed event to a series of events. Without the ability to portray a phenomenon in its full visual multidimensionality, the limitations of Renaissance linear perspective painting and photography's inherently static nature had been long acknowledged. Bois and Shepley's extensive discussion of Giovanni Battista Piranesi's montage technique addresses precisely this issue. Their comparison of Piranesi's 18th-century 'I Carceri' drawings and the cinematic style of Sergei Eisenstein revealed Piranesi's attempt to overcome the technical shortcomings of 2D representation, and, more importantly, its constraints, well before the advent of cinematic technology. Using a strategy similar to the cinematic montage of Eisenstein, these authors argued that Piranesi discarded Eisenstein's 'single continuity of perspective'[35] in favour of independent, autonomous spaces, connected instead by the qualitative intensity of differing depth. They go on to show how techniques common to both artists depart from the linear narrative technique, seen in Eisenstein's disjunctive shots and Piranesi's disjunctive plan and elevation. Both overturn the domination of the ground plan over space, ultimately seeking to rupture the image's narrative structure. 'He seeks to destroy that which has been the age-old foundation of narration, namely its conclusion.'[36]

However, the filmic montage technique of the Soviet cinematographers Eisenstein and Vertov did more than depart from a singular, linear narrative; it also asked the viewer to engage in an extended temporal frame.

According to Deleuze, this new approach is aligned with the more natural biological procedures of human vision, in which the perception of formal space exceeds perspective's limitations; 'where there are no edges, no up or down, no right or left, no in or out ... [there is only] ... universal variation ... universal undulations, universal rippling'.[37] Norman Bryson extended this idea by drawing upon the notion of the frame and the viewer's capacity to intervene within this seamless spatial perception. Referring to the work of Keiji Nishitani, Bryson described how Nishitani disrupted tradition by removing the perspectival frame that detaches the object from the universal visual field and freezes it within a static framework, meaning that 'as soon as that frame is withdrawn, the object is found to exist as part of a mobile continuum that cannot be cut anywhere'.[38] By implication then, it is only through the cinematic framing of the city, and the webcam image's correspondence with this type of framing, that intervention can occur.

Following this idea, Deleuze asserted that the world of universal flux, represented by film, can indeed be cut, and that it is precisely this cut that provides an opportunity for architectural intervention.[39] The deliberate withdrawal of the illusion of continuous space and immersion in a new timeframe has profound implications for the conception of architecture. Drawing upon Eisenstein and Vertov's position that montage juxtaposition gives the image the capacity to transform 3D space, Richard Koeck[40] concluded that film and architecture are inseparable. For Koeck, it is camera technology in the artist's hands – Vertov's roving 'montage eye' – that is truly able to respond to the city's multidimensionality and ambiguity by delivering multiple diverse readings. Furthermore, it is only by exercising the multiplicity of readings that the limitations of static, perspectival snapshots and technocratic modes of representation can be addressed.

The camera's new mobility means that the contemporary imagescape is composite or fragmentary in form. Therefore, resistance to continuity and the connecting of fragments becomes a condition of modern life, and a condition whereby this life is understood through the image-making instrument.[41] The image of the contemporary city is fragmentary and dynamic because of its distributed nature, but also because the image-making network is unable to produce a continuous, comprehensive image of it from any single vantage point. In this respect, the Internet webcam network extends the notion of an imagescape into one of a 'montagescape', in which the image-making process is both composite and constantly developing. The webcam network's new streaming technology means that the distributed city's image is now also an uninterrupted video stream, whose frame-rate capture produces video output indistinguishable from the human perception of real time.

To return to Deleuze and the notion of universal flux, because montage is a cinematic device that influences our natural perception of space and its dynamic properties, by extension, it has implications for the way we engage with architectural space. 'If visual theories, film and cinema influence the design of spaces, does this not suggest that we should consider the use of film and cinematic principles as a natural instrument to facilitate engagement with architectural spaces?'[42] In *Cinema 1*, Deleuze[43] introduced the notion of the cinematic selection of 'blocks' of space-time from matter-flux, in which the block of images is a moment of deliberate intervention, or an 'immobile cut' or slice through flowing matter-flux, that stands in contrast to the architect's traditional 'frozen' orthographic representation of static space.[44] McGrath and Gardner referred to filmmaker Yasijiro Ozu's use of a fixed camera to film scenes at multiple right angles to establish a sense of architectural space and the complex trajectory of bodies within this space and, on this basis, to propose a new hybrid system of architectural drawing. This draws upon Deleuzian ideas of infusing the orthographic system of architectural representation with film stills and timelines that map space, time and movement as intervals or 'blocks' of space-time.[45] Furthermore, the architect's ability to manipulate video technology, introducing a cut or slice through the matter-flux, offers insight into both the range and limitations of architectural space, the human trajectory within this space, and the capacity to represent it in a new way.

Nevertheless, as Bryson (1988) reminded us, the 'block' of space-time is only one of many possible framings. The slice of flowing matter-flux establishes not only a framed field, but the field outside the frame according to precisely that act of intervention. Moreover, with an image-making process propagated by a network system of Internet webcam proportions, these acts of intervention are self-determined and potentially infinite. The new technology of the image facilitates a productive environment in which the architects 'experience themselves as moving centres of indeterminacy in an a-centred world' and can 'make drawings of an architecture that moves in a field of relations'.[46] As far as form-making is concerned, the architect can now escape the static image's limitations and historic formal implications. By allowing the city to be understood as a 'Deleuzian montagescape', the webcam provides new access to its more qualitative and uncontrollable properties, meaning that the image now offers the viewer a new type of engagement with the urban landscape while suggesting a new mode of form.

Responding to the digital city

The digital webcam system's collective effect – non-proprietary software, the introduction of multiple authorships, the open structure of the webcam network, multiple camera viewpoints and the camera's dynamic mechanism – grants the digital image a new generative status. By appropriating the human eye's optical strategies and performance, the open structure of the IP webcam, in association with high-speed image-making processes, releases the viewer to a new type of engagement with the city.

Furthermore, the uninhibited network pathways, composed of horizontal and vertical viewpoints, are new, emerging indices and agents of the redistributed ownership of a civic space that do more than simply uphold the existing relationships between power and place that were the original ambition of this mode of representation. In this respect, the proliferation of viewpoints forestalls exclusionary strategies of representational control, initiating a new reflexive indexicality between the image and viewed physical space. The contemporary, dynamic imagescape overcomes the static image's deterministic limitations with its historic formal implications, while also releasing unseen qualitative properties of the city.

This new type of urban image also continues to raise questions about the type of architectural form and context it represents. In this respect, it is even more appropriate to relocate Nigel's Green's comments on modernist architectural space and its photographic representation within a contemporary frame to conclude this chapter.

> The photographic image is a fiction conditioned by the technological possibilities and the cultural conventions of the present. Photography, then, must be seen as never a stable or fixed entity, but rather a process that is continually subject to technological innovation and change. The consistent aspect of photographic representation is that it is always a conduit through which ideas can take on visual form and, as such, it should continue to embrace its potential as a critical tool that both reflects upon and interrogates the process and legacy of architectural discourse.[47]

The application of the network camera to urban space has implications for form that parallel those established by the manifestation of Brunelleschi's perspective in the Urbino Panels. The imagescapes produced by citycams distributed across a global network are thus demonstrations of a new geometry and a new technology that require redefining the experience and materiality of form itself. Furthermore, they provide a clue to the question of future architectural agency posed by Scott McQuire: 'If the modern city is an event in which the authority of centred perception gives way to perception in motion, how do we gain access to it and develop an understanding of its dynamics?'[48] With the viewer in a new productive role, a new index of urban materiality and modes of form-making for the architect based upon the city's affective, qualitative properties come into play. With this in mind, the following section of this book is a response to just one of the many questions posed by McGrath and Gardner's comprehensive investigation of the moving image's impact upon architectural representation: 'What happens when we view architectural constructions through mobile sections rather than static architectural drawing?'[49] It is devoted to exploring new speculative techniques that, by engaging with dynamic perception mediated by the unique processes and instruments of digital technology, demonstrate and suggest how this system might be exploited to define its new role in urban representation and form-making.

Notes

1. Marc Hansen, 2004. *New philosophy for new media*. Cambridge MA: MIT Press, pp. 96–97.
2. Jurgis Baltrušaitis, 1977. *Anamorphic art*. New York, NY: Harry N. Abrams.
3. Lyle Massey, 2003. Configuring spatial ambiguity: Picturing the distance point from Alberti to anamorphosis. *Studies in the History of Art*, 59, p. 170.
4. Lyle Massey, 2007. *Picturing space, displacing bodies: Anamorphosis in early modern theories of perspective*. University Park, PA: Penn State University Press, p. 39.
5. Hansen, *New philosophy for new media*, p. 108.
6. Hansen, *New philosophy for new media*, p. 203.
7. Hansen, *New philosophy for new media*, p. 202.
8. Mark Monmonier, 2000. Webcams, interactive index maps, and our brave new world's brave new globe. *Cartographic Perspectives*, 0 (37), p. 57.
9. Austin Abrams, Nick Fridrich, Nathan Jacobs, and Robert Pless, 2010. *Participatory integration of live webcams into GIS*. Proceedings of the 1st International Conference and Exhibition on Computing for Geospatial Research & Application. Washington, D.C., USA: Association for Computing Machinery, 9, pp. 1–8.
10. Leonard Shlain, 1993. *Art & physics: Parallel visions in space, time and light*. New York, NY: Quill, p. 127.
11. Earthcam: *About Earthcam* [online]. Available from: https://www.earthcam.com/company/aboutus.php.
12. Keith Broadfoot, 2002. Perspective yet again: Damisch with Lacan. *Oxford Art Journal*, 25 (1), p. 93.
13. Damisch, *The origin of perspective*, p. 53.
14. Damisch, *The origin of perspective*, p. 53.
15. Laura Kurgan, 2013. *Close up at a distance: Mapping, technology, and politics*. New York, NY: Zone Books, p. 24.
16. William Bogard, Surveillance assemblages and lines of flight. In: D. Lyon, ed. *Theorizing surveillance: The panopticon and beyond*. Devon, UK: Willan Publishing.
17. Bogard, Surveillance assemblages and lines of flight, p. 121.
18. Michel Foucault, 1977. *Discipline and punish: The birth of the prison* (trans. Alan Sheridan). New York, NY: Random House.
19. Bogard, Surveillance assemblages and lines of flight.
20. Bogard, Surveillance assemblages and lines of flight, p. 115.
21. Bogard, Surveillance assemblages and lines of flight, p. 113.
22. Bogard, Surveillance assemblages and lines of flight, p. 113.
23. Pascal Pinck, 2000. From sofa to the crime scene: Skycam, local news and the televisual city. In: M. Balshaw and L. Kennedy, eds. *Urban space and representation*. Sterling, VA: Pluto Press, p. 57.
24. Bogard, Surveillance assemblages and lines of flight, p. 116.
25. Gilles Deleuze, 1992. Postscript on the societies of control. *October*, 59, p. 4.
26. Hille Koskela, 2006. The other side of surveillance: Webcams, power and agency. In: D. Lyon, ed. *Theorizing surveillance: The panopticon and beyond*. Cullompton: Willan Publishing, p. 165.

27 John Macarthur, 2000. From the air: Collage city, aerial photography and the picturesque. In: M. Ostwald and J. Moore, eds. *Re-framing architecture: Theory, science and myth*. Sydney: Archadia Press, p. 115.
28 Pinck, From sofa to the crime scene: Skycam, local news and the televisual city, p. 63
29 Alan Weedon, 2019. Why large swathes of countries are censored on Google Maps. Available from: https://www.abc.net.au/news/2019-02-21/why-large-parts-of-earth-are-censored-by-google-maps/10826024 [Accessed 23/10/2021].
30 Kurgan, *Close up at a distance*, p. 30.
31 Kurgan, *Close up at a distance*, p. 32.
32 Kurgan, *Close up at a distance*, p. 35.
33 This software is available at: http://www.appliedautonomy.com/isee.html
34 Brian McGrath and Jean Gardner, 2008. Cinemetrics: Embodying architectural representation in the digital age. *Architectural Theory Review*, 13 (1), p. 41.
35 Sergei Eisenstein, 1997. *Piranesi, or the fluidity of forms* (trans. Roberta Reeder). *Oppositions*, 11, pp. 105–106.
36 Yve-Alain Bois and John Shepley, 1984. A picturesque stroll around 'Clara-Clara'. *October*, 29, p. 53.
37 McGrath and Gardner, Cinemetrics: Embodying architectural representation in the digital age, p. 30.
38 Norman Bryson, 1988. The gaze in the expanded field. In: H. Foster, ed. *Vision and visuality*. Seattle, WA: Bay Press, p. 97.
39 Gilles Deleuze, 1986. *Cinema 1: The movement image* (trans. Hugh Tomlinson and Barbara Habberjam). Minneapolis, MN: University of Minnesota Press, p. 18.
40 Richard Koeck, 2013. *Cine-scapes: Cinematic spaces in architecture and cities*. Abingdon-on-Thames: Routledge.
41 Jonathan Beller, 2006. *The cinematic mode of production: Attention economy and the society of the spectacle*. Lebanon, NH: University Press of New England.
42 Richard Koeck, *Cine-scapes*, p. 71.
43 Deleuze, *Cinema 1*.
44 McGrath and Gardner, Cinemetrics: Embodying architectural representation in the digital age, p. 32.
45 McGrath and Gardner, Cinemetrics: Embodying architectural representation in the digital age, p. 35.
46 McGrath and Gardner, Cinemetrics: Embodying architectural representation in the digital age, p. 37.
47 Nigel Green, 2016. The transformative interface. In: G. Cairns, ed. *Visioning technologies: The architectures of sight*. Abingdon-on-Thames: Routledge, pp. 83–84.
48 Scott McQuire, 2016. Intersecting frames: Film + architecture. In: G. Cairns, ed. *Visioning technologies: The architectures of sight*. Abingdon-on-Thames: Routledge, p. 162.
49 Brian McGrath and Jean Gardner, 2007. *Cinemetrics: Architectural drawing today*. Chichester: Wiley-Academy, p. 33.

Part II
New techniques of intervention and disruption

5 Generative techniques

New modes of practice

Dziga Vertov used camera technology to re-present the city as a complex array of disjunctive yet interrelated visual fragments, showing that the medium of documentary film could deliver more than a singular urban narrative. Vertov's intention was to draw the viewer's attention to the mechanics of the camera and to awaken the unconscious viewer. This technique creates a clear distinction between the artwork and the artist, in the same way, that Walter Benjamin described the new 'pictures' obtained by the cameraman, consisting of 'a large number of pieces, which find their way back together by following a new law'.[1] To extend Benjamin's metaphor, the emergence of a new law for the production of artworks is accompanied not only by new technology and modes of practice that both unveil and depart from those of previous scopic regimes, but by new ways of discovering and applying their disciplinary relevance. Generative techniques to do with how the city might be represented and built according to a new digital law are, therefore, the subject of the following section. By disclosing aspects of the city previously unseen within existing civic narratives, these techniques extend disciplinary representation into a new qualitative realm. This profoundly new approach to urban representation is accompanied by speculative interventions that draw upon digital technology to point to previous modes of control and ownership, while simultaneously proposing a new and different type of disciplinary authorship within the urban domain.

In the contemporary city, the promotional webcam image is one instance of film's numerous modern counterparts. However, the complex structure of the digital image and the modes of manufacture and mediation associated with its technology offer more than new modes of generative practice; they also offer new disciplinary agency. Mario Carpo wrote of 'new and hitherto unimaginable venues and possibilities' presented by the digital that require not only a rethinking of architectural modes of production, but recognition that 'design will increasingly be achieved through visual and pictorial interfaces ... to the detriment of the

DOI: 10.4324/9781003133872-8

traditional formats of architectural notations (plans, elevations, and sections)', and that production will be undertaken by 'even nontechnical agents in all stages of design'.[2]

Hence, just as the accessibility of the digital imaging platform opens up image authorship to a global network of Internet users, so does it open up new pathways for image utility and application according to viewer needs. With image authorship thrown open to the viewing public, the question then remains as to what sort of agency the digital image can feasibly deliver to the architect. The answer may lie in the fact that, while the ordinary viewer can certainly intervene directly within the digital image platform, it is the opportunity and ability to negotiate the relationship between the image platform and its relationship to the city's built fabric that distinguishes the architect's use of the virtual image from that of the general populace. Considering this, if the retention of established representational practices within urban domains circumscribes architectural agency, then so too can the disruption of these practices open new disciplinary conversations and new mechanisms for architectural intervention. Therefore, the geometry and technology of the digital image platform can establish the ground not only for a new mode of urban representation, but pave the way for using the image to create a new type of topological, camera-responsive surface.

Protocols associated with the Internet webcam's image platform reflect the geometry that organises and distributes pixel groups for image synthesis. They also provide the technical pathways for the logic of its construction. The assignation of highly specific and layered data to the basic image unit, the pixel, means that qualitative representational content (colour, contrast and brightness) is foregrounded as the image's primary compositional and structural element. This chapter discusses a range of techniques that draw directly upon digital geometry and technology to establish new ways of generating architectural form. The approach presented here concerns how digital assemblies establish new conditions associated with an object's visibility that could inform architectural design development. The discussion includes examples of live urban contexts in which either high levels of contrast or blending could be managed in an architectural design intervention according to specific material selections, material distribution and façade activation. The application of this kind of technique can deliver the capacity to assist these types of design decisions, and it can do so across a temporal frame.

The new techniques fall into two distinct categories. The first consists of synthesised image sets that use existing visioning technologies and open-source digital software to re-present image data. Open-source software is a key aspect of these visual investigations, because, as the product of collective public research, its development relies upon ongoing manipulation and intervention. Transposed from its original scientific purpose into a projective design-based function, open-source software can also instigate generative procedures unavailable within traditional form-making processes. By drawing upon the digital geometry underpinning image assembly, new productive techniques based upon indexical qualitative image content can be included productively at the forefront of any architectural design procedure. Moreover, with pixel geometry acting in conjunction with the many viewing orientations of the webcam, a new mode of urban documentation that enables architects to design with these previously disregarded visual properties in mind becomes possible.

The second category of generative techniques takes the form of scaled prototype tests that underpin speculative architectural interventions. Once again, these draw upon specific aspects of digital geometry and technology's respective correspondences with the human eye to access the city's qualitative properties as generative material for architectural design. By drawing directly upon key curatorial procedures involved in manufacturing the 'sanitised' city image, the new strategies contest the seamless conveyance of image data through camera procedures and, ultimately, the production of a stable, curated representation of the city. By transposing digital micro-geometry patterns at a vastly increased material scale directly within the material surface as 'hyper-pixel' façade arrangements, the tests explore both the formal and visual consequences of adapting unique digital image properties to operate as formal templates for the design of a 'viewed' surface.

Thus, framed by the similar initiatives that underpinned Vertov's radical image-making techniques, and drawing upon an intensive investigation of the technical and translational protocols of digital network-based camera systems, this section presents a range of approaches to formal generation that are directly linked to unique properties of the digital and that exploit its processes. Indeed, it is only by identifying the 'dimensions of use that are not materially present'[3] within the digital image platform, and by identifying their corresponding formal implications, that the generative potential of the digital can be revealed and put to use. In sum, both the generative representational and speculative formal techniques described here demonstrate that the digital image embodies the very properties that predispose it to dismantling the effects of proprietary-controlled image-making. Furthermore, by engaging with the previously excluded qualitative aspects of urban life to inform the assembly of its fabric, these techniques work to both re-engage a new awareness and criticality in the viewer and fundamentally shift the status of the image within the architectural discipline.

The qualitative image

As previously established, digital image formation entails assigning an integer value to its basic unit, the pixel, to specify colour and brightness. According to these properties, a whole image is formed by assigning values to all pixels in the picture-plane grid. In the case of colour images, pixel values are represented by triples of scalar values such as red, blue and green or hue, saturation and intensity, and these values alone determine the relationships between pixels. In the case of the urban image, this means that image content is represented by an array of pixels, all distributed according to a specific numerical relationship. It also means that complex urban conditions captured by Internet webcam technology are also assigned specific numerical values and locations on the picture-plane grid that can be readily reproduced according to a unique array pattern. Furthermore, because these values are exclusively concerned with form demarcation through values associated with colour and brightness rather than through the line, this foregrounding of the city's qualitative aspects suggests a fundamentally new approach to both the documentation and construction of its 'viewed' physical surfaces.

The digital image's unique numerical arrays can be used to identify specific urban conditions, distinguishable according to the precise contextual distribution of pixel values. These include conditions pertaining to pedestrian and vehicular traffic, urban program and material surfaces. Also, to recall Vertov's belief that the city image should avail the viewer of all rather than selected urban conditions, it includes camera aberrations that produce artefact-affected images. PixelMath open-source software can identify an image's individual pixel values, thus establishing the means to document the complex conditions of urban space in numerical form and establish a reproducible platform that indexes the city's properties according to a new range of qualitative criteria. By extension, this means that the same conditions of colour and light in numerical form within the image can inform the city's fabric as a range of material relationships.

An example of how this procure works can be seen in Figure 5.1, which shows a portion of blurred image content (delineated by the white boundary line) translated into a numerical matrix using PixelMath[4] software. Webcam glitches, or transmission errors, are often highly abstracted

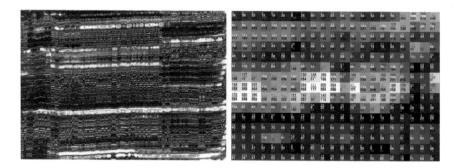

Figure 5.1 Digital glitch broadcasting error blue pixel noise ([golubovy]/Depositphotos.com) (left). Close-up of a section of the transmission error showing RGB pixel values of the artefact (right). (Image by author).

representations of urban conditions and would normally be regarded as disruptive or undesirable in image-making procedures, yet these affective, multiple-exposed images translate the city's landscape into a riot of colour and light. The webcam's automatic inclusion of these images within the daily urban image portfolio further reveals the extraordinary diversity of digital arrays that are potentially translatable into material form.

This numerical matrix serves as the basis for the distribution of numbers that composes this particular represented condition, that of blurring, to be readily transposed into a range of material or structural relationships. For example, the numerical RGB colour values could be transposed into a façade system, which would then mirror the same colour-weighted relationships in the spatial distributions of the city's form. In a hypothetical scenario, the RGB values of the image might inform other material properties such as surface gradient or thickness existing within the camera's field of view.

In this way, the city's material surfaces reflect all the variations revealed by the webcam and suggest how the city's qualitative properties can be embedded as data and represented within its physical surfaces. Even a simple translation of this numerical array in a Microsoft Excel data visualisation chart can indicate the types of spatial distributions of material surface that might arise from this type of approach. For example, numerical colour weightings could inform the lateral displacement of the building's material surface, while its vertical displacement could refer directly to the degree of luminosity distributed across the image. Depending upon the desired effect of the intervention, the resulting surface could operate either in opposition to, or in alignment with, the qualitative conditions of its immediate context.

Diffraction artefacts are another example of aberrant and normally disregarded images that represent the city in its many variable conditions. Even though the diffraction effects of rain on the camera lens are normally rejected and not considered as part of the city's curated 'iconic' repertoire, the webcam's automatic capture of these types of occurrences presents them as just another of the city's many shifting conditions. Also, because the presence of artefacts tends to abstract the traditional notion of image content, under a new digital 'law', these sorts of qualitative urban conditions simply offer further material or data that can be tabulated and transposed into numeric form according to a location and the pixel array's RGB values.

The architectural significance of this is that all of these conditions, aberrant or otherwise, are readily able to be translated into a building's material surface simply because they have a digital numeric attribution. This then initiates a new approach to form-making based not only on a more inclusive understanding of the city in its many conditions, but upon aspects of it that are typically deliberately excluded and discarded as either redundant or unsuitable. For the architect, the intrinsic numerical basis of the image thus opens a vast array of opportunities whereby the qualitative urban conditions associated with colour and brightness unveiled by the digital image can be transposed directly into the city's form. This replication of the numerical relationships between image pixels within material form can thus be seen to provide the wherewithal to tie the geometry of digital image content firmly to its real-time physical counterpart.

Incorporating these conditions directly into a building's physical surface is best understood within a broader disciplinary context. If the architect's role is to interrogate complex urban conditions through disciplinary techniques and their relation to visual apparatuses, then designing new form to obstruct or prevent the emergence and stabilisation of a singular urban narrative is a way of responding to this brief. In a context in which the digital image prevails, the introduction of formal strategies that counter the envisioning of the city as a singular, normative space must involve the incorporation and appropriation of digital properties and behaviours as part of a building's physical surface.

The space within the image

The anamorphic potential of digital technology

While the pixel-based digital array opens vast opportunities for the numerical indexing and inclusion of many diverse urban conditions, it is the webcam's capacity to project the viewer at oblique angles through urban space that provides unprecedented opportunities for rethinking not only how the city is represented and documented but how form might be materialised within that operative space. The zoom trajectory of webcam technology arguably echoes the technique of accelerated and decelerated modes of anamorphic perspective once deployed by Renaissance theatre designers to manipulate the perception of space. The same parallel can be drawn with its PTZ function, which sets up optical viewing conditions that correlate with the effect of other anamorphic techniques, such as when an alternative, secondary image is formed at an oblique angle to the picture plane. However, the formal consequences of digital anamorphic projection are profoundly different from those of earlier analogue image-making practices, because webcam technology enables the viewer to be projected remotely at high velocity and oblique angles across the viewing field. This results in a failure of the camera's capacity to maintain the optical integrity of the representation and the subsequent disclosure of the image's interior pixel architecture. Additionally, motion artefacts begin to assume a new role in the composition of the urban view. So, while this feature opens vast opportunities for the numerical indexing and inclusion of a range of urban conditions dictated by the digital array, the productive and affective potential of the webcam's capacity to move laterally through urban space requires examination.

The dismantling of projective linear space seen in Niceron and Maignan's anamorphic diagrams four centuries ago, and the conflation of the projected and real spaces of viewing, exposed the representational and logical limitations of linear perspective construction. It also advanced the notion of the physical, experiential journey along the surface of the picture plane and the pictorial consequences of this function. Niceron's diagram described previously showing the erasure of the diagrammatic viewing figure in favour of the actual viewer, was a way of simultaneously signalling the experiential limitations imposed by linear perspective geometry. However, this work also unveiled anamorphic perspective's new-found capacity for a heightened, physical viewing experience in the form of an embodied journey along the surface of Maignan's 17th-century fresco (Figure 5.2).

Like Niceron's and Maignan's work, the webcam trajectory across urban space produces oblique views that are at once both profoundly distorted yet highly affective. In this case, however, the viewer's physical journey along the plane of the image's surface, previously undertaken in a bid to assume a 'correct' viewing position, is replaced by the camera's arc, manipulated by the viewer at the site of the computer screen. This results in the production of a new condition of proprioception described by Marc Hansen that heightens the viewer's response to affect, in this case embodied in qualitative aspects of the city: 'proprioception proper designates the body's non-visual, tactile experience of itself, a form directed toward the bodily production of affection (affectivity).'[5] The micro-landscapes that once unfolded in the reflective pauses taken during an embodied journey along the picture-plane of Maignan's *San Francesco di Paola* now find their contemporary counterparts in the stationary moments of focus that occur within the webcam's pan/tilt path. Images from examples of multiple camera installations sites, such as Times Square, New York and Shibuya Crossing, Tokyo, routinely produce a combination of highly resolved as well as artefact-affected images in their prolific output. In these moments, more affective, qualitative aspects of the city operate alongside crisper, higher clarity images. Yet, just as in the case of *San Francesco di Paola*, the coexistence of both is vital to any critical understanding of the city where 'all are allowed to see its conditions'.[6]

Furthermore, the horizontal panning action of the webcam opens a profoundly new set of images based on another type of anamorphic technique: catoptric or reflective cylindrical anamorphosis. Used by Niceron as a mechanism of critical interrogation, the contemporary version of this anamorphic variation generated by the webcam questions traditional ways of representing the city's form. The catoptric anamorphic image is manifest in the relationship between the representational arc of the webcam's horizontal pan action and the elevation of form within this space. In simple terms, the anamorphic projection is a correspondence between a set of Cartesian coordinates and a set of polar coordinates.[7] By comparison, the circular geometry of the webcam arc produces a sequence of Cartesian images that, when redistributed as a horizontal planar

100 *New techniques of intervention and disruption*

Figure 5.2 Emmanuel Maignan's fresco *San Francesco di Paola* (1642) in Trinità dei Monti, Rome, showing distorted image when viewed from frontal position (top left), image when viewed from 'correct' oblique viewing position (top right) and micro-landscapes embedded within the larger image visible from a viewing position perpendicular to the image surface (bottom). (Image by author).

section according to polar coordinates, produces a catoptric anamorphic image. In this scenario, the 'corrected' counterparts of this anamorphic image set, derived from locations along a circular arc (or its elevation in 3D architectural terms), which also form the 'corrected' representation or

Deleuzian 'imagescape' of this space, are at an oblique angle rather than perpendicular to it. Significantly, a key aspect of this type of anamorphic projection is the viewing position. The oblique viewpoint must be above the viewed surface, not perpendicular to it, to produce a 'corrected' view of the distorted image, as in the case of the accelerated and decelerated modes of anamorphism discussed previously. The notion of applying catoptric anamorphic projection to the imaging of urban space, therefore, releases the viewer from what was formerly a privileged, single and fixed viewpoint. In contemporary urban space, where form is highly 'verticalised', the distribution of new webcam viewpoints, which are for the most part oblique and often located in a position more elevated than the viewing field, thus offers the architect an unprecedented range of responsive opportunities.

An example of the potential application of this technique is shown in Figure 5.3, where the catoptric image is generated from a circular mathematical transformation of multiple traditionally oriented vertical views using Cylinder Reflection Generator,[8] a JavaScript open-source software program, to determine the precise angles of the view intersections.

Here the various 'resting' or stationary viewpoints of the webcam are located at various points along the circumference of a circular arc to generate vertically oriented representations or elevations of the urban landscape. The catoptric anamorphic transformation of these views redistributes them as a different type of 2D array, which can only be 'corrected' from an oblique position to this plane on a reflective curved surface, where the distorted anamorphic transformation can be seen in its 'corrected' form (Figure 5.3). This image also reveals how the elevated viewpoint of the observer or camera is crucial to the operation of this particular anamorphic technique. The 'corrected' vertical image's 'other', or its distorted counterpart, then becomes the site plan, automatically investing the 2D image with 3D spatial properties. Importantly, the fact that the composition of the digital array allows the same visual information to be re-presented in alternative versions implies the emergence of a new mode of documenting urban form that interrogates the traditional relationship between elevation and plan.

To explain this further, the catoptric anamorphosis produced by the location of multiple webcams within a single site where multiple fields of view intersect means that the site elevation is determined by intersecting rotational webcams arcs covering a 360° view of the site. A digital data recomposition of multiple intersecting views is thus able to provide a visual transformation of the urban landscape that releases these views from the constraints of traditionally conceived notions of form and time. The reciprocity and interplay between plan and elevation not only question long-held assumptions about the viewer's position in space and the orientation of images arising from such assumptions, but provoke a new disciplinary response to how these types of spaces can be documented to underpin design intervention.

102 *New techniques of intervention and disruption*

Figure 5.3 Stationary camera viewpoints near Customs House, Circular Quay, Sydney (top left); catoptric anamorphic image generated from the same viewpoints (top right); Catoptric cylindrical anamorphic projections of Customs House, Circular Quay, Sydney, showing anamorphic projections, and 'corrected' Cartesian arrays in the reflective surface of the cylinder (bottom images). (Image by author).

The dynamic image

The image as a 3D volume

The following technique draws upon the fragmentary and temporal features of contemporary viewing technology using processed visual data captured from the Internet webcam to reveal the evolutionary pattern of urban conditions. With the distributed nature of the city preventing the formation of either a continuous or comprehensive image from any single vantage point, the image-making process is both complex and constantly evolving. The streaming generation of images recalls Deleuze's concept of the cinematic selection of blocks of space-time from matter-flux, where a block or volume of images is a moment of deliberate intervention, or an 'immobile cut' or slice through flowing matter-flux that stands in contrast to the architect's traditional frozen orthographic representation of static space.[9] In this scenario, the user can manipulate video technology by introducing a cut or slice through the matter-flux that offers insight into urban space and the human trajectory within this space. It also provides an opportunity to offer a disciplinary response to the new spatial conditions that accompany new visual technology's mediation of the city, so comprehensively delineated by McGrath and Gardner:

> When we move planes vertically and horizontally through architecture, much like a CAT scan, we sense a living organism rather than dissecting [sic] an inanimate object. The virtual camera can provide a non-human eye lens for architecture: transparent and able to cut through solid matter. Shooting and the mobile section will be examined not just as a representational technique, but as a new drawing tool and as a means of generating space.[10]

Unlike the traditional static images of the city, the webcam's progressive revealing of the contemporary city can be exploited as a speculative, projective tool to inform design choice directly. The two key determining factors in this procedure are, therefore, time and place.

Open-source Java-based medical image-processing software, ImageJ,[11] was used to 'slice' a selected block of space-time from video footage to initiate a response to the first of these factors. ImageJ offers the capability for organising live streaming video footage into manageable image sets, or 'stacks'. The stacks are multiple spatially and temporally related images or slices displayed in a single window that can be easily manipulated, rotated and reassembled according to user specifications. The 3D visualisation of such a set of images extends its functionality well beyond the realm of 2D analysis into more projective design functions. In these, the evolution of more qualitative aspects of urban activity, in this case, presented in terms of colour and luminosity, can be traced.

104 *New techniques of intervention and disruption*

The selection of New York City as a location addresses the second factor of place. Internet webcams abound in Times Square, offering the capacity to obtain multiple readings, or provide a montagescape, of that place. This location was also selected because webcam image content is primarily geared to reflect the promotional interests of site ownership, therefore presenting an added opportunity to test this new technique's functionality in drawing the viewer's attention to precisely such proprietorial interests.

Figure 5.4 shows a rotated stack of images extracted from time-lapse video footage of the Times Square precinct. The assembled selection clearly shows the evolution of activity in the viewed space over a pre-determined time frame,

Figure 5.4 Rotated time-lapse image stack (top left), intersecting orthogonal slice (top right) and conflated projection of an image stack along z axis (bottom) showing a view of Broadway looking towards Times Square, New York.

Source: Original images: Gavin Hellier.

Generative techniques 105

here taking the form of a progression in colour range distributed across the image stack. A development in degrees of luminosity or brightness can also be seen. The same figure shows a single orthogonal slice through the image stack, revealing how the intersection of digital visual data across multiple axes enables specific time points to be located within a progressive temporal context.

The figure also reveals yet another capability offered by the open-source ImageJ software, the Z Project function. The same image data are presented as a single conflated image according to a range of different urban properties, including brightness and traffic flow. By superimposing all visual data in a single composition, these synthesised images begin to dismantle the traditional criteria applied to the imaging of the city. Here the image's formal properties of clarity and colour coherence are relinquished in favour of the blurred trajectories of form according to motion and time. The presentation of form in terms of colour and brightness made possible by this type of representational technique foregrounds hitherto unseen qualitative conditions operating within the urban precinct.

With urban conditions now visible as a volumetric flow, any intervention made within this space can be easily mapped and made visible in the same qualitative terms. This, therefore, allows the architect to predict a building's 'behaviour' within an urban context across any proposed temporal frame. Most importantly, it offers the opportunity for its built surface to be perceived and understood in the rich and complex qualitative terms that camera viewing technology now makes possible and visible. In other words, the new set of images arising from the application of this technique serves as the means to initiate a new type of design decision that is both qualitative and time-based.

The application of this technique revisits Vertov's use of image content *within* and movement *of* the frame to index processes *outside* the camera frame. To extrapolate the same strategy into a digital context, the ImageJ image stack establishes the means and criteria by which the properties of the city and any intervention made within that immediate space can be perceived and understood, because the stack is but one small part of an evolving continuum. Because both the city and its image-making network are globally distributed, the insertion of this single frame or slice within the universal visual field is only one of an infinite number of framings that might contribute to the establishment of the field outside the frame. Significantly, the viewer's (or architect's) ready accessibility to a 'viewed' world both outside and discontinuous with that within the Internet camera's frame also denies the production of a single, continuous urban narrative. Additionally, it produces a collective montagescape of a newly distributed city, where volumetric representations of qualitative urban space continually cross-pollinate at a global level, and where emerging conditions continue to present themselves for consideration as part of a broader design palette.

The ability to observe the inhabitation of urban space in qualitative terms fostered by this technique also raises the possibility of pre-testing an intervention according to whether it is complementary or dissimilar to the existing site context. For example, how might the colour of a building's material or its shifting brightness levels compare with those of its neighbours? The deliberate insertion of a façade colour standing in high contrast to that of neighbouring façades, combined with strategic activations of program-activated brightness within the building, could profoundly enhance or diminish visibility across a 24-hour webcam cycle.

The visualisation of the city across multiple simultaneously evolving axes of the image stack allows the architect to test the contextual relationship of any intervention at a specific temporal point within the stack. It also facilitates an entirely autonomous viewing experience through the axes of representation. The ImageJ tool that enables this type of visual journey moves the viewer through a series of orthogonally intersecting x, y axes that progressively evolve along a third z-axis to produce a complete reconfiguration of the visual content of the image stack (Figure 5.5). The new image slices synthesise axial cuts that collectively form a new mapping of urban space to question traditional representations of the city and its material surfaces. The visual jolt produced by this tool recalls Vertov's use of jump-cuts to reawaken the viewer's optical processes. Yet here, the procedure of reassembling the city's form and the resulting foregrounding of its affective properties are completely user-determined. The capacity to step inside the image stack releases the city's multiple viewpoints and its conditions to all. To refer once again to the emergence of numerous viewer 'types' proliferated by this image-making platform, on the one hand, the effect of this new mode of urban visualisation profoundly transforms the ordinary viewer's experience and understanding of the city; on the other, it endows the architectural viewer with new generative agency.

The synthesised landscape

Transdisciplinary modes of activating digital colour and luminance (brightness)

The generative capacity of the Deleuzian blocks of space-time made visible by the Internet webcam is again furthered by drawing upon other resources of the versatile ImageJ software platform. Whereas the previous procedure realigns image content along either the image stack's x or y-axis over a specific time frame or its z-axis to establish discrete sectional views of an image set or volume, ImageJ further complexifies the reassembly of the 3D image stack by subjecting it to another 're-slice' process. However, in this case, rather than using the entire image stack, sample images are selected at regular but more extended time intervals. This abstraction of image content departs completely from the conventional modes of representation by allowing complex urban conditions to unfold as temporal patterns of colour

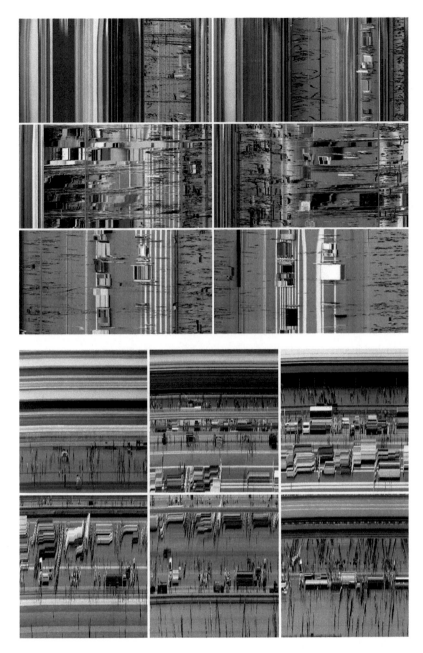

Figure 5.5 Montage of image slices selected from the *xz* (top) and *zy* (bottom) axes of an image stack showing a view of Broadway looking towards Times Square, New York.

Source: Original images: Gavin Hellier.

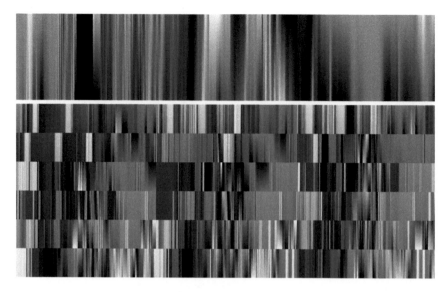

Figure 5.6 A single slice from the image stack (top) and a montage of slices selected from the image stack (bottom) showing a view of Broadway looking towards Times Square, New York.

Source: Original images: Gavin Hellier.

and brightness, as seen in Figure 5.6. Individual slices can also be compiled into a strip or multi-tiered montage to provide a single image of the recomposed urban landscape. A summary of architectural applications associated with this technique and a discussion of some real examples of these applications follows.

Colour and luminance (brightness) profiles as a generative procedure

The conversion of an image stack into a colour and brightness-based temporal representation of the city using ImageJ's Reslice tool introduces the means to map the progression of the city's qualitative content accurately as visual data. Broadly speaking, the development of these properties in a series of images is indicative of corresponding shifts in urban materiality and density. Programmatic transitions of all kinds are represented: urban circulation, such as the density of pedestrian traffic; the patterns of vehicular traffic flow; and the effects of program activation both upon and within building façades. Patterns formed by the reslicing of a sequence of image slices of Times Square provide an insight into the city's new compositional patterns made visible within the image stack. For the architect, this patterning or profiling establishes new conditions to which an intervention might be designed to respond strategically, such as enhancing or diminishing its visibility: its materiality (colour and texture), and changes in its program across a given time frame (brightness). For example, within a webcam's field of view, a building might be designed to stand in direct contrast to its immediate context, in which case the choice of materials and façade activation would be deliberately chosen according to shifts in its program to counteract those of its neighbours.

Conversely, the need for a building to have low visibility would mean a selection of materials and program aligned with those in its immediate context. The colour and brightness profiling technique can deliver the data to make a broad range of new design decisions. It can be used to understand different time spans and provide a more detailed, specific level of information. Furthermore, the global distribution of the webcam network enables it to be used to compare the conditions of either the same location from a range of different angles or different locations globally, meaning that a comparative assessment of the building's performance can be made within the same temporal frame.

These abstract series of urban images ask the viewer to respond to different optical properties in the image. The result is that the city is no longer recognisable in its traditional form. The dominance of linear representation is now relinquished in favour of qualitative aspects in which the internal arrangement and hierarchy of content are organised to allow variations in the transition between pixel edges to be less distinct. Thus, by no longer grouping pixels according to their capacity to enhance linear grouping or any narrative associated with this type of grouping, the urban landscape is converted into a series of fragmentary snapshots that together compose a new type of urban representation. To recall Vertov's innovative cinematic techniques, the translation of the traditional cityscape in this non-traditional way, and the capacity of the webcam's image-making network to support the ready cross-referencing of different conditions at a local and global level, provides the means whereby the complex conditions of modern life in one location can readily index and cross-pollinate those of another. Also, the deliberate inclusion of artefacts, such as blurring and the new pixel grouping hierarchies, distances this type of urban picture from the highly curated properties of the promotional image. Instead, they move it towards Vertov's notion of a common vision of the city, where all are allowed to see its various conditions.

The colour profiles bring a new type of urban visualisation into the architectural arena. The unique assemblies and compositions that form the qualitative representation of the urban landscape connect the architect to correspondingly new and unique types of formal and material assemblies that operate according to their laws. Furthermore, the ability to see the temporal evolution of the same qualitative data transforms how architectural intervention within urban space can be addressed and understood.

Conclusion

The generative capacities of the image sets discussed in this chapter are made possible by two key aspects of digital image-making: the pixel-based structure of the image and the camera's image-making technology. In the first case, the ability to assign a numerical value to all types of urban conditions captured by the webcam image allows those same conditions to be readily duplicated and transposed into their physical counterparts as a series of material and structural relationships. Pixel-based image sets thus provide the architect with a reproducible tool that accurately tabulates a vast range of urban conditions for determining the type of architectural response contextually appropriate to a selected site. In those cases, the same conditions existing in numerical form within the image can be strategically transposed into the city's fabric to operate according to a predictable set of effects underpinned by known material relationships. Furthermore, the new image properties presented by unique pixel arrays supplant the domination of the linear perspective line with the city's qualitative aspects of colour and light. This shift in geometries sets up a comprehensively different hierarchy of image content and, by extension, urban representation and form-making, by which the city's physical properties and conditions are able to be perceived and understood. In response, the technique of colour and brightness profiling establishes new representational techniques in which pixels, no longer being grouped to describe form and, by extension, the traditional city image, are instead recomposed and grouped according to various seemingly random patterns.

A key component of the colour profiling technique is the introduction of a temporal dimension into the new way of visualising the city. It underpins the second key aspect of digital image-making crucial to its generative capability: webcam technology. The Internet camera introduces a temporal factor into the imaging of the city, thus suggesting a vastly different approach to the documentation of urban sites. Also, the webcam's productivity and field of view set a new course for its scope as a generative tool. The technique of organising streaming webcam video footage into 3D volumes, easily manipulated, rotated and reassembled according to user specifications, endows the resulting images with a projective capability that the architect can put to good use. The evolution of the qualitative aspects of a city's activity, now understood as emanations of colour and brightness, can be easily mapped, assessed and predicted. Also, the many transmission glitches or aberrations that occur during the image-making process are now incorporated into the image set to form part of the city's newly comprehensive representation. The interconnected global camera network endows these new representational techniques with indexical properties that are inclusive of all conditions, of 'what always lies beyond the frame, discontinuous with what is framed'.[12] It too recalls Benjamin's[13] observation of the camera's ability to penetrate deeply into the web of reality by revealing the diverse and multifaceted nature of the urban landscape that, by drawing attention to the imperfections within the image-making mechanism itself, ruptures the possibility of any continuous or singular narrative of the city.

Finally, the catoptric anamorphic image sets made available by the webcam's ability to move the viewer through extended lateral arcs of view add further interrogation to the relationship between contemporary urban form and its modes of representation. The ordinary viewer's recent inclusion in what had formerly been a privileged viewpoint poses new questions to the architect, particularly in relation to the anamorphic image sets arising from the many oblique and highly vertical webcam viewpoints. The radical transformation of the data composition of the digital array discussed in this chapter therefore not only privileges image content in a new way, but profoundly interrogates how the city has been traditionally documented. In architectural terms, by redistributing the elevation data into a plan orientation, the catoptric anamorphic image sets suggest a complete inversion of traditional approaches to urban documentation. Similarly, by offering numerous opportunities to intervene along the z-axis of the image stack, the 3D image sets provoke questions about how the traditional section is conceived. All these new urban visualisations are thus more than mere 2D representations of the city. In fact, by releasing the image to a new generative agency, they operate as working drawings for the new digital city.

Notes

1 Walter Benjamin, 1936. The work of art in the age of mechanical reproduction. London: Penguin Books, p. 37.
2 Mario Carpo, 2011. *The alphabet and the algorithm*. Cambridge, MA: MIT Press, p. 125.
3 Martin Hand, 2012. *Ubiquitous photography*. Cambridge: Polity Press, p. 42.
4 PixelMath is an image-processing program developed by the University of Washington that allows the user to access and manipulate the actual pixel values of an image in numeric form. The software is available at: http://pixels.cs.washington.edu/PixelMath/pmdownload/request.php
5 Marc Hansen, 2004. *New philosophy for new media*. Cambridge, MA: MIT Press, p. 229.
6 Thomas Sheehan, 2003. Wittgenstein and Vertov: Aspectuality and anarchy. *Discourse*, 24, p. 100.
7 Anonymous, 2010. *Anamorphic Art: A special instance of perspective* [Online]. Available from: http://anamorphicart.wordpress.com/
8 This software was developed by Nicole Massarelli, under the direction of Dr Don Spickler, Department of Mathematics and Computer Science Henson School of Science & Technology, Salisbury University, Maryland, USA, and is available at: http://facultyfp.salisbury.edu/despickler/personal/Cylinder ReflectionGeneratorMultiImage.asp

9 Brian McGrath and Jean Gardner, 2008. Cinemetrics: Embodying architectural representation in the digital age. *Architectural Theory Review*, 13 (1), pp. 29–51.
10 Brian McGrath and Jean Gardner, 2007. *Cinemetrics: Architectural drawing today*. Chichester: Wiley-Academy, p. 33.
11 This software is available at: http://rsbweb.nih.gov/ij/
12 Sheehan, Wittgenstein and Vertov: Aspectuality and anarchy, p. 98.
13 Benjamin, The work of art in the age of mechanical reproduction.

6 The building surface as a colour modifier

Design templates for the built surface

A second category of generative techniques taking the form of series of physical tests complements those presented in chapter 5. These constitute new strategies for exploiting the technical pathways of key image-making strategies that disrupt image data transmission and, consequently, the ability to sustain a stable promotional image of the city. The tests focus on three aspects of image production: protocols governing colour composition, the management of image artefacts and the privileging of areas of interest. The outcomes reveal how building design incorporating pattern types associated with these technical pathways can modify the perception of the digital image.

Image modification occurs in two ways: a designed surface can either shift the viewing hierarchy of the image by reorganising the prominence of elements within its field of view, or it can directly disrupt the camera's ability to produce a legible representation of the city. These two options underpin a series of potentially generative procedures that allow the architect to design specific effects into a building's physical surface. Conceptually, the tests rely upon a principle of increased scale. In the case of all three test types, elements of the camera's processing procedures are extrapolated from their original micro context within the camera and are reinterpreted and 'mirrored' at a vastly increased scale as speculative building façade elements. The purpose of this is to reveal how the protocols, operating directly as templates for the design of a building's surface, can be applied strategically to any viewed scene. Because the mirrored 'hyperpixel' façade arrangements interfere with the camera's ability to record viewed content, theoretically, they enable the architect to adjust a building's visual effect by assigning designed assemblies of colour and contrast to its surface. By operating as templates, these transposed protocols instigate a vastly different viewing condition, in which the virtual and real experiences of the city's qualitative properties (colour and brightness) are separated. Simultaneously, they provoke the viewer's awareness of the deliberately constructed nature of the image's scene. Furthermore, the tests show that

DOI: 10.4324/9781003133872-9

digital geometry's capacity to be operative across an infinite range of scales, and to be assembled into highly controllable and repeatable pixel patterns, means that these new assemblies can be linked indexically to the optical effects of the built surface.

Test strategies

Colour

The first of the speculative prototype test series (Series 1) deals with the camera's colour receptor mechanism, consisting of a CCD or CMOS sensor and the CFA pattern defined in earlier chapters, located within it. Both CCD and CMOS sensors utilise a scanning process to convert electrical charge into a digital value, but the CCD sensor has 10 times the light sensitivity of the CMOS sensor, which also has a poorer dynamic response. (The human eye can see objects under a light condition of 1 Lux, whereas the CCD sensor requires only 0.1–3 Lux.[1]) Cameras for more complex applications use a CCD sensor; CMOS sensors are normally used for low-end home security. The CFA is located above the pixel sensors to capture colour information and convert it into a full-colour image. The tests associated with this camera mechanism aim to reveal how the performance of selected CFA patterns, some of which are cited as having explicit degrees of effectiveness (clarity) in image-processing,[2] correlates with the results achieved when patterns are transformed to an architectural scale.

Image artefacts

The second test series (Series 2) employs the same scalar translation from micro to macro, but here the scalable subject replaces colour with the image artefact, in this case, a diffraction pattern. Traditionally an unwanted and discarded product of image-making, diffraction patterns are created by an interaction between an obstacle, commonly known as a diffraction grating, and a light source. This test aims to reveal how the deliberate manufacture of image artefacts, such as diffraction patterns seen in the received camera image of a building's surface, might draw attention to the city image's deliberately constructed nature and artifice. This is achieved by incorporating specific pattern arrangements within the city's built surfaces to disrupt the production of a stable image.

Attention tracking

The third and final test series (Series 3) turns again to the camera's image sensor, but in this case involves raster scanning, the pattern created by the encoding, decompression and subdivision of information into sequences of 'scan lines'[3] that are retranslated as architectural elements at hyper-pixel

The building surface as a colour modifier

scale. Scan-order patterns are part of a highly strategic camera process controlled by a predetermined algorithm programmed to prioritise the production of a smooth, moving image. Furthermore, variations of the scan-order code enable the identification and privileging of image regions of specific interest, thereby exposing image content to high levels of curatorial intervention and control.[4] Consequently, this test series aims to show how a strategic transposition and incorporation of selected scan-order patterns within the city's material surfaces can disrupt the camera's capacity to create a coherent, legible image or inscribe it with a viewing hierarchy that privileges selective areas of content. As in the other tests, the capacity to extrapolate this type of information as reusable data is unique to digital geometry.

Validation methods

The results of the tests documented in this section are corroborated by quantitative analysis provided by a range of analytical procedures available in open-source software. Two platforms are used: ImageJ and HyperCube2.[5] ImageJ is a complex and regularly developed open-source JavaScript image-analysis software traditionally used for biological image analysis. This application is used in a parallel mode to assess transitions and differences within image content over defined periods. HyperCube2 is a spectral imagery analysis program developed by the US Army to provide static and dynamic display of the image cube (a technique for examining the cyclic structure of wavelengths in the visible electromagnetic spectrum) and generate spectral classifications.[6]

ImageJ has a range of custom acquisition, analysis and processing plugins that underpin the test outcomes described in this section. The assessment of colour intensity and emission of the image's individual RGB colour channels is achieved using a Colour Histogram plugin, while tools such as the 3D Colour Inspector plugin allow the viewer to understand colour distribution as a 3D model within a colour space.

The second test series, concerning luminance, or a particular pattern's capacity to transmit light, draws upon two ImageJ functions, the first of which is its Interactive 3D Surface Plot plugin. This plugin interprets the luminance of an image as the height for the plot, allowing the articulated 3D surface plot of one image to be visualised and tested against the surface plot of another. The benefit of this function is that it allows the status of the individual colour channels to be observed and the relative luminosity levels of individual pattern types to be compared easily.

A more accurate quantitative analysis of the comparative luminance of each pattern is determined using a second ImageJ function, the Floyd Steinberg Dithering Algorithm, which combines a binary converter and a particle assessment function. Using this algorithm, the images are converted to binary form and subsequently counted and measured according to the maxima of luminance, with the luminance defined as the weighted or unweighted average of the colours.[7] This particle data count procedure operates by scanning the image or selection until it finds an edge to count and measure identifiable objects. In other words, the greater the number of objects, the brighter the selected area of content. However, the measuring of brightness can also be associated with the presence of camera glare artefacts that compromise the delineation of the viewed object. In this case, the particle data counts reflect the formation of particles that bind together into clusters and therefore fewer individual, legible units. The camera then interprets these clusters as a glare artefact.

Finally, it is this software's ability to assemble large numbers of individual images into a single, manageable image stack using its Z Project function, discussed in chapter 5 and seen in Figure 5.6, that enables all image properties and values contained within each volume to be assessed. This function quantifies all image data throughout any selected trajectory of the webcam.

HyperCube2 software contains data visualisation functions with the capacity to produce spectral plots from an image cube, where the vertical axis shows the minimum and maximum reflectance value of all the vectors relative to the wavelength on the horizontal axis. In the Series 1 tests, the software is used to assess the quantum of luminosity emitted at a specific wavelength, in this case the median wavelength emitted by the patterns, to corroborate the data obtained from the ImageJ luminance tests.

Although adapted here from a traditional operating environment, both non-commercial software packages provide a comprehensive test platform for analysing the properties of adapted CFA patterns and assessing their performance at a much larger speculative material scale.

Series 1 tests overview

Using specific CFA pattern types, including those used by commercial manufacturers and other pattern variants, the Series 1 tests project CFA patterns onto a building's surface as vastly scaled-up mirrors of the camera's original CFA mosaic structure. The underpinning assumption is that the mirrored pattern will produce a visible effect upon the quality of the image relayed to the viewer's digital device. Therefore, the tests aim to demonstrate how the geometry of any situated webcam output can be used to modify façade visibility by altering the received image's visual hierarchy.

Different parts of the tests address the two modes of image modification mentioned previously separately. One part draws upon various adapted versions of the camera's CFA pattern to reorganise the hierarchy of the elements within the camera's field of view through the varying ability of the arrays to transmit colour intensity. The second and third parts address the transmission of image legibility, using variations in the arrays' brightness and the effects of their physical superimposition to determine object visibility, respectively.

Test part 1: Strategies of pattern hierarchy

In the CFA pattern mosaic structure, the pixel is positioned as the focus and determinant of image data transmission. It is situated above the CCD pixel sensor as a repetitive array of red, green and blue filter material positioned above every spatial location in the array. The camera lens focuses light from a single point within the image frame directly onto the arrangement of colour filters on the sensor's pixel array, generating a charge that is directly proportional to that light. In this operational context, the pixel is a single scalar element within a multi-component representation in which a direct relationship is established between the patterning and quality of the received image on the digital display device and the patterning of the CFA.[8] However, this technological mode of colour transferal remains an imperfect extrapolation of the capability of human vision.

> A required image-processing step for Bayer pattern sensors is interpolation, during which the missing data is estimated from neighboring pixel data. For example, for a red pixel location, the green and blue data must be interpolated from green and blue neighbors since these values are not directly recorded.[9]

Put simply, if there is no colour information available, then the camera design must perform the task of interpolating missing colour data to create three complete RGB colour image planes. By extension, the translation of chromatic and luminosity-related data from one pixel to its neighbour becomes a process of estimation, in which a perfect simulacrum of the original signal is not possible. This procedural gap exposes the imaging process to many kinds of intervention, including those that work to minimise and normalise the digital visual information field. It also leads to the erasure of potentially interesting visual effects in favour of a pre-enhanced model. The most common CFA pattern type used in cameras is the Bayer filter, with a pattern distribution of 50% green, 25% red and 25% blue. This pattern produces a stable and predictable outcome and happens to be compatible with the numerous commercial software applications used further down the image-processing pipeline. However, multiple alternative array assembly options also exist.

John Savard[10] outlined numerous unexplored CFA pattern variants that warrant further investigation, in view of the fact that the choice of CFA pattern 'critically influences the accuracy of the single-sensor imaging pipeline'.[11] Lukac and Plataniotis revealed that of the 10 patterns they investigated, only one, the traditional Bayer pattern, had been the subject of any further scientific attention.[12] Their investigation of 10 RGB CFA types led them to propose that while there is no 'perfect' CFA, CFA selection does indeed influence the performance of the sensor pipeline, while simultaneously reducing image aberrations. Therefore, by relying upon the

118 *New techniques of intervention and disruption*

(caption on next page)

Figure 6.1 Patterns used in Series 1 tests. Column 1, top to bottom: Pattern 1 – Bayer CFA; Pattern 2 – pattern proposed by Lukac and Plationatis; Pattern 3 – Yamanaka CFA; Pattern 4 – diagonal stripe CFA; Pattern 5 – pseudo-random CFA. Column 2, top to bottom: Pattern 6 – HVS-based CFA; Pattern 7 – non-CFA pattern (red, blue); Pattern 8 – non-CFA pattern (blue, green); Pattern 9 – periodic hexagonal grid CFA; Pattern 10 – non-periodic hexagonal grid CFA. (Image by author).

established efficacy of the CFA patterns used in the authors' tests at an original micro camera scale, it is proposed that their inclusion in the following speculative tests will produce a similar hierarchy of performative attributes when translated to an architectural scale.

Of the ten CFA patterns with test results reported here, Lukac and Plataniotis describe six (Figure 6.1). The patterns can be divided into two distinct types – periodic and pseudo-random – according to the ease with which camera manufacturers can ensure that the sensor is able to reconstruct the image cost-effectively. Although the demosaicing process is far simpler with periodic than pseudo-random patterns, the latter are less likely to produce image artefacts, such as colour moiré effects. Of the five periodic patterns tested, one is the most common pattern (Bayer), and another draws upon a pattern that Lukac and Plataniotis proposed as the most effective CFA pattern. The pseudo-random pattern is based upon the colour responses of the HVS. Its authors refer to an HVS model to characterise perceptual error in an image, then deploy an algorithm to minimise that error.[13] In addition, two non-CFA patterns are included, both having only two of the three RGB colour channels, to observe the effects of pattern shape and distribution upon the transmission of colour and luminosity. These two non-CFA patterns provide a control function for the tests by not conforming to the colour distribution models of the other standard CFA patterns. The remaining two patterns are variations upon the hexagonal grid, known to have several significant perceptual advantages over the square grid.[14]

By incorporating a broad range of pattern types, the tests seek to establish a set of speculative behavioural criteria associated with their transposition from a micro to a macro context at a massively increased order of magnitude. These criteria are determined according to the extent to which each pattern's adaptation and reuse as an element of a building's structure and materiality modify the building's visibility when viewed by the camera.

Test technical data and conditions

The tests were undertaken in a controlled, dark, interior environment using a Sony SX43E Handycam digital video recorder, comparable to the Kintronics long-range IR PTZ surveillance camera.[15] Both cameras have CCD sensors that use interlaced scanning, and both have a 60x zoom capacity. The CFA patterns were cut from 3 mm coloured acrylic, assembled onto a second transparent acrylic base and placed individually in front of a single light source. A 30W Par 64 RGB LED lamp simulated the level of light emission conditions emitted by the interior lighting of a city office building at night, while the adapted array patterns simulate a translucent building façade backlit by interior lighting. The camera's placement at 8 m from the image plane represents a scaled approximation (1:10) of an average Internet camera viewing distance from a brightly lit image source, or in other words, the 8 m length in the test correlates with an 80 m distance in an exterior environment.

Similarly, the CFA patterns were fabricated in 360 mm^2 square elements, correlating with a building façade surface area of 3.6 m^2. The aim was to enable specific effects seen in the captured image to align with the camera's aperture range or f-stop increments, and thus to be identified according to the camera's zoom trajectory.

Test analysis methodology

The images of the tests of individual patterns were processed using ImageJ's Z Project function. This function enables assessment of the relative values of image effects by projecting an image stack along the axis perpendicular to the image plane (the so-called z-axis). It also supports different projection types, including an average intensity projection (AIP) and a maximum intensity projection (MIP), wherein each pixel accumulates the average and maximum intensity levels (respectively) of all images throughout the stack at a corresponding pixel location, according to RGB levels.[16] These two projections were used in the first test series to determine the extent of the patterns' effects upon colour processing. The objective was to identify discrepancies in the transmission capabilities of the patterns to determine whether their translation to a much larger scale and their transposition into material surfaces directly affected the camera's ability to process levels of image colour intensity. Each pattern was tested twice to account for variation in measurements, and the resulting data was compiled into a matrix to enable a detailed quantitative and comparative assessment of all captured footage.

Test results

The tests revealed that of the periodic or regular patterns (patterns 1–4), pattern 2, proposed by Lukac and Plationatis, has the highest AIP level of RGB, followed by pattern 3 (Yamanaka pattern) and then pattern 1 (Bayer pattern). Pattern 4 (diagonal stripe) has the lowest AIP RGB level.

Of the non-periodic or pseudo-random patterns (patterns 5 and 6), pattern 6, based upon the HVS, produces the highest RGB AIP level and is, therefore, the more visible of these pattern types.

Two non-CFA patterns, patterns 7 and 8, each containing only two colour channels, were used as control patterns. Pattern 8 emitted similar RGB MIP levels to pattern 2, the pattern proposed by Lukac and Plataniotis, but the horizontal pattern orientation of pattern 7 with the omission of a green channel produced a much lower MIP level of emission than the vertical format of pattern 8, which has no red channel.

Patterns 9 and 10, based on the HVS and comprising hexagonal elements on a square grid device, were also tested. Pattern 9 is a periodic pattern and pattern 10 is a random pattern with a hexagonal grid. Pattern 10 produced the second-highest overall RGB levels in terms of both AIP and MIP RGB emission levels (Table 6.1).

Test summary and conclusions

The original ambition of this test was to identify CFA pattern types that modify building façade visibility by increasing or diminishing colour intensity levels according to the arrangement of a particular pattern type.

The tests show distinct variation in the camera's ability to process colour intensity according to pattern type (CFA or non-CFA, periodic or non-periodic (random) and square or hexagonal elements). Of the 10 patterns used, those based upon the HVS (patterns 6 and 10) produced higher levels of RGB intensity in the camera readings than the non-HVS-based patterns.

Pattern orientation also affected RGB emission levels, seen in the different readings taken from the two non-CFA patterns (patterns 7 and 8) and the lower MIP intensity readings emitted by the diagonal format of pattern 4.

A discrepancy between the AIP and MIP colour emission levels in some patterns, such as pattern 4, suggests that these produce greater RGB

Table 6.1 The total AVG, MAX RGB intensity, luminosity and particle data count values of Patterns 1–10

	Total AVG RGB Intensity	Total AVG RGB Luminosity	Total AVG Particle Count	Total MAX RGB Intensity	Total MAX RGB Luminosity	Total MAX Particle Count
Pattern 1	21.712	24.23	2614	72.182	72.25	8291
Pattern 2	26.139	28.14	2833	80.919	81.01	7413
Pattern 3	22.6	25.13	2540	76.329	76.4	9478
Pattern 4	17.633	17.74	2554	75.777	75.8	6683
Pattern 5	23.787	25.26	2763	71.734	71.79	8163
Pattern 6	27.228	28.72	3160	84.363	84.43	10323
Pattern 7	26.151	24.73	2180	75.003	75	8647
Pattern 8	25.967	29.02	2845	82.801	82.91	10009
Pattern 9	23.657	24.88	2479	74.449	74.49	7774
Pattern 10	26.83	27.55	2234	83.472	83.5	10212

intensity than others at certain apertures or f-stop increments along the camera's zoom trajectory. Significantly, this feature ties colour intensity emission levels to specific camera f-stops, thus allowing the extent of these effects to be reproduced and predicted.

The deliberate removal of the green colour channel in pattern 7 reduces the overall level of colour emission to a far greater extent than the loss of the red colour channel in pattern 8. This phenomenon confirms the theory that camera colour transmission relies heavily upon the green colour channel, in accordance with the greater capacity of the human eye to resolve green.

Finally, it is interesting to note that pattern 1, the Bayer pattern and the most commonly used CFA, produced only mediocre RGB intensity transmission levels.

Test part 2: Hierarchies of visibility – the shifting function of luminosity (brightness)

The second of the Series 1 tests focuses on assessing an object's luminosity (brightness). The luminosity intensity effects of the 10 array patterns were again analysed using ImageJ's Z Project function using the same video footage as the previous colour intensity tests. This function can accommodate the many thousands of image slices within the image stack of each segment of video footage and conflate the effects into a single piece of analysable data. Image J's Interactive 3D Surface Plot, a luminosity visualisation tool, was added to the analytical toolset to enable comparison of the image luminance levels of the array patterns. The binary converter and particle assessment function were used to convert the image slices to binary form using the Floyd Steinberg Dithering Algorithm.[17]

These tools constitute an arsenal of quantitative measurement functions that can provide a comprehensive, precise assessment of each array pattern's brightness transmission within a hypothetical building façade context at night.

Test results

As with the previous RGB intensity test, the primary objective was to establish whether the array patterns possess discrepant transmission capabilities. In this case, however, the intention was to discover whether their translation to a much larger material scale has an observable effect upon the camera's reception of their luminosity levels.

The luminosity test produced similar results to the previous test. Patterns based upon the HVS, patterns 6 and 10, produced higher luminosity readings than the non-HVS-based patterns, except for patterns 2 and 8.

Of the periodic or regular patterns, pattern 2, proposed by Lukac and Plataniotis, emitted the highest average luminosity levels, while pattern 4 showed the lowest average luminosity levels.

Tests on the remaining patterns largely mirrored the RGB intensity test results, except for the two non-CFA patterns. Pattern 7 (the horizontally oriented pattern) emitted lower luminosity levels than pattern 8 (the vertically oriented pattern), which had the highest emission levels of all patterns (Table 6.1).

The particle data counts reflected similar outcomes. The HVS array pattern (pattern 6) produced the highest AVG and MAX particle data counts of 3,160 and 10,323 units respectively, followed by the other HVS-based pattern, pattern 10 (based on hexagonal elements on a square grid). Pattern 4 produced the lowest overall particle data count (Table 6.1).

Test summary and conclusions

Of the 10 patterns tested, the HVS-based pattern (pattern 6) showed the highest levels of brightness emission and the highest particle data count, suggesting that pattern type (pixel distribution across the array) and pixel shape affect brightness emission and data transmission levels. The discrepancy between the luminosity and particle data counts of pattern 10 (with random hexagonal elements) also suggests that randomly distributed hexagonal shapes generate a high luminosity transmission reading, while simultaneously diminishing camera glare, therefore increasing the pattern's capacity to transmit legible data. In other words, while the pattern emits high luminosity, or brightness levels, it is also highly legible owing to the shape of its pixels. This behaviour differs from the other HVS-based pattern, pattern 6, which, although showing high luminosity, produced higher particle data count levels, and therefore more glare, than pattern 10.

The removal of the green colour channel (pattern 7) profoundly affects luminosity emission levels but not overall RGB intensity levels. This feature is seen in the discrepancy between the high RGB intensity level and relatively low luminosity transmission level and particle data count of pattern 7 (the horizontal non-CFA pattern), which suggests that colour plays a significant role in pattern visibility.

Test part 3: The disruptive potential of additive colour

The third test in Series 1 again draws upon the camera's colour receptor mechanism – the CCD sensor and the CFA pattern located within it. Situated above the pixel sensors to capture colour information for conversion into a full-colour image, the most common pattern array is the Bayer filter with 50% green, 25% red and 25% blue.

As in the previous tests, this transposes the Bayer pattern arrangement into the architectural surface as a scaled-up mirror of the CFA to disrupt or modify the viewed scene. The proposition that different distributions of the three complementary colours of the RGB additive colour model in the Bayer pattern array will produce another set of secondary colours when partially superimposed on each other, and white (zero colour) when completely superimposed, underpins the test. Secondary RGB colours – cyan, magenta and yellow – are formed by the mixture of two primaries: red and green combine to make yellow, green and blue make cyan, blue and red make magenta.[18]

The addition or subtraction of one or more of these patterns then introduces the possibility of altering the image's visual hierarchy, and thus the viewing experience, by linking changes in a building's program to variations of colour. These occur as different planar components of the building's façade and interior come into play as they are backlit and superimposed according to various activations of the building's program (Figure 6.2).

Test technical data and conditions

The final part of the series applied the same physical conditions and constraints as previous tests, although in this case an incandescent light source was used. The lighting sources were three American DJ FS-1000 Followspots with ZBHX600 120V 300W halogen lamps. The tests were conducted in low ambient light conditions (0.27–1.0 lux, equivalent to a full moon on a clear night)[19] to simulate urban night-time lighting conditions.

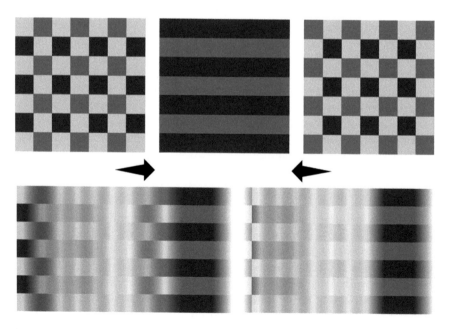

Figure 6.2 Complementary colour variations of the Bayer array pattern, showing the effect of dynamic colour overlay, including areas of white. (Image by author).

The Bayer array pattern and two variations were arranged in front of the three Followspot lamps. The reflection of the collective light emission of the patterns onto a whiteboard was then recorded at a standard 1m distance from the pattern over a range of zoom factors. The camera was then placed in the position previously occupied by the board to observe the correlation between the reflected image previously seen on the board and the image subsequently captured by the camera.

Test results and analysis

When the three patterns were arranged to overlap, the resulting reflected image produced a secondary set of colours in the overlapping zones based on cyan, magenta and yellow. When the camera was placed in the position previously occupied by the whiteboard, the resulting image revealed the emergence of the same secondary colours based on cyan, magenta and yellow. This effect was most prominent at the camera's lowest f-stop range, diminishing as the f-stop range increased towards the furthest extent of the camera's zoom trajectory.

The numbers of unique colours in images of the overlapping patterns at f-1.8 and f-3 were counted using ImageJ's Unique Colour Count function to assess the quantum of colour produced in relation to the camera's f-stop range. This revealed a unique colour count of 396,991 at the lower end of the camera's f-stop range (f-1.8), as well as the emergence of a secondary set of colours. At the higher f-stop of f-3, the unique colour count was lower at 304,208 and there were fewer secondary colours.

Test summary and conclusions

The results of this test reveal that the adapted CFA pattern can alter the viewed scene's hierarchy by introducing a secondary range of colours. The phenomenon modifies the image throughout an observed spectrum of the camera's aperture range, or f-stop increments, that act in conjunction with its zoom trajectory to determine the changeable visibility of a building's surface. The shifts are a response to its different programmatic activities throughout the day and night. Linking a building's visibility and its changes in use or occupation to the camera's f-stop range increases architectural agency by enabling the employment of predictive strategies that are connected to program activation. The camera's zoom function, limited only by the constraints of its trajectory, presents the architect with a new realm of material assemblies that draw directly upon digital technology to destabilise the promotional image and re-present the urban narrative.

The data matrix

The Series 1 tests were intended to discover the relative colour intensity and legibility of a selection of transposed CFA patterns viewed through the

Internet camera at a vastly increased material scale. The transmissive intensities of main image compositional elements of colour and luminosity (brightness) were measured to link any captured idiosyncratic visual effect to a particular pattern array.

However, the ability to align a building's visibility with material assemblies drawn from digital geometry relies upon collating data into a matrix charting the relative pattern transmission intensities. The matrix allows each pattern's behaviour to be linked explicitly to camera f-stop increments. This feature enables any design decision about a building's visibility to be controlled precisely, by aligning its levels of colour and luminosity emanation with the activation of its program over a known period.

To further explain the matrix's functionality, while an object's visibility depends upon its colour intensity and luminosity (brightness), the matrix reveals that these features do not always occur simultaneously. An example of this is pattern 10, the HVS-based hexagonal pattern, with the second-highest overall level of RGB intensity but, paradoxically, with the second-lowest overall level of luminosity. Conversely, pattern 5, the pseudo-random pattern, has a low overall level of RGB intensity and a high level of luminosity. This suggests that object visibility concerning colour is the result of the pattern array.

Furthermore, by aligning colour intensity and luminosity data with the camera's f-stop increments, the matrix provides access to a comprehensive range of pattern effects. For instance, some patterns have much greater levels of colour or RGB intensity at the full extent of the camera's zoom range than others. If the intention were to vary a building's visibility to achieve precise effects across a given time frame, selecting a particular façade pattern type would require its surface to correlate with corresponding values in the matrix. For example, if a pattern's most intense colour effect occurs at the smallest f-stop (the furthest away from the viewed object), with the design intention of being highly visible within this range, then the obvious choice would be pattern 2 or 10, which have the highest RGB intensity and luminosity readings at this distance between camera and object. On the other hand, if the requirement was for high levels of visibility at close range, then the choice might be between patterns 6, 7 or 8, all of which have the highest RGB intensity and luminosity levels. Figure 6.3 shows an extract from an example of this tool.

Other requirements might include the need for low levels of object visibility, in which case pattern 1 would satisfy this requirement at all camera distances. A general point worth noting here is that patterns based upon human optics – pattern 6, with its random distribution of pixels, and pattern 10, with the hexagonal pixel shape – produce the highest levels of visibility. In contrast, those based upon uniform distributions of pixels are the least visible.

The matrix also supports the identification of common pattern behaviours in which a shift in pattern discernibility takes place. An example is

The building surface as a colour modifier 127

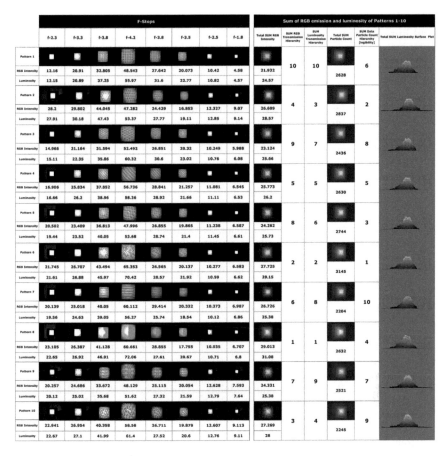

Figure 6.3 Extract from example of an RGB transmission data matrix. (Image by author).

the f-stop range of all patterns between f-2.3 and f-3.3, where pattern legibility diminishes. On the other hand, effects specific to individual patterns can be associated with a particular f-stop increment if they are present. One further point to note, evidenced by the data matrix, is the low intensity levels produced by the most used CFA, pattern 1, the traditional Bayer pattern. This finding queries manufacturer's heavy reliance upon this array over a choice of other, potentially more transmissive options.

The data matrix is only a single example of configurable data's unlimited potential as a design tool. The indexing of pattern array visibility to the built surface means that a building's visual prominence within any viewed scene can be adjusted and predicted by redistributing the visual hierarchy of its colour content. Importantly, it also suggests a new range of material assemblies, tied exclusively to the geometry and technology of the digital, in

128 New techniques of intervention and disruption

which qualitative and quantitative data can be readily and selectively activated as material form according to strategic pattern assemblies of colour and luminosity.

Notes

1. Unifore, 2011. *CCD VS CMOS in video surveillance cameras* [online]. Available from: http://www.hkvstar.com/technology-news/ccd-vs-cmos-in-video-surveillance-cameras.html
2. Rastislav Lukac and Konstantinos Plataniotis, 2005. Color filter arrays: Design and performance analysis. *IEEE Transactions on Consumer Electronics*, 51 (4), pp. 1260–1267.
3. James D. Foley, Andries Van Dam, Steven K. Feiner, John F. Hughes, E. Angel, and J. Hughes, 1997. *Computer graphics: Principles and practice*. Boston, MA: Addison-Wesley Professional.
4. Virginio Cantoni, Stefano Levialdi, and Bertrand Zavidovique, 2011. *3C vision: Cues, context and channels*. Waltham, MA: Elsevier.
5. HyperCube2 software is available at: https://www.erdc.usace.army.mil/Media/Fact-Sheets/Fact-Sheet-Article-View/Article/610433/hypercube/
6. HyperCube is a Macintosh and Windows application program created by the US Army Corps of Engineer Research and Development Center's Geospatial Research Laboratory. The software analyses and displays multi- and hyperspectral imagery, including the static and dynamic display of the image cube and the generation of spectral classifications using both imagery and spectral libraries.
7. Tiago Ferreira and Wayne Rasband, 2011. *The ImageJ user guide*. USA: National Institutes of Health.
8. Lukac and Plataniotis, Color filter arrays: Design and performance analysis.
9. Paul M. Hubel, John Liu, and Rudolph J. Guttosch, 2004. Spatial frequency response of color image sensors: Bayer color filters and Foveon X3. *Proceedings, Volume 5301, Sensors and camera systems for scientific, industrial, and digital photography applications*, p. 402.
10. John J. G. Savard, 2009. *Color filter array designs* [online]. Available from: http://quadibloc.com/other/cfaint.htm
11. Lukac and Plataniotis, Color filter arrays: Design and performance analysis, p. 1260.
12. Lukac and Plataniotis, Color filter arrays: Design and performance analysis, p. 1260.
13. M. Parmar and S. J. Reeves, 2004. A perceptually based design methodology for color filter arrays [image reconstruction]. *2004 IEEE International Conference on Acoustics, Speech, and Signal Processing*, pp. III–473.
14. Richard C. Staunton and Neil Storey, 1990. A comparison between square and hexagonal sampling methods for pipeline image processing. *Optics, Illumination, and Image Sensing for Machine Vision IV*, 1194, pp. 142–151.
15. Kintronics, 2014. *Night vision and long-range IR PTZ camera system* [online]. Available from: http://www.kintronics.com/night-vision-ir-ptz-camera-with-long-rangecapability/-2
16. Ferreira and Rasband, *The ImageJ user guide*, p. 90. Each value recorded for RGB emission is an intensity value between 0 and 255, which is used for total image intensity evaluation. This can be further subdivided into values either for each channel or for total RGB intensity.

17 R. W. Floyd and L. Steinberg, 1976. An adaptive algorithm for spatial greyscale. *Proceedings of the Society of Information Display,* 17, pp. 75–77.
18 Theresa-Marie Rhyne, 2017. Applying color theory to digital media and visualization. *Proceedings of the 2017 CHI Conference Extended Abstracts on Human Factors in Computing Systems,* pp. 1264–1267.
19 Paul Schlyter, 1997. *Radiometry and photometry in astronomy* [online]. Available from: http://stjarnhimlen.se/comp/radfaq.html

7 Re-viewing diffraction

Series 2 tests overview

The webcam's ability to produce a coherent, legible image is vital to the optimum promotional success of viewed sites. Consequently, anything that works against the ability to achieve this end is either minimised or eliminated altogether. A casualty of this strategy is the digital image artefact. Artefacts of many kinds are present throughout many digital image-making procedures, but diffraction is one of the most challenging for camera manufacturers and users. Diffraction is a phenomenon associated with optical science. It occurs throughout the camera's aperture range when a beam of light is partially blocked and split by an obstacle, causing it to pass through a small opening, such as a camera lens. In automated webcam trajectories, these phenomena cannot be controlled, and they appear regularly as a result of climatic conditions such as rain or fog. However, when the slit or lens focusing the light passing through it is a considerable distance from the plane on which the light waves fall, Fraunhofer or far-field diffraction occurs. This effect produces different patterns according to the shape of the aperture.[1]

The ambition of the Series 2 tests is to capitalise on diffraction's disruptive effects by destabilising the production of enhanced re-presentations of the city associated with the proprietary interests of site ownership. The tests involve applying transposed Fraunhofer patterns, again upscaled by a vast order of magnitude, as an external material 'skin' over a building's façade. In this scenario, the Fraunhofer pattern, fabricated as a material grid overlaid on the building's surface, acts as a giant disruptive grating by transmitting diffracted light to the camera lens. This strategy then allows the architect to predict and control the extent and nature of a building's visibility by exploiting the peculiarities of digital geometry. Furthermore, by using these effects to draw the viewer's attention to the disparity between the virtual and real experiences of the city, it positions the image as the central agent in provoking the viewer to apprehend the deliberately constructed nature of the urban visual narrative.

DOI: 10.4324/9781003133872-10

Re-viewing diffraction 131

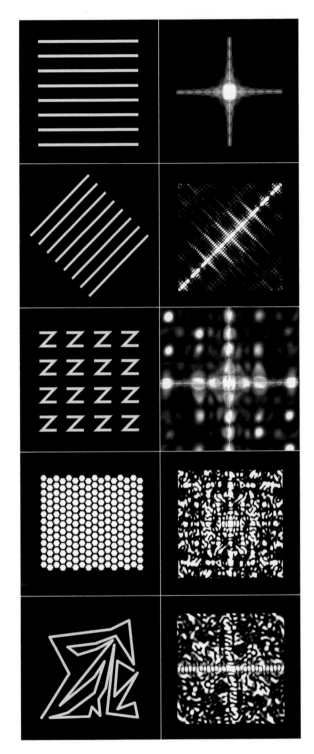

(caption on next page)

Figure 7.1 Patterns used in Series 2 tests. Column 1, top to bottom: Pattern 1 – standard horizontal raster scan-order pattern; Pattern 2 – standard horizontal raster scan-order pattern in a 45° rotated orientation; Pattern 3 – recursive Z scan-order pattern; Pattern 4 – hexagonal, HVS-based pattern; Pattern 5 – random or non-periodic pattern. Column 2, top to bottom: Patterns 1F–5F – Fraunhofer patterns produced from each of the Column 1 patterns. (Image by author)

Patterns of disruption

The Series 2 tests, comprising five pattern types, are designed to investigate the comparative impact of digitally and non-digitally derived diffraction grating patterns on the camera's ability to form a coherent image (Figure 7.1).

Three digital patterns are derived from the camera's internal data-scanning or raster-scanning procedure.[2] A fourth pattern is based on the HVS, comprising the hexagonal elements described by Michael Deering: 'the human retinal cones generally form a triangular lattice of hexagonal elements, with irregular perturbations and breaks.'[3] A fifth random pattern is based on the randomly generated type referred to by Cantoni et al.[4] Fraunhofer patterns derived from each of the five patterns mentioned above were also created using the open-source software Fresnel Diffraction Explorer[5] and a Fast Fourier Transform algorithm. These patterns form the full complement of the tests in this series.

The aim is to observe how the five patterns affect camera reception when compared with five Fraunhofer versions produced by using the parent pattern as a diffraction grating. The Fraunhofer versions are thus produced by capturing them as reflected versions of their parent pattern and transferring them onto a physical template. Again, the intention is to enlarge the patterns by a vast order of magnitude and eventually transpose them as part of a building surface. The aim is to test for any disruption the patterns cause in the webcam's capacity to process image data. A further objective of the tests is to observe the disruptive effect of the patterns in relation to the camera's f-stop increments, enabling accurate application of this data to real-world situations.

Test technical data and conditions

Series 2 tests were conducted using the same camera equipment as the Series 1 tests, and two separate series of tests were conducted to corroborate the findings. The diffraction grating patterns were cut from 2 mm opaque black acrylic. They were then placed in front of an American DJ FS-1000 Followspot with a ZB-HX600, 120V 300W halogen lamp to simulate the level of light emission conditions emitted by a brightly lit interior of a city office building at night. The diffraction grating patterns were intended to simulate a perforated building façade skin overlaid across the building's surface and backlit by interior lighting.

The camera was placed 8 m from the image plane, with the light source located 0.5 m directly behind it. This represents a scaled approximation of the standard Internet camera viewing distance from a brightly lit image source where a relative scale of 1:10 operates; that is, the 8 m image plane distance in the test correlates with an 80 m distance in an exterior environment. Similarly, the grating elements used were 500 mm^2, to correlate with a typical building façade surface area of 5 m^2. The aim of this was to enable specific image effects to be associated with specific camera f-stop increments, and thus to be identified according to the camera's zoom trajectory.

Test analysis methodology

The results of the individual patterns were processed in two ways: by empirical observation and by using ImageJ quantitative analysis tools. ImageJ's Reslice tool was used because a comparative assessment of the effects of non-Fraunhofer and Fraunhofer pattern types was required, and because their respective quanta of diffracted light varied considerably. This tool allowed all video stills to be reassembled into quantifiable data by reconstructing an orthogonal slice through the image volume.[6] Therefore, a comparable result could be obtained by converting the video of each grating pattern into a dataset with the same constraints.

ImageJ analysis was used to assess the number of unique colours produced by each pattern, because the number of unique colours is directly linked to the effects of diffraction. The same tool was used to measure each pattern's level of luminosity emission. Because the objective was to see the effects of the diffraction grating upon the webcam's image-processing function, the quantum of unique colours produced by each grating and the luminosity (brightness) of each was critical to assessing the camera disruption. Therefore, for each grating pattern, the image at the high end of the camera's aperture or f-stop range was selected to observe the number of diffraction artefacts present, because this is the point at which these are most likely to occur.

ImageJ's Z Project function was used to synthesise multiple images into a single image showing the Sum (SUM) and Standard Deviation (STD) values of all the combined pixel intensities in the stack. Both the SUM (a real image that is the sum of the slices in the stack) and the STD (a real image containing the standard deviation of the slices in the stack) functions produce a single image that is the conflated projection of an image stack along the axis perpendicular to the image plane (the z axis).[7] In this case, the SUM tool allowed the total effects of the reprocessed images to be evaluated according to the number of unique colours present across the total aperture range and zoom trajectory. At the same time, the STD function revealed the extent of variation or range of unique colours present within the aperture range and trajectory of each individual grating pattern.

134 *New techniques of intervention and disruption*

ImageJ's Particle Data Count function was also used as a supplementary tool to corroborate the results. This command counts and measures objects in binary or thresholded images and operates by scanning the image until it finds the edge of an object. Therefore, the greater the number of objects, the higher the luminosity of the selected area of image content.

Test results and analysis

Unique colours

All patterns produced strong diffraction effects at f-6 aperture, which is the furthest extent of the camera's zoom trajectory. Of these, the horizontal slit grating pattern (pattern 1), and the Fraunhofer pattern derived from the rotated version of the slit grating pattern (pattern 7), produced the highest number of diffraction artefacts; 96,172 and 91,986 units respectively. This was observed empirically in both tests and evidenced by the number of unique colours produced by each of these grating patterns.

The Fraunhofer patterns derived from digital-based patterns (6, 7 and 8) all produced diffraction effects profoundly different from their parent patterns. In other words, each of the Fraunhofer grating patterns extracted directly from digital geometry demonstrated a vastly different diffractive capability from that of its derivative pattern. This effect was measured by the unique colour count of each pattern. Conversely, while the non-digital-based grating patterns (4 and 5) also produced strong diffraction artefacts, the Fraunhofer grating patterns derived from them (9 and 10) produced a similar quantum of unique colours to their parent patterns (Table 7.1).

Table 7.1 Unique colour count and particle data count values of Patterns 1–5 and 1F–5F

	Unique colours in total STD of reslice	Particle data count of total STD of reslice	Unique colours in total SUM of reslice	Particle data count of total SUM of reslice	Unique colours at mid-point	Particle data count at mid-point of reslice
Pattern 1	49111	4484	31792	798	96172	2712
Pattern 2	23217	5238	17348	734	44536	1175
Pattern 3	18147	13435	57851	2246	72724	3583
Pattern 4	33102	10290	16847	2011	91986	5066
Pattern 5	29818	2030	21029	1093	67378	1656
Pattern 1F	29079	9563	31973	3635	53317	1916
Pattern 2F	24874	9381	24033	3149	75315	3878
Pattern 3F	21321	11132	27008	5790	76160	6780
Pattern 4F	27811	8106	27966	2493	87687	5065
Pattern 5F	27017	11217	20459	3822	86074	5164

Particle data count

Particle data counts were taken to corroborate or supplement the measurements of the numbers of unique colours produced by diffraction effects. Using ImageJ's Floyd Steinberg Dithering Algorithm, the images were first converted to binary form and subsequently counted and measured according to the maxima of luminance, with the luminance defined as the weighted or unweighted average of the colours.

The results confirmed the unique colour measurements, in terms of both empirical observation and quantitative analysis. However, the results also showed a large discrepancy between the diffraction artefacts produced by pattern 4 (the HVS based pattern) and its Fraunhofer sibling pattern 9. Notwithstanding this, the non-digital pattern, pattern 5, produced similar results to the unique colour analysis for both the parent and Fraunhofer versions of the pattern (Table 7.1).

Test summary, conclusions and the data matrix

The Series 2 tests show that digitally derived Fraunhofer grating patterns reverse the light diffraction capabilities of their parent patterns, while Fraunhofer grating patterns derived from non-digital sources produce a similar quantum of unique colours to their parent patterns. Furthermore, as in the Series 1 tests in chapter 6, collating the results into a data matrix links pattern effects to the camera's f-stop increments, thus enabling them to be linked to precise distances between the camera and the viewed surface.

In this collision between optical science and the properties of digital data, the diffraction data matrix allows the eccentricities of digital image data to be identified readily. For the architect, it means that a calculable effect can be achieved by controlling a building's disruptive potential within any viewed scene. By embedding compositional and structural elements of digital image-making into a building's material surface to subvert promotional ambitions, this new 'enabling of the digital' allows the qualitative properties of urban life to define the contemporary representation of the city.

Notes

1 Leno S. Pedrotti, 2008. Basic physical optics. *Fundamentals of Photonics*, 1, pp. 117–167.
2 A detailed investigation of these patterns and their implications for the camera's hierarchical reading of the built surface is the subject of the Series 3 tests in chapter 7.
3 Michael F. Deering, 2005. A photon accurate model of the human eye. *ACM Transactions on Graphics*, 24 (3), pp. 649–658.

4 Virginio Cantoni, Stefano Levialdi, and Bertrand Zavidovique, 2011. *3C vision: Cues, context and channels*. Waltham, MA: Elsevier.
5 This software is available at: http://daugerresearch.com/fresnel/index.shtml
6 Tiago Ferreira and Wayne Rasband, 2011. *The ImageJ User Guide*. USA: National Institutes of Health.
7 Ferreira and Rasband, *The ImageJ User Guide*.

8 New readings of the city

Series 3 tests overview

The third series of tests uses the camera's image sensor to investigate the adaptation of patterns created by the encoding, decompression and subdivision of image data into sequences of scan lines (raster scanning).[1] The aim is to observe how the application to a building façade of different scan order patterns at hyper-pixel scale affects the image of the captured scene.

As discussed in chapter 2, digital camera protocols assemble the basic image unit into pixel groups to which integer values of both colour and luminosity are assigned.[2] The camera's image sensor uses various architectures to convert the analogue electrical light charge into a digital value; all of these processes involve the procedure of raster scanning.[3] The function of ordering pixels by rows is a highly strategic process with direction and vertical retrace action controlled by a pre-determined scanning algorithm programmed to prioritise the production of a smooth, dynamic image. Many variations of the scan-order code enable the process to isolate and privilege image regions of specific interest, thus providing opportunities for high levels of manipulation.[4]

Digital cameras focus incoming light onto a light-sensitive, solid-state sensor, either a CCD or CMOS device. The sensor is composed of a rectangular array of equidistant discrete light-sensing elements or photo-sites, each of which becomes electrically charged in direct proportion to the amount of light that strikes it over a given period.[5] The three Series 3 tests refer to camera technology using CCD rather than CMOS image sensor architectures for image processing because the CCD sensor has 10 times the light sensitivity of the CMOS sensor.

Two types of CCD designs transfer the accumulated charges from a CCD array: frame-transfer (FT) and interline-transfer (IT). The technology referred to in this test series, the IT-CCD design, incorporates legible strips of photo-sites located either horizontally or vertically between the lines of active photo-sites in the array. The IT-CCD achieves much faster data transfer rates than the FT-CCD due to the distribution of the array, thus facilitating faster frame rates and higher accuracy.[6] The IT sensor uses either 2:1 interlaced scanning

DOI: 10.4324/9781003133872-11

or progressive scanning to display a video image on an electronic screen, which it does by scanning each row of pixels in a particular order and orientation. The interlaced scanning technique used by the camera referred to in these tests uses two fields to create a frame: one containing the odd lines and the other containing the even lines of the image.[7]

Scanning variants

The precise scanning strategies proprietary camera hardware and software manufacturers use for specific image-making applications are difficult to access. Klette and Rosenfeld[8] referred to at least six varieties, including a version of the standard zigzag raster scanning sequence used in interlaced scanning. In addition, Cantoni et al.'s discussion of artificial vision technology procedures presents a diverse range of scanning patterns based upon two distinct strategies: deterministic space-filling paths and random paths. The latter is based upon the way saccadic eye movements work in natural vision.[9] Three deterministic scan-order patterns and one other random pattern were selected for the Series 3 tests, to represent a cross-section of standard image-scanning procedures designed to deliver the most legible image with the fewest unwanted image artefacts. They also can target specific areas of interest, with the added possibility of revisiting cells for further image enhancement.

The tests aim to investigate how the four patterns described by Cantoni et al.,[10] and variations of these in different orientations, affect camera reception when applied as scaled-up elements of a building façade (Figure 8.1). The 'mirroring' of the scan-order pattern in the viewed façade is designed to test for any conflict with, or enhancement of, the camera's pre-determined scanning algorithm, with the idea that this would subsequently be observed in the legibility of the captured image.

Pattern 1 represents a standard raster scanning sequence correlating with the scanning sequence of IT-CCD sensors. Pattern 2 visits only adjacent cells on a 4- or 8-connected neighbourhood where the scanning sequence commences from the centre of the image. This pattern array ensures that pixels with high autocorrelation values are covered, leading to image compression. Pattern 3 is a recursive Z-pattern linked by the basic Peano curve; it is based upon a hierarchical approach corresponding to the projection of the binary tree data structure.[11] Finally, pattern 10 is random. The intention is to link the extent of the mirrored scan-order patterns' legibility to the camera's f-stop increments so that their relative capacity to disrupt or enhance the resulting image can be predicted.

Test technical data and conditions

The scan-order patterns were cut from 3 mm opaque black acrylic squares and then placed in front of a single light source (a 30W Par 64 RGB LED) to simulate the level of light emission conditions emitted by a brightly lit

New readings of the city 139

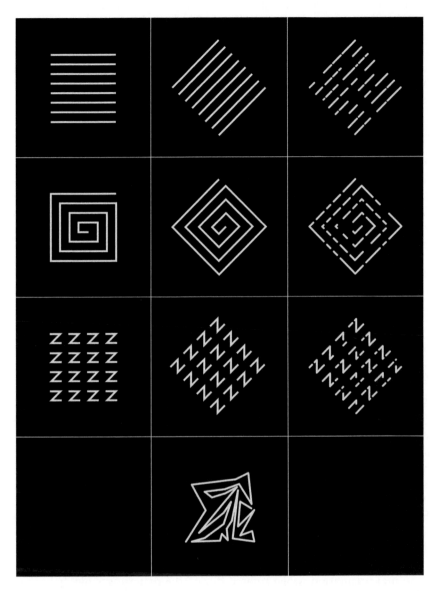

Figure 8.1 Patterns used in Series 3 tests. Top row, left to right: Pattern 1 – standard raster scan-order pattern; Pattern 2 – standard raster scan-order pattern (45° rotated orientation); Pattern 3 – standard raster scan-order pattern (45° rotated and discontinuous); Pattern 4 – outward spiral; Pattern 5 – outward spiral (45° rotated orientation); Pattern 6 – outward spiral (45° rotated and discontinuous); Pattern 7 – recursive Z-pattern; Pattern 8 – recursive Z-pattern (45° rotated orientation); Pattern 9 – recursive Z-pattern (45° rotated and discontinuous); Pattern 10 – random or non-periodic pattern. (Image by author).

interior of a city office building at night. As in the previous tests, the camera was placed 8 m from the image plane, with the light source located 0.5 m directly behind it. The scan-order pattern elements used were 360 mm^2, correlating with a building façade surface area of 3.6 m^2. Once again, the aim is to enable specific effects seen in the captured image to align with the camera's aperture range or f-stop increments and thus to be identified according to the camera's zoom trajectory.

Test analysis methodology

Drawing upon ImageJ's Z Project function to synthesise multiple images, images were selected from the test video footage at precise moments according to each f-stop increment. The result was individual images showing the average, sum and maximum values of the combined pixel intensities within the stack, thus allowing variations between the different weightings to be assessed.

The results of the pattern tests were initially assessed using empirical observation. They were also measured using Photoshop's luminosity assessment function, while ImageJ's Particle Data Count function was used to corroborate the results obtained from Photoshop.

Test results and analysis

Pattern legibility

The results showed that both pattern type and orientation are critical factors in pattern legibility. Of the 10 patterns tested, pattern 1, based on the standard raster scanning sequence, appeared the least legible and the most unstable when viewed in horizontal orientation. At the higher end of the camera zoom trajectory, between f-5.5 and the f-6 aperture stops, the camera could not resolve the image. This led to a persistent fluctuation of the focusing mechanism and an inability to deliver a stable image (Figure 8.2). The test was repeated several times to verify this result. The same pattern also produced quite extensive colour artefacts, with a distinct blue colour present at the upper end of the f-stop range.

In contrast to the illegible and unstable images produced by pattern 1 in a horizontal orientation, when rotated by 45° the pattern was highly legible, creating a crisp image with no colour artefacts throughout the camera's aperture range and zoom trajectory. This result was also true for the discontinuous rotated version of this pattern.

Both orientations of pattern 4, based on the spiral 4- or 8-connected neighbourhood scanning sequence, and pattern 7, the recursive Z-pattern scanning sequence, produced fewer legibility problems than the horizontal version of pattern 1. However, pattern 7 did produce some blurring in horizontal orientation, but to a lesser extent than pattern 1.

New readings of the city 141

Figure 8.2 F-stop sequence of pattern 1 in horizontal orientation showing progression of visual blurring at f-6 aperture. (Image by author).

Pattern 10, based on a random or non-periodic scanning sequence, produced results similar to pattern 1. The camera had difficulty resolving the image at the high end of the f-stop range and creating a blue colour artefact. However, unlike pattern 1, the image eventually stabilised.

As in the case of the CFA pattern tests described in chapter 6, a specific f-stop range emerged in all patterns between f-2.3 and f-3.3, in which legibility was much higher (Table 8.1).

Luminosity

Images sampled from the full f-stop range and zoom trajectory of both orientations of patterns 1–9 (pattern 10 is random and has no correct orientation) were assessed quantitatively using Photoshop's luminance measurement tool to corroborate the information gathered by observation. The results confirmed the empirical observations, showing a significant variation between pattern luminosity emission levels according to orientation. They also showed that pattern legibility and luminosity levels were sometimes inversely related in certain pattern types: the higher the level of luminosity, the poorer the legibility, and vice versa. This suggests that in some patterns, such as pattern 10, high luminosity readings are associated with glare and a blurred image. In contrast, a lower reading means that the pattern is more delineated. In other words, a highly delineated pattern may not necessarily be the most luminous, such as pattern 8, the rotated version of the Z pattern.

In summary, in most test cases, the total luminance emission level produced by the patterns for all measurements (average, sum and maximum levels) was far greater when the pattern was captured in a horizontal orientation than in a rotated orientation. The tests also showed that luminance emission level was influenced by pattern type (Table 8.1).

Test summary, conclusions and the data matrix

The Series 3 tests show that pattern type and orientation affect the image's legibility and luminosity emission level. In all cases, the horizontal orientation of each pattern produced consistently higher levels of disruption to the camera's image production than the rotated orientation. This effect was particularly evident in pattern 1 (the television raster scanning sequence) at the high end of the f-stop range, where the camera could not resolve the image. This phenomenon was also present to a lesser degree in pattern 4, the random pattern.

The horizontal orientation of the pattern to the camera also produced consistently higher levels of luminosity emission than the rotated orientation. This suggests that pattern legibility and luminosity are inversely related, meaning that high levels of image definition are associated with lower levels of luminosity and vice versa.

Table 8.1 The total AVG, SUM and MAX luminosity and particle data count values of all versions of Patterns 1–10

	Total AVG Luminosity	Total AVG Particle Count	Total SUM Luminosity	Total SUM Particle Count	Total MAX Luminosity	Total MAX Particle Count
Pattern 1	37.02	494	39.16	524	152.59	10523
Pattern 2 (rotated 45°)	36.61	126	49.12	1194	149.74	678
Pattern 3 (rotated and discontinuous)	26.96	1	42.9	436	129.2	783
Pattern 4	35.3	1	54.8	2324	159.56	6295
Pattern 5 (rotated 45°)	33.21	177	38.48	585	143.64	2857
Pattern 6 (rotated and discontinuous)	25.74	1	41.57	453	125.01	709
Pattern 7	41.49	998	42	1022	166.32	6388
Pattern 8 (rotated 45°)	28.87	212	29.8	218	134.16	3558
Pattern 9 (rotated and discontinuous)	35.11	624	35.54	622	155.45	4962
Pattern 10	35.92	762	39.91	1095	114.39	12763

In summary, the combined effect of pattern type and orientation contributes to the achievement of optimum camera disruption, manifested in its inability to focus and the production of strong colour artefacts. As in the case of both the CFA pattern and the diffraction pattern tests (Series 1 and 2), the collation of Series 3 test data into a matrix ties the effects of optical scan order patterns to the camera's f-stop increments. This visible interlinking of data unveils a complex relationship between a viewed object's legibility and luminosity that is highly specific to pattern type and orientation. This projective tool thus provides the architect with the means to both interrupt and draw the viewer's attention to promotional strategies associated with site ownership currently at play within the city.

Concluding comments on the test series and the data matrices

The test results show that key processes associated with digital imaging can also be used to develop new approaches to form-making. Just as the consequences of the application of linear perspective to material form had included the establishment of a set of material protocols that exploited its geometry to foster political ideals, so too does the application of digital geometry to the built surface present unique opportunities for the city's material composition and political agency. The opportunities are manifested in new tactics that harness digital geometries and technologies to the patterns composing building surfaces, utilising the qualitative aspects of the city and allowing different aspects of urban space to be unleashed and understood.

The data matrices are, therefore, the key outcomes of the three test series. The geometric idiosyncrasies of associative pixel data form the basis of the Series 1 test results matrix. They enable a tabulation of the operative colour and luminosity emission hierarchies of different pixel distributions, with clear outcomes for their strategic application to a building's surface. In this series, issues of visibility, brightness and contextual relations relating to camera reception (extrapolated from the operation of the HVS) are key factors driving the selection of one or more of these arrangements to a viewed surface, with high degrees of variation available according to pattern type and combination.

The highly affective properties of the image artefact form the basis of the second data matrix. The fact that an image artefact can be productively exploited as generative data releases the image from any deterministic constraints. Its inclusion in the city's fabric opens up a vast range of new material possibilities peculiar to digital geometry. The collision of optical science and digital geometry seen in the Series 2 tests produced results that emphasise the uniqueness of digital geometry as a material generator underpinned by an untapped array of interactions between material behaviour and viewed surface.

The data matrix relating to the Series 3 tests results from a technical camera procedure that is, again, an appropriation of human optical processes. This second-generation extrapolation of optical scan paths underpins the assessment of the legibility of a viewed object in a scene. The results reveal how the ordering, distribution and orientation of non-colour-related elements can affect the camera's shape reception profoundly. Accordingly, their inclusion within a tabulated matrix ensures that the range of resulting material possibilities able to be derived from them is indexable to precise and predictable degrees of legibility based on the unique behaviour of digital geometry.

Nor can the representational significance of the digital zoom lens for the contemporary city be overstated. The ability to tie the city's projective materiality to the f-stops of imaging technology accesses a previously untapped repository of material surfaces that are inextricably linked to the unique properties of the digital. It also establishes the data matrix as the projective 'timetable' of material performance. Therefore, the capacity to access this data vastly extends the range and influence of the digital over the city's materiality and the extent to which it reinforces the status quo.

With the matrix as a projective tool for the organisation and implementation of the city's fabric, there emerges a question about the type of transformative architectural strategies that can result from applying such tactics. A new type of materiality must emerge by positioning the pixel as the pivotal generative unit of the urban surface. The new structural pixel unit, now in material form, directly addresses the very representational devices that normalise it and disable its affective status. When applied, the new strategies would use an unprecedented range and combination of material surfaces to either transform the hierarchy of objects within the view or dismantle the manufacture of iconic city views. In either case, their success ultimately resides in the tension set up between the real and the virtual representations of urban space. It also resides in the reinstatement of architectural agency that comes from directing this tension towards the recognition of the vast and uncurated dynamic qualities of urban space.

Notes

1 James D. Foley, Foley Dan Van, Andries Van Dam, Steven K. Feiner, John F. Hughes, Edward Angel, and J. Hughes, 1996. *Computer graphics: Principles and practice*. Boston, MA: Addison-Wesley Professional.
2 John Zeimbekis, 2012. Digital pictures, sampling, and vagueness: The ontology of digital pictures. *The Journal of Aesthetics and Art Criticism*, 70, pp. 43–53.
3 Herman Kruegle, 2007. *CCTV surveillance: Analog and digital video practices and technology*. Amsterdam: Elsevier Butterworth Heinemann.
4 Virginio Cantoni, Stefano Levialdi, and Bertrand Zavidovique, 2011. *3C vision: Cues, context and channels*. Waltham, MA: Elsevier.
5 National Instruments, 2006. *Anatomy of a camera* [online]. Available from: https://www.ni.com/en-au/innovations/white-papers/06/anatomy-of-a-camera.html

6 Adept Turnkey Pty Ltd. 2012. *Sensor comparison I: Interlaced scan, non-interlaced scan, progressive scan.* Available from: http://www.adept.net.au/news/newsletter/200809sep/sensors.shtml
7 AXIS Communications, 2021. *Technical guide to network video* [online]. Available from: http://www.axis.com/products/video/camera/progressive_scan.htm
8 Klette, Reinhard, and Azriel Rosenfeld, 2004. *Digital geometry: Geometric methods for digital picture analysis.* Boston, MA: Elsevier.
9 Cantoni, Levialdi, and Zavidovique, *3C vision: Cues, context and channels.*
10 Cantoni, Levialdi, and Zavidovique, *3C vision: Cues, context and channels.*
11 Cantoni, Levialdi, and Zavidovique, *3C vision: Cues, context and channels,* p. 14.

9 *'La città ideale'*: Design drawings for the digital city

The digital Urbino Panel

Drawings that draw upon the architectural possibilities arising from applying the research described in this book must be exclusively aligned with their native geometry and technology if they are to delineate new disciplinary territory. Therefore, as a way of describing the nature of the paradigm shift instigated by digital representation, the following design speculations directly reference Hubert Damisch's proposition that the linear perspective technique is best explained by the 16th-century representations known as the Urbino Panels.[1] A group of three works presenting the linear perspective technique applied to different urban contexts, these paintings openly declare their own representational function; they are, according to Damisch, 'the representation of a representation'.[2] Being pictorial works, their relevance to this book's research resides in the fact that they demonstrate the blending of linear perspective representation and the architectural form aligned with it: 'perspective, whether the work of a painter or an architect, was inseparable from architecture.'[3] In other words, they reveal that the application of a visual geometry to projective real-world contexts has explicit formal consequences.

A further relevance of the Urbino Panels to the research described here lies in an entirely hypothetical suggestion by Damisch concerning the possible existence of a fourth, and yet undiscovered, member of the existing group of three.

> Thus we cannot be sure, a priori, that other paintings, other works, obscure or previously unknown, won't eventually become part of the group, though they can only do so on condition that they put into play all the requisite features and introduce a new transformational twist, correcting, modifying, or rearranging the model.[4]

These drawings, therefore, are a response to the open-endedness of Damisch's speculation. Like the Urbino Panels, they are a demonstration of how the application of a representational regime – in this case, that of the digital – has

DOI: 10.4324/9781003133872-12

unique consequences for urban form. In this sense, they are a demonstration of the diverse capacity of binary digital image data to inflect the city's form towards the full spectrum of its qualitative properties, understood as colour and brightness. And, inasmuch as they explicate the consequences of digital geometry for the city in this way, drawings such as these allow both the idiosyncrasies and broad visual range offered by technology's multiple viewpoints to be incorporated within the urban built form.

Preliminary digital site mapping procedures

The development of this chapter's design drawings began with a digital spatial analysis of the site of a series of proposed interventions in Times Square, New York. Under constant surveillance by situated webcams and promoted globally as an iconic tourist venue, Times Square presents a discrete urban opportunity to speculate upon the effectiveness of applying disruptive optical patterns to its many viewed surfaces.

The initial site analysis was undertaken within a digital analytical framework using ImageJ software to process segments of video footage of Times Square captured from webcams and tourist devices. The three axes of the resulting three-dimensional image stack allowed regions of specific interest to be precisely located, identified and quantified according to variations of colour, brightness and clarity (legibility). A representation of this kind identifies explicit moments, clearly visible along the z-axis of time and space, at which the pixel's numerical properties establish an indexical link between qualitative image content and the city's material surfaces. In sum, this link allows the architect to make predictive and precise design decisions based on context as it unfolds across a temporal frame. Figure 9.1 shows an example of the application of this process to a single location in Times Square revealing the temporal shifts of colour and brightness along the multiple axes of the image stack.

The digital mapping techniques described here are therefore proposed as the new digital counterpart to the traditional orthographic plan, section and elevation of the digital city. Consequently, camera technology procedures relating to colour transmission, diffraction artefacts and shape recognition become the new digital 'rules' that position the ephemeral and constantly emerging qualitative properties of urban space as the organising and generative principles of urban form.

The digital Urbino Panel: A summary of visual effects

The second component of design drawings takes the form of a series of 'snapshots' that compose a dynamic fly-through of Times Square. Each series demonstrates an intervention based on the three types of speculative applications of digital data extracted from the research test series, now realised as the material composition of a building façade.

Design drawings for the digital city 149

Figure 9.1 Rotated time-lapse image stack (top) and combined orthogonal view of image stack (bottom) showing a busy intersection in Times Square, New York.

Source: Original images: VIA Films.

Given the numerous situated camera locations in Times Square and the transient, highly mobile nature of its tourist population, each potentially equipped with a camera device, the proposed drawings are not linked to any of the existing situated public camera sites. Instead, they represent locations that together demonstrate how the effects might best be accomplished through various viewer experiences captured from multiple viewpoints. In this respect, the images are presented as a montage of moving images that exploit both the anamorphic capabilities of the PTZ webcam and the pedestrian. They show the ensuing effects achievable from the many diverse angles presented to the camera.

Furthermore, it is important to note that the patterns are integrated into the building surface, forming part of the façade itself. In other words, the proposal is not a dynamic media façade attached to the building and relying on a power source, but an external 'skin' or material screen. This can be finely perforated, in the case of the diffraction gratings, or composed of translucent material and backlit as in the CFA patterns, or a combination of both, as in the scan-order patterns. Additionally, these effects rely heavily upon an evening timeframe for their potency, as does the promotional branding content of Times Square façades. That is not to say that they do not operate in daylight, but they are designed to compete with the promotional branding associated with site ownership and to draw the viewer's attention to these contrivances.

Intervention 1

Intervention 1 uses an adaptation of the camera's CFA pattern to identify specific pattern types that modify building façade visibility by causing variations in its intensity and brightness in the captured image or video. Based on the outcome of the Series 1 tests, the pattern selection refers to the data matrix results,[5] which show that the HVS-based CFA pattern produces greater RGB intensity than other tested patterns across the camera's zoom trajectory. The selection of this pattern means that the heightened colour intensity of its distributed elements makes it more visible and legible.

The location of Intervention 1 is the New York Marriott Marquis Hotel at 1535 Broadway between West 45th and West 46th Streets on the western side of Times Square. Designed by architect John C. Portman Jr. and opened in 1985, the Marriott was the first of the Times Square revitalisation projects and is believed to have initiated its regeneration. The application of the CFA pattern is aligned with the existing building's fenestration and floor levels to strengthen the effect of the colour distribution and to maximise the strength of the interior backlighting from the offices (Figure 9.2). Situated at the very heart of the Times Square advertising precinct, the CFA pattern overrides the barrage of neighbouring images located just above street level, relying for its potency not upon the camera's

Design drawings for the digital city 151

Figure 9.2 HVS-based CFA pattern building façade.
Source: 3D Visualisation – zspace.com.au.

anamorphic projection or zoom functions to draw the viewer's attention, but the intensity of the pattern's colour and brightness and its clearly defined edges. Furthermore, the pattern's repetitive nature creates the disruptive and disorienting effect of flattening the building's angles, transforming its 3D surface into a visually dominant 2D graphic billboard.

Intervention 2

This intervention refers to the Series 2 tests in which an image artefact is integrated into the building surface. Designed to contest the production of iconic cityscapes associated with the promotion of site ownership, digitally derived diffraction patterns produce powerful glare artefacts in image production when the camera aperture and the zoom factor vary. Based upon results taken from the data matrix,[6] Fraunhofer patterns produced from two types of slit gratings – a pattern of horizontal slits, derived from the digital raster scan-order pattern, and a pattern of z-shaped slits, derived from the digital horizontal version of a recursive 'z' scan-order pattern – have strong disruptive effects.

Two sites are associated with Intervention 2, again on the western side of Times Square. The first is 3 Times Square, alternatively known as the Thomson Reuters Building, a 32-story skyscraper located on 7th Avenue between 42nd and 43rd Streets. Situated in the heart of the theatre district, the lower façades of the building support numerous large electronic advertising displays. The building was part of a large redevelopment project

152 New techniques of intervention and disruption

built by Tishman Construction in 2000. The second site is the Riu Plaza Hotel on West 46th Street. Located on a large podium base that sets its mass back from Times Square, the Riu Plaza was built in 2016 and is one of a global chain of hotels.

The application of diffraction pattern templates to both buildings takes the form of a perforated external skin attached to the existing surface. The disruptive effects of the Fraunhofer patterns are caused by the interior light from the building passing through the attached screen to the viewer, who receives the image through either a mobile device or webcam technology transmitted via the Internet. The level of disruption varies according to the distance of the camera from the building surface; the closer the camera, the higher the intensity of glare and brightness. The camera's zoom function plays a key role in determining the extent of the disruptive effect, which is determined by varying increments of viewing proximity.

Just as the adapted CFA pattern in Intervention 1 resets the hierarchy of the viewed scene by dominating its distribution of colour intensity, so does the Fraunhofer pattern in Intervention 2 achieve a similar outcome by exploiting glare as a promotional disruptor. While both distract the viewer from the local scene of competing constructed electronic billboards, the magnified diffractive effect of the Fraunhofer pattern possesses even greater potency because it operates dynamically. The disruptive effect gathers intensity in two ways: as the viewing distance is increased or diminished, and according to the anamorphic angle of the camera view (Figure 9.3).

Furthermore, the clear identification of the relationship between the extent of disruptive effects caused to the situated camera and its PTZ trajectory also calls for a pattern that responds to this ever-changing condition. A recursive pattern embedding scales corresponding to the camera's zoom, and therefore aperture increments, ensures the quantum of camera disruption is maximised across a temporal frame. Using a commonly avoided by-product of camera technology in this way not only provokes an extremely disruptive image through its visual domination of the scene, but incorporating the city's qualitative properties within the viewed scene subverts any attempt to curate its global representation.

Intervention 3

The third intervention operates in a similarly dynamic way, using the varying effects caused by adapted optical scan patterns drawn from the camera's scanning and shape-identification procedures to capture the viewer's attention throughout the camera's zoom trajectory. Referring directly to the Series 3 tests and based upon results from the data matrix,[7] the raster-scan or horizontal slit pattern becomes extremely blurred and

Design drawings for the digital city   153

Figure 9.3 Fraunhofer diffraction pattern derived from rotated raster-scan pattern used as building façade diffraction grating (left-hand column). Fraunhofer diffraction pattern derived from rotated recursive Z-pattern (right-hand column).

Source: 3D Visualisation – zspace.com.au.

increases in brightness as the camera aperture and proximity to the façade increase. This pattern also produces many diffraction artefacts at the full extent of the camera's aperture. By contrast, the rotated version of the recursive Z-pattern, defined in chapter 8, remains highly legible and distinct throughout the full range of the camera's aperture settings and its zoom trajectory (Figure 9.4).

Two adjacent sites are associated with Intervention 3, on opposite corners of West 43rd Street on the eastern side of Times Square. The Condé Nast Building at 4 Times Square is the home of the Times Square Multimedia Group and Nasdaq's MarketSite, and the other is the location of the US Marine Corps and Army Recruiting Centre. Both are skyscrapers that devote their lower floors to media façades providing live updates of the US Stock Exchange indices and entertainment advertisements, respectively.

154 *New techniques of intervention and disruption*

Figure 9.4 Raster-scan pattern façade diffraction grating (left-hand column). Recursive Z-pattern façade diffraction grating (right-hand column). (Image by author.

Source: 3D Visualisation – zspace.com.au.

This intervention is designed with two strategies in mind. In the first case, the adjacency of two patterns of opposing legibility strengthens their combined effect. Secondly, they both compete with existing signage at the buildings' street level, with the result that the viewer's attention is distracted from any existing media message. The image fluctuation caused by the camera's attempts to resolve the focus of the horizontal slit (raster-scan) pattern, combined with the varying effects of the anamorphic camera angles, only exacerbates its disruptive effect, and works in contrast to the high clarity of the adjacent Z-pattern.

The three interventions presented in this chapter represent only a few of the many unique consequences of digital technology for the design of urban form. They draw upon the complexity of the city's qualitative properties and exploit the idiosyncrasies and multiple viewpoints of its technology to interrupt existing narratives. Like their analogue counterparts six centuries earlier, they demonstrate the inextricable link between the geometry and technology with which we view and understand the world and the form we build. Furthermore, they demonstrate that disciplinary agency resides not only in the design of form but the making of images.

Notes

1 Hubert Damisch, 1994. *The origin of perspective*. Cambridge, MA: MIT Press.
2 Damisch, *The origin of perspective*, p. 226.
3 Damisch, *The origin of perspective*, p. 270.
4 Damisch, *The origin of perspective*, p. 317.
5 Table 6.1.
6 Table 7.1.
7 Table 8.1.

10 Conclusion

When speculating upon the nature of digital technology's impact on disciplinary agency, Mario Carpo predicts a grim future: 'The modern process of architectural design, and the architect's authorial role in it, may not survive the digital turn.'[1] However, if Carpo's prediction is interpreted within the broader framework of Walter Benjamin's thesis[2] – that the evolution of visioning technology is accompanied by the emergence of a corresponding series of conditions relating directly to how the world is perceived, experienced and inhabited – then recalibration and adaptation delineate the way forward. It has been the task of this research to speculate upon what form or forms recalibration and adaptation might take, in terms of both the tools and techniques of architecture and the future trajectory of the discipline itself. The speculations are therefore framed within the unique functions of digital geometry and the mechanical procedures and idiosyncrasies of the visioning systems that deploy it to view our world. In sum, they present the realignment of newly defined architectural tools and techniques with the many shifting conditions associated with inhabiting the digital city.

The new tools and techniques of architecture

To engage with the architecture of the contemporary city is to engage with the relationship between its built surfaces and the viewing technologies that preside over them. A profoundly different toolset is at work in this new bi-fold operational frame, where intervention is physical and viewing both physical and virtual. As the base operational unit of the image and its technological procedures, the pixel is the cornerstone of all processes relating to the perception of built form within a camera's visual field. Key modes of architectural intervention are therefore contingent upon the reciprocity – and indeed the discrepancy – between digital geometry, camera technology, the HVS and the vast array of material surfaces that can be linked to visioning systems through the numerical array of the pixel. This requires the individual techniques associated with this toolset's deployment and the operational conditions that influence

DOI: 10.4324/9781003133872-13

Conclusion   157

and determine their effect to be readily identifiable. A review of these techniques and conditions follows.

The pixel radically shifts the rules by which representation is constructed and perceived by positioning the qualitative properties of urban space – colour, contrast and brightness – as the principal determinants of image assembly and perceptual hierarchy. In an unprecedented architectural manoeuvre, the pixel's numerical array allows these properties to be indexically linked to the city's material surfaces. Furthermore, in the case of both situated cameras and handheld devices, the distributed physical nature of the network and the viewer means that image artefacts to do with the city's shifting emanation of colour and brightness become incorporated into the canon of city views, and thus form part of any future design intervention framework. The inclusion of camera 'aberrations' such as these within the city view ensures that its image is a heterogeneous and complex trace of multiple spaces and conditions.

Secondly, the extrapolation of the optical procedures of shape recognition into the core processes of digital image data transmission means that associated patterns can be selectively applied to either serve or disrupt the viewed site's existing representational ambitions. The extrapolation of human perceptual scanning procedures and their subsequent transposition into image pattern data exposes digital visioning technology to interventions of all kinds. In architectural terms, its data-based nature establishes conditions under which, once again, these types of procedures can be numerically linked to the production of the city's form. With the architect's newfound capacity to modify the visual hierarchy of a building by referring to projective tools like the test data matrix, the critical question then becomes: what transformative architectural strategies can result from the application of these tactics?

Positioning the pixel as the pivotal generative unit of the urban surface directly addresses procedural strategies embedded within visioning devices on their terms. Therefore, counterstrategies to image normalisation and 'cleansing' would entail using a new range of material surfaces that either transform the visual hierarchy of objects within the scene, or disrupt the production of iconic promotional views, or both. In either case, their potency ultimately resides in the tension between the real and the virtual representations of urban space, and in the instigation of new architectural agency arising from directing this tension towards recognising the broad and highly heterogeneous spectrum of the city's dynamic qualities.

Finally, the new viewing conditions brought about by digital camera technology profoundly affect how urban space can be experienced. The anamorphic effect of the camera's zoom trajectory transforms the city image from that generated by a single, predetermined viewing position into the highly interactive and abstracted product of the numerous locations and angles captured by the camera lens. For the architect, this provides the opportunity to precisely align the camera's technical capability with the

158 Conclusion

various tabulated effects of a vast range of material surfaces. In this scenario, the viewer's ability to operate the camera mechanism and the effects of pixel distribution in the image cooperate to inform design decisions about the strategic siting of any architectural intervention within viewed urban space.

The disciplinary shift

The realignment of architectural tools and techniques with the challenges and opportunities presented by digital technology has inevitable disciplinary implications. In the same way that Djiga Vertov's montage technique superseded the existing didactic narrative of the early 20th-century city, so do the visual manoeuvres made possible by the digital image demand nothing less than a profound redistribution of disciplinary tools and techniques and a reorientation of disciplinary knowledge to address the dynamic conditions of a digital city.

To return to Walter Benjamin, the dissection of the city through technology sets out the new terms by which it should be represented (and by extension, constructed) and the terms by which it should be experienced.[3] The pixel grid's data array positions the laws, processes and effects of digital geometry and technology at the centre of generative architectural procedures. Moreover, it presents a unique range of criteria with which architecture can be read and understood. With the city's qualitative properties (colour, brightness and shape) now operating as the core data according to which it is perceived and represented, these same properties set the new terms by which intervention is understood. To realign disciplinary knowledge with the digital frame thus requires the relinquishing of traditional linear-based modes of spatial apprehension in favour of an expanded operation, in which a building's visual potency resides in the tension between its virtual and real presentations. By exploiting digital technology's own generative procedures, disciplinary realignment is undertaken at the level of Benjamin's surgeon, now transformed into the architect who uses technology to penetrate and reveal the city's complex spatial properties. In this new scenario, it is the management of a building's visibility and its capacity to draw attention to both the city's uncurated aspects and the artifice of proprietary and promotional city views that become the new operational criteria for urban design within a digital frame.

The foregrounding of the city's qualitative properties also presents an entirely new formal language to the discipline. Drawing upon the procedures of the HVS as the terms of reference for formal discussion is a radical departure from traditional linear-based architectural language. Instead, it is now the language associated with the relationship between an object's colour, brightness and shape that informs design decisions and the documentation that transforms them into built form. With pixel assembly rather than linear coordinates as the point of departure for disciplinary practice, architectural discourse now revolves around relational issues of proximity, connectivity and grouping rather than around an object's placement on a perspectival grid, where its qualitative properties are secondary afterthoughts.

Yet disciplinary realignment means that the role and identity of the architect must also be interrogated and shift in accordance with the new scopic regime of the digital. The multiplication of viewpoints in urban space produces unique conditions for the procedures governing its designers. Mario Carpo argues that digital visioning technology blurs the traditional hierarchical boundaries that existed between artist and viewer, writing that 'the traditional divide between sender and receiver, or author and audience, is fading',[4] and that this means architectural agency is at stake: 'with the transition from mechanical to digital technologies ... a recast of architectural agency will also be inevitable.'[5] Recognition of the increasing slippage between 'anybody' and 'the architect' as the designer of contemporary urban space is therefore a disciplinary responsibility. The charting of an adaptive path to new agency is its necessary outcome.

The tools and techniques presented in this book suggest in practical terms how the reinstatement of architectural agency might occur within the new digital frame. They reveal that the architect now needs to be both an image-maker and a maker of surfaces and forms in the city if the latest incarnation of this generative role is to respond comprehensively to the complex, bi-fold conditions instigated by the digital. They suggest too that newfound agency is best found by addressing technology on its own procedural terms, allowing proprietary strategies to be unveiled and singular ambitions dismantled. In sum, the capacity of these new tools and techniques to release the qualitative and reinforce the ambiguous endows the architect with new agency. In so doing, it realigns the trajectory of the discipline with the frame of the digital. Furthermore, it is the discipline's readiness to acknowledge the increasing status of the image – and thus its own capacity to engage with the visioning technology of the incumbent scopic regime – that will ensure its survival, not only of the digital turn, but of the challenges presented by other future visual paradigms.

Notes

1 Mario Carpo, 2011. *The alphabet and the algorithm*. Cambridge, MA: MIT Press, p. 127.
2 Walter Benjamin, 1936. *The work of art in the age of mechanical reproduction*. London: Penguin Books.
3 Benjamin, *The work of art in the age of mechanical reproduction*.
4 Carpo, *The alphabet and the algorithm*, p. 113.
5 Carpo, *The alphabet and the algorithm*, p. 44.

Glossary

Anamorphic/anamorphosis (digital anamorphosis)

The two principal operational procedures of this counter-technique to linear perspective projection have a counterpart in a contemporary image-making process that is unique to the digital environment. The geometric distortions that operate perpendicular to the picture plane to either increase or decrease the perception of depth correlate with the effect of the webcam's zoom mechanism. The zoom device allows the viewer to accelerate towards or decelerate from an object, but the difference now is that the viewer's trajectory can exceed the image's resolution or the 'ideal' viewing position.

The second type of early anamorphic technique, which forms an alternative, secondary image at an oblique viewing angle to the picture plane, corresponds with the effect of the pan/tilt mechanism of the webcam. Digital public webcams enable the viewer to rotate the camera lens remotely to capture a wide field of view. The unique effect of the oblique views of the city that comes with the webcam's multiplication of viewpoints is that a primary view does not exist. Instead of a single privileged vantage point by means of which the 'ideal' image of the city is presented, the camera views are all primary, yet they also form other secondary oblique landscapes.

F-stop and zoom

The camera's f-stop relates to its aperture setting. Aperture and shutter speed are ways of controlling exposure. Aperture (which relates directly to the camera's f-stop numbers) controls the diameter of the lens' diaphragm that lets light into the camera and onto the image sensor. The lower the f-stop number, the more light enters the camera lens. Diffraction artefacts also tend to appear at both low and high ends of the camera's aperture range. There is, however, no difference in exposure during the zoom trajectory, because the camera's zoom or magnification mechanism is designed to compensate for any change in aperture.

While the f-stop numbers of digital cameras vary to the extent that half stops or even third stops of exposure are possible, this scale nevertheless still provides a reliable numerical index of the effects of light upon the camera's image-making procedures.[1] The camera's f-stop is thus a means of establishing not only an exact numerical link between an object's surface, the effects of this surface upon the camera and the increments of the camera's f-stop settings acting in conjunction with its zoom trajectory, but a behavioural matrix that delineates the conditions of this digital visioning environment.

Indexical/raster or pixel grid

A raster is a matrix of cells (or pixels) arranged in rows and columns, or a grid, in which each cell contains a data value. The cell or pixel values represent the condition portrayed by the raster dataset, such as colour (RGB) or luminance. For most data, the cell or pixel value represents a sampling of a condition and the value represents the entire cell square. The location of each cell is defined by its xy location within the raster matrix in which the rows of the matrix are parallel to the x-axis and the columns to the y-axis of the Cartesian plane.[2] In terms of the RGB values of a pixel data array, this then means that the pixel has a limitless capacity to link data to a range of explicit visual effects that are associated with numerical weightings and a location within the array. Furthermore, in contrast to earlier notions of indexicality that 'tied design notations to their material result in an object',[3] the digital index instead draws upon the numerical grid of the pictorial pixel array to assign qualitative properties to the viewed surfaces of the city.

Instrumentalisation

The type of mathematical construct or theory that underpins visioning technology, in this case either linear perspective geometry or digital geometry.

Notes

1 Spencer Cox, 2021. What is f-stop and how does it work? [Online]. Available from: https://photographylife.com/f-stop/amp
2 ArcMap. 2021. What is raster data [Online]. Available from: https://desktop.arcgis.com/en/arcmap/latest/manage-data/raster-and-images/what-is-raster-data.htm
3 Mario Carpo, 2011. *The alphabet and the algorithm*. Cambridge, MA: MIT Press, p. 43.

Bibliography

Abrams, Austin, Nick Fridrich, Nathan Jacobs, and Robert Pless, 2010. *Participatory integration of live webcams into GIS*. Proceedings of the 1st International Conference and Exhibition on Computing for Geospatial Research & Application. Washington, D.C., USA: Association for Computing Machinery, 9, pp. 1–8. 10.1145/1823854.1823867

Ackerman, James S., 1994. *Distance points: Essays in theory and Renaissance art and architecture*. Cambridge, MA: MIT Press.

Adept Turnkey Pty Ltd. 2012. *Sensor comparison I: Interlaced scan, non-interlaced scan, progressive scan*. Available from: http://www.adept.net.au/news/newsletter/200809sep/sensors.shtml

ADOBE. 2000. Adobe Technical Guides. Available from: http://dba.med.sc.edu/price/irf/Adobe_tg/models/rgbcmy.html

Alleysson, David, Sabine Süsstrunk, and Jeremy Hérault, Jeremy, 2002. Color demosaicing by estimating luminance and opponent chromatic signals in the Fourier domain. *Proceedings of Society for Imaging Science and Technology, 10th Color Imaging Conference*, 10, pp. 331–336.

Anonymous, 2010. *Anamorphic Art: A special instance of perspective* [online]. Available from: http://anamorphicart.wordpress.com/.

ArcMap, 2021. What is raster data [Online]. Available from: https://desktop.arcgis.com/en/arcmap/latest/manage-data/raster-and-images/what-is-raster-data.htm.

Atencia, Anais, Vinxcent Boyer, and Jean-Jacques Bourdin, 2008. From detail to global view, an impressionist approach. In *2008 IEEE International Conference on Signal Image Technology and Internet Based Systems*, pp. 366–374.

AXIS Communications, 2021. *Technical guide to network video* [online]. Available from: http://www.axis.com/products/video/camera/progressive_scan.htm

Baltrušaitis, Jurgis, 1977. *Anamorphic art*. New York, NY: Harry N. Abrams.

Barasch, Moshe, 1998. *Modem theories of art, 2: From impressionism to Kandinsky*. New York, NY: New York University Press.

Barneva, Reneta P., and Valentin Brimkov, 2009. Digital geometry and its applications to medical imaging. In: João Manuel R. S. Tavares and R. M. Natal Jorge, eds. *Advances in computational vision and medical image processing*, pp. 77–92. Dordrecht: Springer. 10.1007/978-1-4020-9086-8_4

Beller, Jonathon, 2006. *The cinematic mode of production: Attention economy and the society of the spectacle*. Lebanon, NH: University Press of New England.

Benjamin, Walter, 1936. *The work of art in the age of mechanical reproduction*. London: Penguin Books.
Benjamin, Walter, 1979. *A small history of photography. One-way street and other writings*. Brooklyn, NY: Verso.
Bhowmick, Partha, 2009. Evolution of geometric figures from the Euclidean to the digital era. *Proceedings of the First International Conference on Intelligent Human Computer Interaction*, pp. 19–36.
Blake, Edwin, 1990. The natural flow of perspective: Reformulating perspective projection for computer animation. *Leonardo*, 23 (4), pp. 401–409. doi: 10.2307/1575343
Bogard, William, 2006. Surveillance assemblages and lines of flight. In: D. Lyon, ed. *Theorizing surveillance: The panopticon and beyond*. Devon, UK: Willan Publishing, pp. 111–136.
Bois, Yve-Alain, and John Shepley, 1984. A picturesque stroll around 'Clara-Clara'. *October*, 29, pp. 33–62.
Bois, Yve-Alain, and Amy Reiter-McIntosh, 1988. Piet Mondrian, 'New York City'. *Critical Inquiry*, 14 (2), pp. 244–277. doi: 10.1086/448437
Bolter, Jay, and Richard Grusin, 1999. *Remediation: Understanding new media*. Cambridge, MA: MIT Press.
Bordwell, David, Keith, Thompson, and Jeff, Ashton, 1997. *Film art: An introduction*. New York, NY: McGraw-Hill.
Boring, Edwin, 1946. The perception of objects. *American Journal of Physics*, 14 (2), pp. 99–107. doi: 10.1119/1.1990807.
Boyer, Christine, 1996. *CyberCities visual perception in the age of electronic communication* (1st ed.). New York, NY: Princeton Architectural Press.
Boyle, Jen, 2010. *Anamorphosis in early modern literature: Mediation and affect* (1st ed.). Abingdon-on-Thames: Routledge. 10.4324/9781315262598.
Broadfoot, Keith, 2002. Perspective yet again: Damisch with Lacan. *Oxford Art Journal*, 25 (1), pp. 71–94. http://www.jstor.org/stable/3600421
Brown, Theodore M. 1965. Rietveld's egocentric vision. *Journal of the Society of Architectural Historians*, 24 (4), pp. 292–296.
Bruce, Vicki, Patrick Green, and Mark Georgeson, 2010. *Visual perception: Physiology, psychology & ecology*. Hove: Psychology Press.
Bryson, Norman, 1988. The gaze in the expanded field. In: H. Foster, ed. *Vision and visuality*. Seattle, WA: Bay Press, pp. 86–113.
Cairns, Graham, 2013. *The architecture of the screen: Essays in cinematographic space*. Bristol: Intellect Books.
Cairns, Graham, ed., 2016. *Visioning technologies: The architectures of sight*. Abingdon-on-Thames: Routledge.
Cambridge in colour, no date. Digital camera diffraction, part 2. Available from: https://www.cambridgeincolour.com/tutorials/diffraction-photography-2.htm
Cantoni, Virginio, Stefano Levialdi, and Bertrand Zavidovique, 2011. *3C vision: Cues, context and channels*. Waltham, MA: Elsevier.
Cardoso Llach, Daniel, 2015. *Builders of the vision: Software and the imagination of design* (1st ed.). Abingdon-on-Thames: Routledge.
Carpo, Mario, 2011. *The alphabet and the algorithm*. Cambridge, MA: MIT Press.
Carpo, Mario, 2017. *The second digital turn: Design beyond intelligence*. Cambridge, MA: MIT Press. doi: 10.7551/mitpress/9976.001.0001

Carullo, Valeria, 2016. The great publicist of modern building. In: G. Cairns, ed. *Visioning technologies: The architectures of sight*. Abingdon-on-Thames: Routledge, pp. 87–104.
Cassirer, Ernst, 1968. *The philosophy of symbolic forms* (trans. Ralph Manheim), Yale University Press.
Chard, Nat, 2003. Positioning and the picture plane. *The Journal of Architecture*, 8, pp. 211–220. doi: 10.1080/13602360309587.
ColorSchemer, no date. Available from: https://www.apponic.com/developer/colorschemer-11646/
Cox, Spencer, 2021. What is f-stop and how does it work? [Online]. Available from: https://photographylife.com/f-stop/amp
Crary, Jonathan, 1992. *Techniques of the observer: On vision and modernity in the nineteenth century*. Cambridge, MA: MIT Press.
Damisch, Hubert, 1994. *The origin of perspective*. Cambridge, MA: MIT Press.
Davies, Nigel P., and Antony B. Morland, 2002. The Hermann-Hering grid illusion demonstrates disruption of lateral inhibition processing in diabetes mellitus. *British Journal of Ophthalmology*, 86, pp. 203–208. doi: 10.1136/bjo.86.2.203
Deering, Micahel F., 2005. A photon accurate model of the human eye. *ACM Transactions on Graphics*, 24 (3), pp. 649–658.
Deleuze, Gilles, 1986. *Cinema 1: The movement image* (trans. Hugh Tomlinson and Barbara Habberjam). Minneapolis, MN: University of Minnesota Press.
Deleuze, Gilles, 1992. Postscript on the societies of control. *October*, 59, pp. 3–7. http://www.jstor.org/stable/778828
De Quincy, Antoine Quatremere, 1832. *Dictionnaire historique d'architecture: Comprenant dans son plan les notions historiques, descriptives, archéologiques ... De cet art. Tome 1*, Le Clère et Cie Paris.
Diffraction, 2021. CCD versus CMOS: Which is better? [Online] Diffraction. Ottawa. Available from: https://diffractionlimited.com/ccd-versus-cmos-which-is-better/feature-image/
DiPaola, Steve, Caitlin Riebe, and James Enns, 2010. Rembrandt's textural agency: A shared perspective in visual art and science. *Leonardo*, 43 (2), pp. 145–151. doi: 10.1162/leon.2010.43.2.145
Durand, Fredo, and Julie Dorsey, 2002. Fast bilateral filtering for the display of high-dynamic-range images. *ACM Transactions on Graphics*, 21 (3), pp. 257–266. 10.1145/566654.566574
Durão, Maria Joao, 2011. Sketching the Ariadne's Thread for alchemical linkages to painting. *Fabrikart*, 8, pp. 106–123.
Dyce, Matt, 2013. Canada between the photograph and the map: Aerial photography, geographical vision and the state. *Journal of Historical Geography*, 39, pp. 69–84.
Eisenstein, Sergei M., 1997. Piranesi, or the fluidity of forms (trans. Roberta Reeder). *Oppositions*, 11, pp. 84–110.
Elliott, Eugene Clinton 1960. Some recent conceptions of color theory. *Journal of Aesthetics and Art Criticism*, pp. 494–503.
Evans, Brian, 1990. Temporal coherence with digital color. *Leonardo*, 23 (6), pp. 43–49. doi: 10.2307/1557894
Farago, Claire J., 1991. Leonardo's color and chiaroscuro reconsidered: The visual force of painted images. *The Art Bulletin*, 73 (1), pp. 63–88.

Ferreira, Tiago, and Wayne Rasband, 2011. *The ImageJ User Guide*. USA: National Institutes of Health.

Floyd, Robert. W. and Louis Steinberg, 1976. An adaptive algorithm for spatial grey scale. *Proceedings of the Society of Information Display*, 17, pp. 75–77.

Foley, James D., Andries, Van Dam, Steven K., FeinerJohn F., Hughes, 1996. *Computer graphics: Principles and practice*. Boston, MA: Addison-Wesley Professional.

Foucault, Michel. 1977. *Discipline and punish: The birth of the prison* (trans. Alan Sheridan). New York, NY: Random House.

Fuller, John, 1976. Atget and Man Ray in the context of surrealism. *Art Journal*, 36 (2), pp. 130–138.

Gage, John, 1982. Colour at the Bauhaus. *AA Files*, 2, pp. 50–54.

Gage, John, 1990. Color in Western art: An issue? *The Art Bulletin*, 72, pp. 518–541.

Gage, John, 2013. *Shadowy figures*. Available from: https://wengam.com/PDFs/john_gage_light_from_shadow.pdf.

Gibson, James, 1979. *The ecological approach to visual perception*. Boston, MA: Houghton Mifflin.

Gillam, Barbara, 1980. Geometrical illusions. *Scientific American*, 242, pp. 102–111.

Gillam, Barbara, 2007. Hochberg: A perceptual psychologist. In: M. A. Peterson, B. Gillam and H.A. Sedgwick, eds. *In the mind's eye: Julian Hochberg on the perception of pictures, films, and the world*, Kettering: Oxford University Press, pp. 405–419.

Gordon, Ian E., 2004. *Theories of visual perception* (1st ed.). Hove: Psychology Press. 10.4324/9780203502259

Gorse, George L., 1997. A classical stage for the old nobility: The Strada Nuova and sixteenth-century Genoa. *The Art Bulletin*, 79, pp. 301–326.

Green, Nigel, 2016. The transformative interface. In: G. Cairns, ed. *Visioning technologies: The architectures of sight*. Abingdon-on-Thames: Routledge, pp. 73–86.

Gregory, Richard L., 1997. *Eye and brain: The psychology of seeing*. New York, NY: Princeton University Press. doi: 10.2307/j.ctvc77h66

Gregory, Richard L., 1997. Knowledge in perception and illusion. *Philosophical Transactions of the Royal Society B*, 352 (1358), pp. 1121–1127. 10.1098/rstb.1997.0095

Gurtner, Lilla M., Mathias Hartmann, and Fred Mast, 2021. Eye movements during visual imagery and perception show spatial correspondence but have unique temporal signatures. *Cognition*, 210, 104597. 10.1016/j.cognition.2021.104597

He, Xiangjian, and Jianmin Li, 2007. Linear interpolation for image conversion between square structure and hexagonal structure. *PAMM: Proceedings in Applied Mathematics and Mechanics*, 7 (1), pp. 1011001–1011002. Berlin: WILEY-VCH Verlag.

Hirsch, Robert, 2008. *Seizing the light*. New York, NY: McGraw-Hill.

Hand, Martin, 2012. *Ubiquitous photography*. Cambridge: Polity Press.

Hansen, Marc, 2004. *New philosophy for new media*. Cambridge, MA: MIT Press.

He, X. and Li, J., 2007. Linear interpolation for image conversion between square structure and hexagonal structure. *PAMM: Proceedings in Applied Mathematics and Mechanics* 7 (1), pp. 1011001–1011002. Berlin: WILEY-VCH Verlag.

Hochberg, Julian, 2007. Looking ahead (one glance at a time). In: M. A. Peterson, B. Gillam and H. A. Sedgwick, eds. *In the mind's eye: Julian Hochberg on the perception of pictures, films, and the world*. Kettering: Oxford University Press, pp. 396–414.

Hubel, Paul M., John Liu, and Rudolph J. Guttosch, 2004. Spatial frequency response of color image sensors: Bayer color filters and Foveon X3. *Proceedings, Volume 5301, Sensors and camera systems for scientific, industrial, and digital photography applications*. doi: 10.1117/12.561568

Humphrey, Katherine Anne, 2010. *Eye movements and scanpaths in the perception of real-world scenes*. Thesis (PhD). University of Nottingham.

Itti, Laurent, and Christof Koch, 2001. Computational modelling of visual attention. *Nature Reviews Neuroscience*, 2 (3), pp. 194–203. 10.1038/35058500

Jameson, Dorothea, and Leo M. Hurvich, 1975. From contrast to assimilation: In art and in the eye. *Leonardo*, 8 (2), pp. 125–131. 10.2307/1572954

Jay, Martin, 1988. Scopic regimes of modernity. In: H. Foster, ed. *Vision and visuality*. Seattle: Bay Press.

Julesz, Bela, 1991. Early vision and focal attention. *Reviews of Modern Physics*, 63 (3), pp. 735–772. doi: 10.1103/RevModPhys.63.735

Kanizsa, Gaetano, 1979. *Organization in vision: Essays on Gestalt perception*. New York, NY: Praeger Publishers.

Kaplan, Louis, 2003. Where the paranoid meets the paranormal: Speculations on spirit photography. *Art Journal*, 62, pp. 18–27. doi: 10.1080/00043249.2003.10792167

Kapoula, Zoï, Qing Yang, Marine Vernet, and Maria-Pia Bucci, 2009. Eye movements and pictorial space perception: studies of paintings from Francis Bacon and Piero della Francesca. *Cognitive Semiotics*, 5 (Fall), pp. 103–121. doi: 10.1515/cogsem.2009.5.fall2009.103

Kemp, Martin, 1990. *The science of art: Optical themes in western art from Brunelleschi to Seurat*. New Haven, CT: Yale University Press.

Kingdom, Frederick A., 2014. Mach bands explained by response normalization Frontiers in human neuroscience 8:843 [online] Available from: https://pubmed.ncbi.nlm.nih.gov/25408643/

Kintronics, 2014. *Night vision and long-range IR PTZ camera system* [online]. Available from: http://www.kintronics.com/night-vision-ir-ptz-camera-with-long-rangecapability/-2

Klette, Reinhard, and Azriel Rosenfeld, 2004. *Digital geometry: Geometric methods for digital picture analysis*. Boston, MA: Elsevier.

Koeck, Richard, 2013. *Cine-scapes: Cinematic spaces in architecture and cities*. Abingdon-on-Thames: Routledge. doi: 10.4324/9780203721186

Köhler, Wolfgang, 1967. Gestalt psychology. *Psychologische Forschung*, 31(1), pp. XVIII–XXX.

Koskela, Hille, 2006. The other side of surveillance: Webcams, power and agency. In: D. Lyon, ed. *Theorizing surveillance: The panopticon and beyond*. Cullompton: Willan Publishing.

Kruegle, Herman, 2007. *CCTV surveillance: Analog and digital video practices and technology*. Amsterdam: Elsevier Butterworth Heinemann.

Kurgan, Laura, 2013. *Close up at a distance: Mapping, technology, and politics*. New York, NY: Zone Books.

Lawton, Anna, 1978. Rhythmic montage in the films of Dziga Vertov: A Poetic use of the language of cinema. *Pacific Coast Philology*, pp. 44–50. doi: 10.2307/1316363.
Leck, B. van der, 1917. De plaats van het moderne schilderen in de architectuur. *De Stijl*, 1, pp. 6–7.
Lehar, Steven M., 2003. *The world in your head: A gestalt view of the mechanism of conscious experience*. Mahwah, NJ: Lawrence Erlbaum Associates.
Livingstone, Margaret S., 1988. Art, illusion and the visual system. *Scientific American*, 258, pp. 78–85. doi: 10.1038/scientificamerican0188-78
Lotringer, Sylvère, and Paul Virilio, 2005. *The accident of art*. New York, NY: Semiotext(e) Foreign Agents.
Lu, Yue M., and Martin Vetterli, 2009. Optimal color filter array design: Quantitative conditions and an efficient search procedure. *Digital Photography V*, 7250, p. 725009. doi: 10.1117/12.807598
Lukac, Rastislav, and Konstantinos Plataniotis, 2005. Color filter arrays: Design and performance analysis. *IEEE Transactions on Consumer Electronics*, 51(4), pp. 1260–1267.
Macarthur, John, 2000. From the air: Collage city, aerial photography and the picturesque. In: M. Ostwald and J. Moore, eds. *Re-framing architecture: Theory, science and myth*. Sydney: Archadia Press, pp. 113–120.
Mannan, Sabira, Ruddock, Keith, and Wooding, David, 1996. The relationship between the locations of spatial features and those of fixations made during visual examination of briefly presented images. *Spatial Vision*, 10 (3), pp. 165–188. doi: 10.1163/156856896×00123
Marr, David, and Herbert Keith, Nishihara, 1978. Representation and recognition of the spatial organization of three-dimensional shapes. *Proceedings of the Royal Society of London. Series B. Biological Sciences*, 200, pp. 269–294. doi: 10.1098/rspb.1978.0020
Massey, Lyle, 2003. Configuring spatial ambiguity: Picturing the distance point from Alberti to anamorphosis. *Studies in the History of Art*, 59, pp. 160–175. doi: 10.1086/426295
Massey, Lyle, 2007. *Picturing space, displacing bodies: Anamorphosis in early modern theories of perspective*. University Park, PA: Penn State University Press.
Massumi, Brian, 2002. *Parables for the virtual: Movement, affect, sensation*. Durham, NC: Duke University Press.
Maxim, Juliana, 2011. Developing socialism: The photographic condition of architecture in Romania, 1958–1970. *Visual Resources*, 27, pp. 154–171.
McCann, John J., 2007. Art, science, and appearance in HDR. *Journal of the Society for Information Display*, 15 (9), pp. 709–719. doi: 10.1889/1.2785204
McCann, John J., and Alessandro, Rizzi, 2007. Camera and visual veiling glare in HDR images. *Journal of the Society for Information Display*, 15 (9), pp. 721–730. doi: 10.1889/1.2785205
McCann, John J., and Rizzi, Alessandro, 2009. Retinal HDR images: Intraocular glare and object size. *Journal of the Society for Information Display*, 17(11), pp. 913–920.
McCann, John J., and Rizzi, Alessandro, 2007. Spatial comparisons: The antidote to veiling glare limitations in image capture and display. *Proc.IMQA*.
McGrath, Brian, and Jean Gardner, 2007. *Cinemetrics: Architectural drawing today*. Chichester: Wiley-Academy.

McGrath, Brian, and Jean Gardner, 2008. Cinemetrics: Embodying architectural representation in the digital age. *Architectural Theory Review*, 13 (1), pp. 29–51. doi: 10.1080/13264820801915104

McLeod, Saul A., 2018. Visual perception theory. *Simply Psychology* [online]. Available from: http://www.simplypsychology.org/perception-theories.html.

McQuire, Scott, 2016. Intersecting frames: Film + architecture. In: G. Cairns, ed. *Visioning Technologies*, Routledge, pp. 167–180.

Melcher, David, and Patrick Cavanagh, 2011. Pictorial cues in art and in visual perception. In: F. Bacci and D. Melcher, eds. *Art and the senses*. Oxford: Oxford University Press, pp. 359–394.

Minsky, Marvin, 1988. *Society of mind*. New York, NY: Simon and Schuster.

Mitchell, William J., 1992. *The reconfigured eye. Visual truth in in the post-photographic era*. Cambridge, MA: MIT Press.

Monmonier, Mark, 2000. Webcams, interactive index maps, and our brave new world's brave new globe, *Cartographic Perspectives*, (37), pp. 51–64. doi: 10.14714/CP37.809

Morgan, Luke, 2005. The early modern 'trompe-l'oeil' garden. *Garden History*, pp. 286–293.

Nagel, Alexander, 1993. Leonardo and sfumato. *RES: Anthropology and Aesthetics*, 24 (1), pp. 7–20. doi: 10.1086/RESv24n1ms20166875

Nalwa, Vishvjit S., 1994. *A guided tour of computer vision*. Boston, MA: Addison-Wesley, p. 4.

National Instruments, 2006. *Anatomy of a camera* [online]. Available from: https://www.ni.com/en-au/innovations/white-papers/06/anatomy-of-a-camera.html

Norman, Joel, 2002. Two visual systems and two theories of perception: An attempt to reconcile the constructivist and ecological approaches. *Behavioral and Brain Sciences*, 25, pp. 73–96. doi: 10.1017/S0140525X0200002X

Noton, David, 1970. A theory of visual pattern perception. *IEEE Transactions on Systems Science and Cybernetics*, 6 (4), pp. 349–357.

Noton, David, and Lawrence Stark, 1971. Eye movements and visual perception. *Scientific American*, 224 (6), pp. 34–43.

O'Connor, Zena, 2010. Colour harmony revisited. *Color Research & Application*, 35 (4), pp. 267–273. doi: 10.1002/col.20578

Panofsky, Erwin, and Christopher Wood, 1991. *Perspective as symbolic form*. Brooklyn, NY: Zone Books.

Papet, Edouard, 2012. Permanent colour: The revival of polychrome sculpture in late 19th century France (trans.Judith Hayward). *Apollo Magazine*. CLXXVl (601) [online]. Available from: https://www.thefreelibrary.com/Permanen-colour: experiments with stoneware revived the...-a0302463263.

Parmar, Manu and Stanley J. Reeves, 2004. A perceptually based design methodology for color filter arrays [image reconstruction]. *2004 IEEE International Conference on Acoustics, Speech, and Signal Processing*, pp. III-473–III-476. doi: 10.1109/ICASSP.2004.1326584

Pedrotti, Leno S., 2008. Basic physical optics. *Fundamentals of Photonics*, 1, pp. 117–167.

Pinck, Pascal, 2000. From sofa to the crime scene: Skycam, local news and the televisual city. In: M. Balshaw and L. Kennedy, eds. *Urban space and representation*. Sterling, VA: Pluto Press.

Poynton, Charles, 2012. *Digital video and HD: Algorithms and interfaces.* San Francisco, CA: Morgan Kaufmann Publishers.

Quatremere De Quincy, Antoine, 1832. *Dictionnaire historique d'architecture: Comprenant dans son plan les notions historiques, descriptives, archéologiques ... de cet art. Tome 1* [online]. Le Clère et Cie Paris. Available from: https://gallica.bnf.fr/ark:/12148/bpt6k1045594m

Quiroga, Rodrigo Q., and Carlos Pedreira, 2011. How do we see art: An eye-tracker study. *Frontiers in Human Neuroscience*, 5, p. 98. doi: 10.3389/fnhum.2011.00098

Ramanath, Rajeev, Wesley Snyder, Griff Bilbro, and William Sander, 2002. Demosaicking methods for Bayer color arrays. *Journal of Electronic Imaging*, 11 (3), pp. 306–315. doi: 10.1117/1.1484495

Reynolds, Bryan, 2006. *Transversal enterprises in the Drama of Shakespeare and his contemporaries.* New York, NY: Palgrave Macmillan.

Rhyne, Theresa-Marie, 2017. Applying color theory to digital media and visualization. Proceedings of the *2017 CHI Conference Extended Abstracts on Human Factors in Computing Systems*, pp. 1264–1267.

Rice, Charles, 2007. Critical post-critical: Problems of effect, experience and immersion. In: J. Rendell, J. Hill, M. Dorrian and M. Fraser, eds. *Critical architecture*, Abingdon-on-Thames: Routledge, pp. 261–268.

Rietveld, Gerrit, 1955. Mondrian en het nieuwe bouwen. *Bouwkundig Weekblad*, 73 (11).

Rizov, Vladimir, 2021. Eugène Atget and documentary photography of the city. *Theory, Culture & Society*, 38 (3), pp. 141–163. doi: 10.1177/02632764210942804

Rock, Irvin, and Stephen Palmer, 1990. The legacy of Gestalt psychology. *Scientific American*, 263 (6), pp. 84–91.

Saleh, Nadia T., 2010. Demosaicing of true color images using adaptive interpolation algorithms. *Journal of Education and Science*, 23 (1), pp. 64–83. doi: 10.33899/edusj.2010.57984

Savard, John J. G., 2009. *Color filter array designs* [online]. Available from: http://quadibloc.com/other/cfaint.htm

Schlyter, Paul, 1997. *Radiometry and photometry in astronomy* [online]. Available from: http://stjarnhimlen.se/comp/radfaq.html

Schütz, Alexander, Doris Braun, and Karl Gegenfurtner, 2011. Eye movements and perception: A selective review. *Journal of Vision*, 11 (5), pp. 1–30. doi: 10.1167/11.5.9

Seigworth, Gregory J., and Melissa Gregg, 2010. An inventory of shimmers. In: G. Seigworth and M. Gregg, eds. *The affect theory reader.* Durham, NC: Duke University Press, pp. 1–27.

Sheehan, Thomas, 2003. Wittgenstein and Vertov: Aspectuality and anarchy. *Discourse*, 24, pp. 95–113. doi: 10.1353/dis.2003.0034

Shi, Yun-Qing, and Sun, Huifang, 2017. *Image and Video Compression for Multimedia Engineering: Fundamentals, Algorithms, and Standards*, 2nd Edition, CRC Press.

Shlain, Leonard, 1993. *Art & physics: Parallel visions in space, time and light.* New York, NY: Quill.

Sontag, Susan, 1977. *On photography.* London: Penguin Books.

170 Bibliography

Staunton, Richard C., and Neil Storey, 1990. A comparison between square and hexagonal sampling methods for pipeline image processing. *Optics, Illumination, and Image Sensing for Machine Vision IV*, 1194, pp. 142–151. doi:10.1117/12.969847

Tanimoto, Steven L., 2012. *An interdisciplinary introduction to image processing: Pixels, numbers, and programs*. Cambridge, MA: MIT Press.

Tkalcic, Marko, and Jurij F. Tasic, 2003. Colour spaces: Perceptual, historical and applicational background. *The IEEE Region 8 EUROCON 2003. Computer as a Tool*, pp. 304–308. doi: 10.1109/EURCON.2003.1248032

Torcellini, D., 2010. Painting and photographing the sunlight. A comparison between old-school and avant-garde techniques. *Proc.CREATE*, pp. 353–358.

Turvey, Malcolm, 1999. Can the camera see? Mimesis in 'Man with a Movie Camera'. *October*, pp. 25–50. doi: 10.2307/779138

Unifore, 2011. *CCD VS CMOS in video surveillance cameras* [online]. Available from: http://www.hkvstar.com/technology-news/ccd-vs-cmos-in-video-surveillance-cameras.html

Van Doesburg, Theo, 1924. Towards a plastic architecture. *de Stijl*, 12 (6/7), pp. 78–83.

Van Zanten, David, 1982. Architectural polychromy: Life in architecture. In: R.D. Middleton, ed. *The Beaux-Arts and Nineteenth-Century French Architecture*, London: Thames and Hudson, pp. 197–215.

Venturi, Robert, Martino Stierli, and David B. Brownlee, 1977. *Complexity and contradiction in architecture* (2nd ed.). London: Architectural Press.

Verstegen, Ian, 2010. A classification of perceptual corrections of perspective distortions in Renaissance painting. *Perception*, 39, pp. 677–694. doi: 10.1068/p6150

Vertov, Dziga, 1984. *Kino-eye: The writings of Dziga Vertov*. Berkeley, CA: University of California Press.

Weedon, Alan, 2019. Why large swathes of countries are censored on Google Maps. Available from: https://www.abc.net.au/news/2019-02-21/why-large-parts-of-earth-are-censored-by-google-maps/10826024

Wertheimer, Michael, 2012. *On perceived motion and figural organization*. Cambridge, MA: MIT Press.

Womack, Peter, 2008. The comical scene: Perspective and civility on the Renaissance stage. *Representations*, 101, pp. 32–56. doi: 10.1525/rep.2008.101.1.32

Wood, Aylish, 2008. Encounters at the interface: Distributed attention and digital embodiments. *Quarterly Review of Film and Video*, 25, pp. 219–229. doi: 10.1080/10509200601091490

Yarbus, Alfred L., 1967. Eye movements during perception of complex objects. In: A. L. Yarbus, ed. *Eye movements and Vision*. Boston, MA: Springer, pp. 171–211.

Zakia, Richard D., 2013. *Perception and imaging: Photography – a way of seeing*. New York, NY: Taylor & Francis.

Zeimbekis, John, 2012. Digital pictures, sampling, and vagueness: The ontology of digital pictures. *The Journal of Aesthetics and Art Criticism*, 70, pp. 43–53. doi: 10.1111/j.1540-6245.2011.01497.x

Index

Note: Italicized and bold page numbers refer to figures and tables. Page numbers followed by "n" refer to notes.

Adobe Creative Suite's Photoshop 51
affective anamorphic network 76–77
affective space 22–24
affective virtuality 22
Alberti, L. B.: *De pictura* 47
Alpers, S. 83
Ambassadors, The (Holbein) 15, 22, 76, 79
analog 4, 6, 11, 16, 19, 21, 28–32, 36, 39–41, 65, 67, 74, 76, 77, 98, 137, 154
anamorphic/anamorphosis 6, 15–16, 20, 22, 24, 111, 150–152, 154, 157; affective anamorphic network 76–77; digital 74–80, 98–102; pre-digital anamorphic techniques 74–76; techniques 77–80
Annunciation (Francesca) 63, 64, 72n106
Aquinas, T. 46
architectural event-space theory 19
Aristotle 46
Assumption of the Virgin (Correggio) 56, 57
Atget, E. 14
attention tracking 114–115
authorship 4, 5, 13, 20, 29, 30, 32, 42, 43, 86, 93, 94
avant-garde 10

Baltrušaitis, J. 74
Barneva, R. P. 51
Battle of San Romano, The (Uccello) 40
Benjamin, W. 3, 4, 12, 14, 21, 93, 110–111, 156

Bentham, J. 81
Berlin-Symphony of a Great City (Ruttman) 17
Bogard, W. 81
Bois, Y.-A. 16, 49
Boring, E. 33, 34, 36–37
Borromini, F.: San Carlo alle Quattro Fontane 12
'bottom-up' or data-driven processing 34, 63
Braque, G. 49
brightness 23, 27n75, 35, 98, 157; as an artefact 58–59; digital mediation of 35–41; digital perception of 55–60; Fraunhofer diffraction, as productive aberration 59–60; profiles, as generative procedure 108–109; register, shifting 55–58; shifting function of 122–123; transdisciplinary modes of activating 106, 108, *108*
Brimkov, V. 51
Broadfoot, K. 79
Brunelleschi, F. 10, 28, 87
Bryson, N. 85
building surface, as colour modifier 113–128; design templates 113–114; Series 1 tests *see* Series 1 tests; test strategies 114–115; validation methods 115–116

camera obscura model 47
Camp David, November 15, 1986, Reagan/Thatcher (Johnson) 68
Cantoni, V. 132, 138

172 Index

Carpo, M. 4, 42, 54, 93, 156, 159
Cavanagh, P. 62, 63
CCD *see* couple charged device (CCD)
CCTV *see* closed-circuit television (CCTV)
Center of gaze (Molina) 65
CFA *see* colour filter array (CFA)
chiaroscuro technique 56, 71n63
CIE *see* Commission International de l'Éclairage (CIE)
cinematic selection of blocks 103
città ideale 47
closed-circuit television (CCTV) 83, 84
CMOS *see* complementary metal-oxide-semiconductor (CMOS)
CMYK (cyan, magenta, yellow and key) model 37, 50
'coarse-to-fine' procedure 62
Color Blender 53
ColorSchemer Studio 51
colour 35, 98, 157; additive, disruptive potential of 123–128, *124*, *127*; digital 36–38; digital manipulation of 50–53; digital mediation of 35–41; as form 47–49; by guesswork 52–53; modifier, building surface as 113–128; non-proprietary 53–54; profiles, as generative procedure 108–109; proprietary 50–51; test strategies for 114; transdisciplinary modes of activating 106, 108, *108*; transformation 46–47
colour filter array (CFA) 52, 114, 116, 117, *119*, 119–123, 125, 127, 144, 152; exploiting 54–55; HVS-based 150, *151*
Commission International de l'Éclairage (CIE) 50
complementary metal-oxide-semiconductor (CMOS) 29, 67, 114, 137; sensor 52
context 34
contrast 17, 27n75, 28, 29, 33, 37, 41, 47–49, 52, 60, 63, 83, 86, 94, 103, 106, 109, 113, 126, 140, 142, 153, 154, 157; perception 38–40; spatial 55–59
core 34
Correggio, A. da: *Assumption of the Virgin* 56, 57
couple charged device (CCD) 29, 52, 67, 114, 117, 137, 150; frame-transfer (FT) 137; interline-transfer (IT) 137–138; sensor 123
Crary, J. 46; *Techniques of the observer* 47
Cylinder Reflection Generator 101, *102*

Damisch, H. 16, 80, 147; critical task of image retrieval 17–18
de Caus, S. 11
decision-making process 43
Deering, M. 132
Degas, E. 63
Deleuze, G. 81, 82, 85–86, 101; *Cinema 1*, 86; 'rhizomic' model 80
De pictura (Alberti) 47
de Quincy, Q. 48
De Stijl form 46, 48
diffraction: artefacts 97; re-viewing 130–135, *131–132*, 134
digital anamorphosis 74–80; affective anamorphic network 76–77; pre-digital anamorphic techniques 74–76; techniques 77–80
digital artefacts, productive inclusion of 67–68
digital assembly, unique modes of: discontinuous digital line 30–31; pixel relationships, predictability of 32–33; qualitative content 31
digital city, responding to 86–88
digital geometry 5, 6, 20, 21, 30–32, 40, 41, 76, 94, *95*, 114, 115, 126, 130, 134, 144, 145, 148, 156, 158; intersection with optical science 33–35; perceptual behaviours 33–35
digital image-making technology: brightness, digital perception of 55–60; colour as form 47–49; colour's transformation 46–47; digital manipulation of colour 50–53; new digital opportunities 53–55; shape 60–68
digital mediation of colour, brightness and shape: contrast perception 38–40; digital colour 36–38; luminosity 38–40; perception 40–41; pixel geometry, contextual advantages of 38–40; pixel geometry, inherent imperatives of 40–41; technological disruption 35–36
digital technology 28–30; *see also individual entries*

digital Urbino Panel 87, 147–155; Intervention 1, 150–151, *151*; Intervention 2, 151–152, *153*; Intervention 3, 152–155, *154*; preliminary digital site mapping procedures 148; visual effects 148–150, *149*
Diller, E. 18
DiPaola, S. 63
disciplinary shift 158–159
discontinuous digital line 30–31
distributed attention 19
distributed digital networks, new agency of 74–88; digital anamorphosis 74–80; expanded image 80–88; virtual picture plane 74–80
Drewry, W. 12–13
Durer, A. 10
Dyce, M. 12
dynamic image 103–106; as a 3D volume 103–106, *104*

Ecological Approach to Visual Perception, The (Gibson) 34
Eisenstein, S. 8–10, 17, 65, 81, 84, 85; 'Montage of Attractions' 9
Elliott, E. 48
expanded image 80–88; distributed network 80–84; responding to digital city 86–88; temporal frame 84–86; viewpoints, multiplication of 80–84

Farbenlehre (Goethe) 47
Figgis, M.: *Timecode* 19, 21
filmic space/architectural space 18–19
Floyd Steinberg Dithering Algorithm 115, 122
Foucault, M. 81
fragmentary spaces of representation: anamorphosis 15–16; filmic space/architectural space 18–19; qualitative image and affective space 22–24; reversal of logic 15–16; Vertovian image 16–18
Francesca, P. D.: *Annunciation* 63, *64*, 72n106; *Polyptych of St. Anthony* 63
Fraunhofer diffraction, as productive aberration 59–60
Fresnel Diffraction Explorer 132
f-stop 120, 122, 125–127, 132, 133, 135, 138, 140, *141*, 142, 144, 145
Fumiani, G.: *Il Martirio di San Pantaleon* 56

Gage, J. 47
Gardner, J. 86, 87, 103
gaze trajectory 64–65
generative techniques 93–112; dynamic image 103–106; new modes of practice 93–95; qualitative image 95–98, *96*; space within the image 98–102; synthesised landscape 106–111
Genoa 11
Gestalt principles 41
Gestalt theory 40
Gibson, J.: *Ecological Approach to Visual Perception, The* 34
Gillam, B. 36
GIMP 53
Goethe, J.W.: *Farbenlehre* 47
Google Earth 39, 75, 79, 82
Green, N. 13, 15, 87
Gregg, M. 22
Gregory, R. L. 33
Groner, R. 72n91
grouping 40
Guattari, F. 81; 'rhizomic' model 80
Gurtner, L. 62

Hand, M. 20
Hansen, M. 22, 79, 99; *New Philosophy for New Media* 76
Haussmann, B. 13, 14
HDR *see* high dynamic range (HDR)
Helmholz, H. von 33
Hermann–Hering grid illusion 38
herringbone technique 28, 41
high dynamic range (HDR) 58
Hochberg, J. 60–61
Holbein, H. 74; *Ambassadors, The* 15, 22, 76, 79; anamorphic skull 78
homogeneous space 42
human visual system (HVS) 4–6, 22–24, 38, 39, 50, 51, 56, 57, 59–66, 68, 120–123, 126, 132, 135, 144, 156, 158; -based CFA pattern 150, *151*; colour receptor mechanism 55
Hurvich, L. M. 55
HVS *see* human visual system (HVS)
HyperCube2 115, 116, 128n6

Il Martirio di San Pantaleon (Fumiani) 56
image: as a 3D volume 103–106, *104*, *107*; artefacts 114
ImageJ 54, 103, 105, 106, 108, 115; Particle Data Count function 134,

174   Index

140; Reslice tool 133; Unique Colour Count function 125; Z Project function 120, 122, 133, 140
image of the city, problem of 6–27; fragmentary spaces of representation 15–24; singular or narrative spaces of representation 10–15; spatial representation, disruptive techniques of 8–10
indexical/raster 4, 6, 13, 21, 23, 33, 83, 87, 95, 110, 114, 148
Institute of Applied Autonomy 83
instrumentalisation 80
Internet protocol (IP) network 29
IP *see* Internet protocol (IP) network
i-See program 83

Jameson, D. 55
Johnson, A. E.: *Camp David, November 15, 1986, Reagan/Thatcher* 68
jolt technique 9, 16, 19, 20, 22, 65, 106
jump cut 9, 17–19, 26n48, 65, 67, 106

Kandinsky, W. 48
Kanizsa, G. 34
Kapoula, Z. 64
Kemp, M. 46
Klette, R. 138
Koeck, R. 9, 85
Köhler, W. 34
Koolhaas, R. 19
Kuler 51
Kurgan, L. 83

LAN *see* local area network (LAN)
Last Judgement (Michelangelo Buonarotti) 74
Last Supper, The (Michelangelo Buonarotti) 75
lateral inhibition 38
Lazzarini, R.: *Skulls* 22, 76, 77
Leonardo da Vinci: *sfumato* technique 46, 47, 56, 71n64
Lissitzky, E. 17
Livingstone, M. S. 35, 50–51
local area network (LAN) 29
Lukac, R. 117, 119–122
luminosity 27n75, 35, 38–40, 97; profiles, as generative procedure 108–109; Series 3 tests 142, **143**; shifting function of 122–123; transdisciplinary modes of activating 106, 108, *108*

Macarthur, J. 82, 83
Maignan, E. 74, 98–99; *San Francesco di Paola* 15, 75, 99, *100*; San Trinità fresco 78
Manhattan Transcripts (Tschumi) 19
Mannan, S 74n91
Man Ray 14
Man with a Movie Camera (Vertov) 3, 9, 17
Marville, C. 13
Massarelli, N. 111n8
Massey, L. 15, 76
Massumi, B. 22–23; *Too Blue* 23
Maxim, J. 14
McGrath, B. 86, 87, 103
McQuire, S. 18, 87
Melcher, D. 62, 63
Michelangelo Buonarotti: *Last Judgement* 74; *Last Supper, The* 75
Miró, J. 63
Mitchell, WJT 29
Modernism 48
Moholy-Nagy, L. 16
Molina, M.: *Center of gaze* 65
Mondrian, P.: *New York City I* 49
Monet, C.: *Rouen Cathedral* series 58
Monmonier, M. 77
'Montage of Attractions' (Eisenstein) 9
montage technique 8–9
Morgan, L. 11

Nagel, T. 83
New Philosophy for New Media (Hansen) 76
new tools and techniques of architecture 156–158
New York City I (Mondrian) 49
Niceron, J.-F. 15, 74, 76, 98–99
Nishitani, K. 85
non-proprietary colour 53–54
Norman, J. 34
Noton, D. 61, 62
Nouvel, J. 19; Culture and Congress Centre 19
Nuova, S. 11, 12

open-source code 53–54
open-source software 94–95
optical 'suppression' process 36
Ozu, Y. 86

Palmer, S. 33
Panofsky, E. 10, 11

pan-tilt-zoom (PTZ) function 36, 67, 77, 78, 98, 119, 150
Pedreira, C. 64
perceptual behaviours 33–35
perceptual saliency 63
perspectival city 11–12
photography: as bearer of truth 12–15; spirit 13
Picasso 49, 63
Pipette 53
Piranesi, G. B. 16, 84
pixel geometry: contextual advantages of 38–40; inherent imperatives of 40–41
pixel grid 7, 35, 158
PixelMath 39, *39*, 44n37, 96, 111n4
pixel relationships, predictability of 32–33
pixel's visual territory 28–43; digital assembly, unique modes of 30–33; digital geometry's intersection with optical science 33–35; digital mediation of colour, brightness and shape 35–41; representation 41–43; symbolic form 41–43
Plataniotis, K. 117, 119–122
Polyptych of St. Anthony (Francesca) 63
Pozzo, A.: *Perspectiva pictorum et architectorum* 42; *Transmission of the Divine Spirit, The* 42
pre-digital anamorphic techniques 74–76
proprietary colour 50–51

qualitative content 31
qualitative image 22–24, 95–98, *96*
Quiroga, Q. 64

radical approach 3
Raw Therapee 53
register, shifting 55–58
Renoir, P.-A. 63
representation 4, 5, 16–18, 20–23, 28, 31, 32, 34, 35, 38–40, 49, 51, 54–56, 58, 60, 61, 63, 64, 74, 76–80, 82–88, 93–95, 97–101, 103, 105, 106, 108, 109–111, 113, 117, 130, 135, 145, 147, 148, 152, 157; fragmentary spaces of *see* fragmentary spaces of representation; pixel's visual territory 41–43; singular or narrative spaces of 10–15; spatial representation, disruptive techniques of 8–10

reversal of logic 15–16
Reynolds, B. 16
RGB (red, green and blue) model 37, 59, 97, 117, 120, 123–124, 126, *127*, 128n16; colour filter array 54; colour space 50, 51
rhizomic network system 82
Riefenstahl, L.: *Triumph of the Will* 17
Riu Plaza 152
Rock, I. 33
Rodchenko, A. 16
Rosenfeld, A. 138
Rouen Cathedral series (Monet) 58
Rubens, P. P. 11
Ruddock, K. 74n91
Ruff, T. 59
Ruttman, W.: *Berlin-Symphony of a Great City* 17

saccadic motion 63
saccadic scanning 8
San Francesco di Paola (Maignan) 15, 75, 99, *100*
Sant'Andrea della Valle, Rome 56
Savard, J. 117
scaled prototype tests 95
scanning 63; saccadic 8
scan path theory 61–65
Scofidio, R. 18
'seeing' versus 'thinking' 35
Sehen, N. 16
Seigworth, G. 22
Series 1 tests: additive colour, disruptive potential of 123–128, *124*, *127*; data matrix 125–128, *127*; hierarchies of visibility 122–123; overview 116; pattern hierarchy, strategies of 117–122, *118–119*, **121**; unique colour count 134, **134**
Series 2 tests: analysis methodology 133–134; conclusions 135; data matrix 135; disruption, patterns of 132–135, **134**; overview 130–132, *131–132*; particle data count **134**, 135; results and analysis 134–135; summary 135; technical data and conditions 132–133
Series 3 tests: data matrix 144–145; luminosity 142, **143**; overview 137–138; pattern legibility 140–142, *141*; scanning variants 138–145, *139*, *141*, **143**
Serlio, S. 10, 11

Severini, G. 63
sfumato technique 46, 47, 56, 71n64
shape: digital artefacts, productive inclusion of 67–68; digital mediation of 35–41; human perception of 60–61; human visual system 61–65; saliency 65–67; scan path theory 61–65
Shed, The 18–19
Shepley, J. 16
Shibuya Crossing, Tokyo 99
singular or narrative spaces of representation: perspectival city 11–12; photography, as bearer of truth 12–15; 'symbolic' intent of linear perspective geometry 9–10
*Skulls*n (Lazzarini) 22, 76, 77
Sontag, S. 13, 20
space within the image 98–102
spatial representation, disruptive techniques of 8–10
Spickler, D. 111n8
spirit photography 13
Stark, L. 61, 62
'symbolic' intent of linear perspective geometry 9–10
synthesised landscape 106–111; colour and luminance (brightness) profiles, as generative procedure 108–109; digital colour and luminance (brightness), transdisciplinary modes of activating 106, 108, *108*

Techniques of the observer (Crary) 47
technological transition 4
3D Colour Inspector 115
Timecode (Figgis) 19, 21
Times Square webcam network (aka Thomson Reuters Building) 7, 36, 78, 99, 104, *104*, 107, 108, *108*, 148, *149*, 151–152
Tishman Construction 152
Too Blue (Massumi) 23
'top-down' theory 33–34
Triumph of the Will (Riefenstahl) 17

Tschumi, B.: *Manhattan Transcripts* 19
Turner, J. M. W. 46–48, 56, 59

Uccello, P.: *Battle of San Romano, The* 40
universal flux 85

Van der Leck, B. 69n22
Van Doesburg, T. 48
Vertov, D. 8–10, 14, 15, 24, 65, 81, 82, 84, 85, 93, 105, 158; digital image: contemporary city, envisioning 19–21; critique 16–18; form-making 16–18; representation 16–18; jolt technique 20, 22; *Man with a Movie Camera* 3, 9, 17; radical approach 3–4, 18
viewpoints, multiplication of 80–84
Vignola, G. B. da 10
virtual picture plane 74–80

webcam 6, 7, 21, 22, 35, 36, 59, 68, 79–82, 93–99, 101, 109–111, 116, 130, 132, 133, 148, 150, 152; advantages of 65–67; anamorphic capacity of 24; automatic capture 97; commercial 67; digital webcam network 79; glitches 96; high-definition 60–61; Internet 85, 86, 94, 96, 103, 104, 106; PTZ mechanism 67, 78; public urban 19–20; saliency of 65–67; user-based, spatial effects of 4; zoom mechanism 22, 37, 67, 76, 77, 98
Wertheimer, .N 34
'winner-take-all' network 63
Wood, A. 19
Wooding, D. 74n91

zoom 6, 20, 22, 41, 59, 66, 119–120, 122, 125, 126, 133, 134, 140, 142, 145, 150–153, 157; Google Earth 39; PTZ 36, 67, 77, 78, 98, 119, 150; webcam 22, 37, 67, 76, 77, 98